Sport and Society

A list of books in the series appears at the end of this volume.

Minor League Baseball and
Local Economic Development

Minor League Baseball and Local Economic Development

Arthur T. Johnson

University of Illinois Press
Urbana and Chicago

Illini Books edition, 1995
© 1993 by the Board of Trustees of the University of Illinois
Manufactured in the United States of America
1 2 3 4 5 C P 5 4 3 2 1

This book is printed on acid-free paper.

Library of Congress Cataloging-in-Publication Data

Johnson, Arthur T.
    Minor league baseball and local economic development / Arthur T.
Johnson.
        p.   cm. — (Sport and society)
    Includes bibliographical references (p.   ) and index.
    ISBN 0-252-01865-6 (cloth : alk. paper). — ISBN 0-252-06502-6
(pbk. : alk. paper)
        1. Minor league baseball—Economic aspects—United States.
2. Urban renewal—Economic aspects—United States. 3. Stadiums—
Economic aspects—United States. I. Title. II. Series.
GV880.J64   1993
338.4'7796357'640973—dc20   92-15713
                                                                CIP

To Robert Cahill,
Citizen, Community Leader, and Sportsman

Contents

Preface

Minor league baseball evokes a vast array of colorful images: small-town America; the purity of baseball; grown men and teenagers pursuing their dream in the "bush leagues," hoping to make it to "the bigs" or "the show"; crazy antics of players, managers, umpires, and fans; run-down ball parks, perhaps in a corn field or behind an abandoned high school; long and tortuous bus rides; shoestring business operations. These and other images have been portrayed wonderfully in film (e.g., *Bull Durham*), fiction, and nonfiction (e.g., Roger Kahn's *Good Enough to Dream*). The news media and popular magazines also have done their share to reenforce such images (e.g., *Washington Post, National Geographic, Sports Illustrated*).

Minor league baseball is prime fodder for those who glamorize and mythologize sport; on the other hand, minor league baseball is an inconsequential activity for those who know and care little about baseball. Ironically, both of these perspectives serve to reenforce the myths and legends of minor league baseball. Both emphasize the fact that minor league baseball is "sport." Most of us understand that sport is big business, that it has important sociological functions, and that it often is a tool of public policy with political consequences. These conclusions are derived, however, from analyses of major league sports, big-time college athletics, and significant international amateur athletic events. Little attention has been given to the thriving "secondary" sports market in the United States, of which minor league baseball is a part.

Minor league baseball is a recovering, but relatively healthy industry facing a number of challenges. It is a highly prized industry that is made possible, as are major league sports, by the investment of millions of dollars of taxpayers' money in playing facilities and other subsidies. Unlike major league sports, it is a policy option that cities of medium and small size believe they can afford to pursue. These cities do so in the expectation that economic growth will be advanced.

Whereas twenty-six cities host major league baseball teams, and approximately two dozen more host major league teams in basketball, hockey, and football, more than 150 communities host minor league baseball teams in the United States and Canada. That number will increase by nearly twenty when the major leagues complete their expansion plans for four new teams by the late 1990s. Minor league baseball thus is much more national than is major league baseball in terms of citizens' geographical (and financial) ability to attend a game in person.

This book treats minor league baseball as an object of public policy. The reader looking for sports trivia or more myth making should read no further. The book addresses three thematic issues throughout: the political process by which stadium decisions are made, the presence or absence of a development strategy to guide decision making, and the value of a minor league team and its stadium to a community. Case studies are used to analyze these three issues. The case studies are presented according to the substantive issues of the use of a "sports strategy," franchise relocation, and the use of minor league stadiums for downtown development and for opening up new land for development. Analyses of survey data and of the economics and structure of minor league baseball provide a foundation for understanding the case studies and the political economy of minor league baseball. Appendix A provides details of the methods used to collect the survey and case study data.

This book should be of value to local officials, economic development practitioners, planners, and leaders of chambers of commerce and of other community organizations who want to understand the risks and potential value of hosting a minor league baseball team and want to gain insight into the dynamics of city-team relations. I hope those in the business will see the book as a fair treatment of the industry and as a valid assessment of its role in local economic development. For the academic, the book provides cases that, taken together, provide another example of the politics of local economic development. It also provides another approach to the question of whether public investment in sports is "worth it."

The perspective of the author is important in writing case studies, and the reader has a right to some insight into that perspective. Am I a fan or not? I lost my innocence as a fan many years ago when the Dodgers abandoned Brooklyn. I remain a semi-interested spectator of the game, who can root for the home team, but I am not a fanatic. Did I find a research project that would be a summer's entertainment and a lark? Traveling from city to city in a limited period of time with hardly a break is not fun. I attended games in each case study community if the team was at home, but, with one exception, I never stayed for an entire game. My attention was more on the fans, the physical quality of the stadium, the types of entertainment, concession prices, and many other nonsport concerns, than on the game. Am I someone who had major league dreams? Although I played baseball into my college years, I cannot recall having delusions of grandeur. I do admit to a growing curiosity about fantasy camps as the years pass. Am I a friend or foe of the industry? I see myself as neither. I was active in the attempt to have Baltimore's Memorial Stadium renovated instead of building a new stadium for the Orioles, but I claim, as I did then, the role of objective analyst. The reader must judge my success.

My research and this book were made possible by the assistance and support of many. The University of Maryland Baltimore County (UMBC) provided financial assistance through the President's Faculty Research Travel Award and its SRIS program. These awards allowed me to determine the feasibility of the project and to begin the case studies. The support of UMBC's Political Science Department and its former chairperson, Nicholas Miller, is what every scholar hopes for. The International City Management Association (ICMA) financed a survey of cities that hosted minor league teams. The results of that survey confirmed that minor league baseball was a subject of some importance to local officials and worth serious study. The support and encouragement of Steve Mountain, the former director of ICMA's Sports Consortium, was invaluable in conducting the survey as well as the case studies. Other support and hospitality came from the city of Visalia, Indiana University–Purdue University at Fort Wayne, and the Center for Governmental Research and Public Service at Bowling Green State University.

The planning of the case studies posed a series of complicated logistical problems. I was able to go about my work efficiently in each city only because of the generous cooperation and assistance of key individuals in each city and the willingness of scores of individuals to meet with me and answer my questions. In most cases, the interviews went well beyond the amount of time the interviewees had agreed to give me. Although space does not allow me to acknowledge all of those I interviewed, I do wish to thank those who took care of arrangements and helped in other ways in each city: Scott Carter, Jerry Mileur, Charles Coss, John Pedersen, Jr., Jim Owen, Tara Barney, Curt Seditz, Suzanne Utley, Gary Cuddeback, Ed LaMonte, J. Clay Kilian, Boyd Cauble, and Ron Primavera. The numerous reference librarians in the public libraries of the case study communities also deserve my thanks.

My thanks to James Milroy, a senior legislative assistant with the Buffalo Common Council and a visiting instructor at SUNY Buffalo's

Center for Applied Public Affairs Studies; James Owens, associate professor in the School of Public and Environmental Affairs (SPEA) at
Indiana University–Purdue University at Fort Wayne; Mark Rosentraub,
dean of SPEA at Indiana University at Indianapolis; David Swindell, a
graduate student at SPEA at Indiana University at Bloomington; Robyne
Turner, assistant professor of political science at Florida Atlantic
University; and Harry Wessel, associate professor of political science at
Merrimack College, who agreed to contribute case studies of their own
for this book and then so cooperatively tolerated my suggestions and
editing.

I am also grateful to Don Norris, Neil Sullivan, Mike Moore, Roy
Meyers, Benjamin Rader, John Wendel, and Robert Whelan for their
comments on earlier drafts of chapters and their advice on specific
issues.

I am certain that different interpretations of events described in the
book are held by some in the case study communities, especially those
participants I was unable to interview. I, of course, accept responsibility
for the contents of the book, including any inaccuracies or errors that
might appear.

Minor League Baseball and
Local Economic Development

Introduction

The Politics of Development and the Stadium Issue

Professional sports entrepreneurs have proven themselves successful at capturing the attention of public officials and attracting the investment of public dollars for playing facilities by identifying themselves with communities and their economic well-being. The acquisition or retention of a professional sports team (the "sports issue") has become a common objective for communities across the nation, regardless of their size, geographic location, or economic health. Many local officials and economic development practitioners believe that a professional sports team has a direct positive impact on the local economy and helps the host community project a positive image. In essence, sports teams are valued because it is believed they promote economic growth.

The relationship between a team and its host community is defined by the arrangements by which the team's owner obtains a playing facility. A series of public policy decisions, primarily related to financing, siting, and constructing a playing facility for the team, is triggered when local officials decide to host a professional sports team. Public officials and stadium advocates advance their stadium proposal in terms of an economic growth rationale and justify their stadium plans and the team's presence in a community by the number of jobs that will be created, new businesses that will be attracted to the community, and increased prosperity for existing businesses. The team's contribution to the community's quality of life is put forth as an additional benefit for local economic development. Opponents press their own concerns but are forced to confront the economic development arguments of the stadium advocates.

The "sports issue," which, at first, appears to be a safe issue for local politicians to support, very quickly becomes a controversial "stadium issue." The politics of the stadium issue as it is played out in large cities with major league teams (Henderson, 1980; Klobuchar, 1986; Sullivan, 1987) is very much the politics of development, which is so well described in the urban development literature (Molotch, 1976; Peterson, 1981; Mollenkopf, 1983; Fainstein et al., 1986; Logan and Molotch, 1987; Stone and Sanders, 1987; Kantor, 1988; Judd, 1988; Sharp, 1990). This has been the case since the turn of the century (Riess, 1980, 1989).

Local Economic Development and the Economic Impact of Stadiums

Intercity competition is a prime motivator of local economic development activities. Community-based economic development policies and plans are adopted in response to, and in anticipation of, actions taken by competitor cities and other external challenges to local economic health.

Providing public subsidies to private interests is a principal means by which local and state governments compete with one another. These subsidies take many forms, including tax abatements, low-cost capital in the form of subsidized loans, loan guarantees or grants, expensive but necessary infrastructure, and in-kind services. In the case of professional sports, municipal governments offer teams similar inducements that result in publicly owned stadiums, new roads to the stadiums, highway interchanges nearby, guaranteed ticket revenue, and undeveloped real estate for the team's future use. Providing public subsidies for privately owned sports teams is not unique, however, and should be analyzed within the context of a community's overall economic development plan.

Barnekov and Rich (1989: 232) allege that the "competition among city governments for economic resources has turned the promotion of economic development into a new full-time vocation that redefines urban governance as civic marketing." Levy (1990; see also Rubin, 1988) found that local economic development agency directors emphasize "high visibility activities with political payoff," such as sites and structures, rather than less tangible improvements in human resources and capital. Local officials' attention consequently is riveted to economic growth as the primary goal of local economic development activities.

Economic development activities in pursuit of economic growth are designed to attract dollars from outside the community and to increase the amount of spending and income earned within the locality. Development efforts are made to attract new industries and activities to the community as well as to retain and strengthen existing establishments. Judd (1988: 376-77) has identified and illustrated the assumptions of the pro-growth strategy (see Figure 1):

investment leads to more jobs and an improved tax base. This, in turn, raises the incomes of city residents and provides more resources to city governments so that they can improve public services. Higher incomes lead to increased spending and consumption by city residents. Better public services are evidenced by good streets, lighting, parks, and public buildings and in better schools, police protection, and public health, all of which improve the quality of neighborhood life. Rising spending and consumption create a favorable business environment, which, of course, encourages investment, and on around the cycle again.

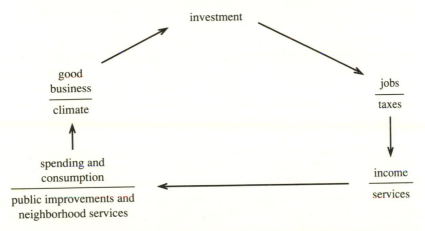

Figure 1: The Growth Model as a Logical Statement

Source: Dennis R. Judd, *The Politics of American Cities: Private Power and Public Policy,* 3d ed. (New York: HarperCollins, 1988), p. 376. Copyright 1988 by Dennis R. Judd; reprinted by permission of HarperCollins Publishers.

These development outcomes commonly are attributed to the presence of a professional sports team and its stadium (Fulton, 1988; Johnson, 1985). However, just as the urban development literature tends to be critical of the economic development practices and trends of local government, there is significant disagreement between academic observers on the one hand and public officials and economic development practitioners on the other concerning the economic impact of sports teams and stadiums.

Specific projects are championed for their expected direct and secondary impacts. Direct impact is the direct infusion of new dollars into the local economy. Secondary impact is the project's indirect effect on other economic activities in the community. This additional activity produces increased circulation of dollars within the local economy, which is the project's "multiplier effect." The multiplier effect is a concept commonly used to measure the expected secondary impact of an economic development activity, such as the construction of a new stadium.

All too often, however, the projected economic impact figures are pure guesswork or are based on overly optimistic assumptions. These assumptions fail to calculate costs associated with a project, including foregone opportunity costs of alternative uses of the site, lost tax dollars, jobs lost, and dollars spent elsewhere during construction. As a result, estimates of economic impact most often are those of "gross impact" rather than of net benefit.

Advocates also commonly assume that citizens have no alternative spending options within the locality in the absence of the project. They often falsely assume that all the benefits of the project are new benefits that otherwise would not occur. This error inflates the positive impact of the project. It is misleading, therefore, to equate economic impact with economic growth when discussing development projects (see Rosentraub and Swindell's case study of Fort Wayne, Indiana, for further discussion).

Economic impact studies of sports teams and their stadiums that have been done for teams and host communities universally show a positive impact (e.g., Shils, 1985; Peat, Marwick, Mitchell and Company, 1987; Chicago Department of Economic Development, 1986; Schaffer and Davidson, 1985; Malloy, 1977; Touche Ross, 1988). Attempts by academic researchers to verify this relationship have been less positive, however. Johnson (1986: 430) and Okner (1974: 346-47) question the economic value of a sports franchise to a community and conclude its value hinges on evaluating indirect and intangible benefits and costs. Baim (1990: 14) reports finding in his early research a positive correlation between the number of jobs and the presence of a major league franchise but, based on his later research findings, concludes "each case is unique and any attempt at generalization is likely doomed to failure." Baade (1987), using regression analysis, offers evidence that the presence of a major league baseball franchise is correlated with a decline in personal income of city residents. Baade and Dye (1988: 274) contend the economic development rationale for stadiums is "made of straw" and dub as naive public policy that approves a stadium and then waits for promised growth.

The Issues of Public Benefits and Popular Control

Critics and advocates alike recognize that development projects may assist a community in achieving its economic development goals in less direct ways than creating jobs and producing a large multiplier effect. For example, a positive quality of life is an intangible that makes a community more attractive to businesses considering relocation and provides individuals and businesses already situated within the community reason to remain. Such projects as theaters, convention centers, civic centers, sports facilities, and symphony halls are defended in terms of not only their economic impact, but also the activities enhancing the community's quality of life.

This type of project is expected to help create, improve, or reinforce a community's image or to focus attention on a community (Bowman and Pagano, 1991). Advocates of such projects as the acquisition of a professional sports franchise assert that they enhance the "prestige" of the city and demonstrate it is now "major league." In doing so, advocates insist, these projects assist a city's marketing efforts (Haider, 1990) and facilitate its ability to attract external dollars through increased tourism, corporate relocation, or some other means.

Writing about the relationship between the arts and economic development, Hendon and Shaw (1987: 210; see also Whitt, 1987) state, "Creating an environment that will appeal to the new generation of technicians and managers, as well as to the corporate elite who direct the flow of development capital has brought the arts (and the necessary structures to house the arts) to center stage as a tool in economic development." Although Hendon and Shaw intend to portray this as a positive result, the implication is that not all firms will be responsive to a sales pitch about the quality of life. Hart, Denison, and Henderson (1989) find that cultural amenities are more important to employees of certain types of companies, such as those in high-technology industries, than to others, such as those who work for manufacturing companies.

Advocates of pro-growth strategies and defenders of specific economic development projects argue that economic growth benefits the entire community (Peterson, 1981: 22–24). Critics of public subsidies for private interests, however, assert there are losers even within the successful cities (Feagin, 1988; Fainstein et al., 1986: 3). They cite the uneven impacts of development and reject the assumption that what is good for the private sector is good for the community (Barnekov and Rich, 1989; Moore and Squires, 1991).

Critics argue that local governments favor "growth machine" values (especially those tied to land and its use) that benefit developers and other assorted business interests at the expense of others in the community, especially the disadvantaged (Molotch, 1976; Logan and Molotch, 1987; Mollenkopf, 1983). Judd and Parkinson (1989: 6), for example, assert that "large scale developments constitute important amenities for the white-

collar professionals and affluent shoppers who use them, but the benefits are not shared by low income groups in surrounding neighborhoods."

The construction of sports stadiums does not escape this criticism
(Robinson and Wright, 1990). Stadium advocates, who often favor a
downtown "corporate center strategy," are pitted against those who
argue that resources invested in the stadium have been diverted from the
neighborhoods or that other priorities have been sacrificed for the
benefit of the wealthy team owner. Levy, Meltsner, and Wildavsky (1974:
124) describe, for example, the construction of an access road to the
Oakland Coliseum so wealthier (and white) sports fans could travel
"more quickly through a poverty area."

The media frequently comment on the high cost of tickets to sporting
events in publicly financed facilities. It is claimed that it is not only the
poor who are prevented from attending these events, but also the average citizen. Major League Baseball traditionally has drawn attention to
its affordability, but as the economics of the game changes, this claim
becomes increasingly hollow.

Buss and Redburn (1987: 290-94) attribute misuse and abuse of
public subsidies for private interests to local governments' lack of strategic planning capacity, private sector dominance of subsidy programs
and the decision-making process, the increased blur of the distinction
between public sector and private sector objectives (i.e., the assertion
that any new investment advances the goal of revitalization), and the
tendency to finance projects with "off-budget" mechanisms that do not
require legislative authorization. In each case, organized and influential
private sector interests can fill a void or take advantage of conditions to
control or to shape decisions.

It cannot be assumed that those favoring growth have complete
hegemony, however (Fainstein et al., 1986; Kantor, 1988; Sanders, 1987).
Although local governments seek to insulate development projects
from widespread popular debate (Kantor, 1988: 250; see also Peterson,
1981: 148-49; Elkin, 1987: 42; J. Grant, 1990; Jones and Bachelor,
1986), opposition to specific development projects does arise. As with
most large development projects, opposition to stadium proposals
springs from those who claim to represent taxpayers' concerns about
cost and competing priorities and those whose neighborhoods and
business interests are threatened by the proposed location of the
stadium.

In some cases, public opposition merely complicates the implementation of a project; in others, it kills the project. Referenda proposing the
construction of major league stadiums have failed in Miami (1988), New
Jersey (1987), San Francisco (1987 and 1989), Phoenix (1989), San Jose

(1990 and 1992), and Cuyahoga County (1984), though they have been approved in Cleveland (1990), Denver (1990), and San Antonio (1989).

Minor League Baseball and Major League Sports

Professional sports franchises of all types, epitomized by major league teams, have evolved into one of the more popular pursuits of local officials and economic development practitioners. Whatever we know about the politics of the "stadium issue," however, has been drawn from the experience of large cities with major league sports. A large "secondary sports market" exists and increasingly is becoming a component of the local economy of communities of all sizes. Minor league baseball is the most visible of the professional sports within the secondary sports market and, from a public policy perspective, is the most important.

Minor league baseball is present in nearly two hundred American and Canadian communities in thirty-seven states and three provinces and is being sought by dozens of other communities. It is the one sport in the secondary sports market that requires costly infrastructure for its economic viability. Just as public investment in a major league stadium is controversial, so too is public investment in a minor league baseball stadium. Even though the cost of a minor league stadium is much less than that of a major league stadium, smaller communities find the necessary $10-12 million burdensome. Not only is the projected return on a public investment in a minor league stadium debatable, but the benefits for a community's image can be questioned as well. All cities want to be perceived as being "major league," but should cities risk being perceived as "minor league" or "bush league"?

The distinction between the economics of major league sports and the reality of the business of professional baseball at the minor league level must be understood when considering economic development options and their expected impacts. A major league team is capable of attracting millions of fans to a stadium in one season, whereas even a successful minor league team rarely draws more than a few hundred thousand fans. A major league team attracts many fans from beyond its local jurisdiction, especially for postseason play, but this is not the case with a minor league team. Employee salaries of a major league team are significantly higher than those of a minor league team, most of whose employees are seasonal. A major league team brings national recognition to a city, but it is arguable that the average minor league team brings even regional recognition to its host community. Local officials and stadium advocates often do not make these distinctions when offering justifications for investing public funds in a minor league baseball stadium.

This study examines the role of minor league baseball in local economic development and the politics of development that encompasses proposals to build minor league stadiums. The case studies address substantive public policy issues relevant to the public ownership of stadiums and the relationship between local government and minor league baseball. They also provide another context within which to examine the themes of the politics of development literature reviewed in this introduction. Part I examines why the economics and structure of minor league baseball make the stadium the crux of the relationship between a minor league team and its host community. Part II addresses the issue of developing a "sports strategy" and the different approaches to the use of minor league teams by local and state governments. Part III examines the causes of franchise relocation and the extent to which minor league teams are able to influence local governments. Parts IV and V examine the potential role of minor league stadiums in downtown redevelopment and in opening up new development opportunities, respectively. They provide examples of the different development rationales for such projects and the potential development value of minor league stadiums, but they also demonstrate that there is no guarantee of success.

Two persistent themes of the urban development and sports policy literatures are intertwined throughout the case studies and provide a common focus for each section. The first relates to the political process and the tension that exists between the ideal of popular control of public policy and the promotion of the local economy: "How are economic development decisions made?" The second theme focuses on the value of development projects to the community: "Is a project worth the investment of public resources?" The conclusion addresses these two themes more generally.

PART I

The Business of Minor League Baseball, the Major Leagues, and Community Ownership of Stadiums

Local officials must understand the structure and economics of the industry with which they deal if they are to be able to assess the likelihood that a proposed partnership will achieve specific development goals and if they are to negotiate reasonably and successfully with potential partners. A knowledge of the industry also is required to understand the strength of the city's negotiating position vis-à-vis competing communities and to estimate the stability of the industry and its long-term health.

Forming private-public partnerships to pursue economic development without thoroughly understanding the economics of the industry for which the partnership is designed is not unusual. On the basis of a review of the literature concerning the influence of publicly offered incentives on corporate location and expansion decisions, Sharp (1990: 245), citing Wolman and Ledebur, concludes, "In general, the inducement strategy works best when public sector officials have very strong information about private sector locational considerations, so that the relevance, appropriate level, and likely impact of any incentives offered by government can be accurately judged. Unfortunately, in many cases public officials do not have good information about private sector motivations and likely behavior." Even though much attention has been given to major league franchise relocations and to major league expansion criteria, it remains doubtful that public officials have the knowledge of major league sports that Sharp suggests is desirable. It is certain that public officials lack such knowledge of minor league baseball.

Interviews with community leaders and local officials in the case study communities revealed that public policy decisions related to minor league teams and stadiums commonly are based on faulty assumptions or inadequate information about the business of minor league baseball and its future market conditions. For example, although many of those interviewed were knowledgeable about the business of minor league baseball, several had the impression that their communities' minor league teams were owned by their major league affiliates, though they were not. Also, officials frequently referred to economic impact studies of major league teams in discussing the importance of their communities' minor league teams. They failed to distinguish between major league and minor league baseball and appeared to believe that public investment decisions regarding minor league teams and facilities can be based on what is known about the economic impact of major league teams.

Blakely (1989: 127) observes that local officials also often make local economic development decisions in reaction to current fads: "High technology, tourism, and convention centers dominate current municipal economic strategies. These faddish approaches are adopted by communities on scanty economic evidence and without any particular ability to achieve them. A substantial body of recent research indicates that there is little support for most communities' aspirations for a high-technology, tourism, or convention scenario."

It is difficult to evaluate, even with a thorough understanding of the business, whether minor league baseball in the 1990s is just another fad. A fundamental understanding of the structure and economics of minor league baseball, however, is essential to understanding why stadiums are the crux of the relationship between minor league baseball teams and their host communities and why the investment of public funds in a stadium involves political and financial risks.

Governance and Structure of Minor League Baseball

The National Association of Professional Baseball Leagues governs nineteen professional baseball leagues that are popularly referred to as the minor leagues. Each league has its own officers, who manage their league's affairs under the jurisdiction of their league's bylaws, the National Association Agreement, and the Professional Baseball Agreement (PBA).

The PBA governs the relationship between the major leagues and the minor leagues as well as certain specified actions of minor league clubs, the minor leagues, and their governing body. A new PBA was signed in December 1990, after bitter negotiations between the major leagues (i.e., the National League of Professional Baseball Clubs and the American League of Professional Baseball Clubs) and the minor leagues, represented by the National Association of Professional Baseball Leagues.

This PBA is scheduled to expire September 30, 1997, but it may be terminated September 30, 1994, by either the major leagues or the minor leagues.

The minor leagues are organized according to the level of the players' skills. Leagues are classified, from highest to lowest: AAA (four leagues, including the Mexican League), AA (three leagues), A (seven leagues), and Rookie (five leagues, including two complex-based leagues and a summer league in the Dominican Republic). Single A–level leagues are subclassified by the 1990 PBA as A-Advanced (three leagues), A (two leagues), and short-season A (two leagues). Rookie leagues also are subclassified as Rookie-Advanced (three leagues) and Rookie (two complex-based leagues).

As can be seen in Table I.1, which identifies each minor league at the Rookie-Advanced level and higher that is based in the United States, cities hosting minor league teams vary greatly in size. This diversity in size exists within leagues and within each level of play. With the exception of the AAA leagues, especially the American Association, minor leagues tend to be geographically compact. This reduces the travel costs of league members.

In 1992, a total of 134 teams played in A (82), AA (26), and AAA (26) leagues (exclusive of the Mexican League). The minor league season is approximately 142 games, which are played between early April and August 31. Teams in short-season A leagues and Rookie-level leagues play approximately half as many games. As of the 1994 season, the maximum number of regular season games each team will be permitted to play will be 140 at the AAA, AA, and A levels, 76 at the short-season A level, and 68 and 60 at the Rookie-Advanced and Rookie levels, respectively.

Nearly all minor league games are played in the evening, except those played on Sundays. The weather is extremely important financially to minor league teams. Rained-out games are difficult to make up because there are few open dates in the teams' schedules. As a result, many teams do not play their full schedule of revenue-producing home games in a season.

The Renewed Popularity of Minor League Baseball

Interest in minor league baseball on the part of fans, prospective owners, and local governments was rekindled in the 1980s. Attendance in 1987, which topped 20 million fans, was the highest overall attendance since 1951, when just over 25 million fans attended games played by nearly twice as many minor league teams (Orange Book, 1990: 14). Minor

Table I.1: Profiles of Minor Leagues, 1992 Season

League	Teams (N)	Smallest / Largest Cities	Geographic Area of League
AAA			
American Association	8	Des Moines / Indianapolis (193,187) / (741,952)	NY, CO, IN, IA, KY, TN, OK, NE
International League	8	Pawtucket / Columbus (72,000) / (632,910)	OH, NY, PA, VA, RI
Pacific Coast League	10	Tacoma / Phoenix (176,664) / (983,403)	NM, NV, AZ, CO, OR, WA, AB, BC
AA			
Eastern League	8	Hagerstown / London (35,445) / (276,000)	NY, OH, PA, CT, MD, ON
Southern League	10	Zebulon / Jacksonville (2,000) / (672,971)	SC, AL, TN, NC, FL
Texas League	8	Midland / San Antonio (98,000) / (935,933)	TX, AR, LA, KS, MS, OK
A			
California League	10	Adelanto / San Jose (10,402) / (782,248)	CA, NV
Carolina League	8	Salem / Winston-Salem (24,000) / (143,485)	NC, VA, MD
Florida State League	14	Vero Beach / St. Petersburg (17,000) / (239,000)	FL
Midwest League	14	Burlington / Rockford (28,000) / (139,426)	WI, IA, IL, IN
South Atlantic	14	Myrtle Beach / Greensboro (27,000) / (183,521)	SC, NC, GA, WV
A (Short Season)			
New York–Penn League	14	Oneonta / Hamilton (13,000) / (308,000)	NY, PA, MA, ON
Northwest League	8	Bend / Spokane (19,000) / (177,196)	WA, ID, OR
Rookie-Advanced			
Appalachian	10	Princeton / Johnson City (7,493) / (44,000)	WV, VA, NC, TN

Table I.1 (Continued)

League	Teams (N)	Smallest / Largest Cities	Geographic Area of League
Pioneer	8	Helena / Salt Lake City (24,000) / (159,936)	MT, ID, UT, AB

Sources: *Municipal Year Book, 1988* (Washington, D.C.: International City Management Association, 1988) and 1990 Census Data. Unincorporated areas are excluded.

Note: The Arizona and Gulf Coast Rookie leagues are organized around the Arizona and Florida training complexes of major league teams, with some teams sharing sites. They are not included.

league attendance has increased each year since 1987, reaching a level of 25,244,569 in 1990 and 26,590,096 in 1991.[1]

Minor league baseball suffered severe financial problems and loss of fan interest in the 1950s (see Figure I.1, which provides annual minor league attendance figures for the period of 1949 to 1990). This was a consequence of several factors, including more telecasts of major league games into minor league territories, relocation of major league franchises into minor league territories, and increased leisure-time options for the public (Sullivan, 1990; Davis, 1974). The number of minor league teams declined from 448 teams (in fifty-nine leagues) in 1949 to 152 teams in 1960. Since 1960, the total number of teams remained stable for two decades but in 1982 began to increase slowly.

Table I.2 demonstrates the recent pattern of renewed fan interest in minor league baseball by comparing league attendance levels in 1986 and 1990. These figures reveal the extent of attendance increases in this five-year period as well as the wide variation in attendance within and between leagues, even at the same league level.

Renewed fan interest in minor league baseball is largely due to the team owners' emphasis on the entertainment aspects of the business. It was not surprising, therefore, that team representatives (general managers and owners) who were interviewed for this study described their business as entertainment, not baseball, when asked what business they were in.[2] As one interviewee explained, they do not scout, draft, or sign players. A team's managers and coaching staff are assigned by the major league club and take their instructions from that organization, not from the minor league team's owner or general manager. In fact, the latter have little to do with what happens on the field of play.

Team representatives stated uniformly that they provide family

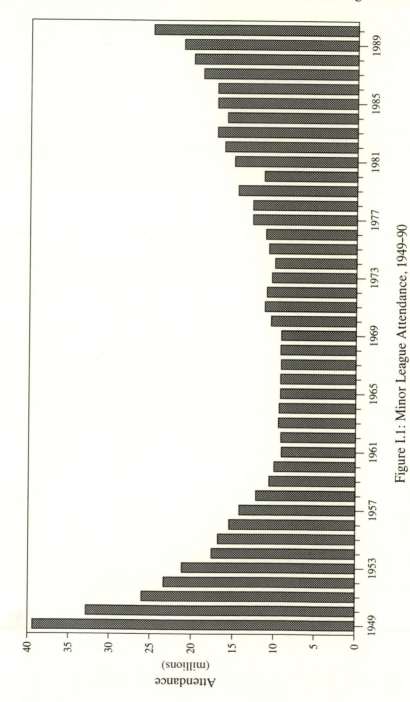

Figure I.1: Minor League Attendance, 1949–90

Source: *Orange Book. 1990* (St. Petersburg, Fla.: National Association of Professional Baseball Leagues, 1990).

Table I.2: Comparison of League Attendance Levels,
1986 and 1990

League	1986	1990
American Association (AAA)		
Highest	660,200	1,156,661
Lowest	220,285	270,215
Total	2,768,027	3,971,859
Average per team	346,003	496,482
Average per game	4,873	6,806
International League (AAA)		
Highest	548,417	584,010
Lowest	105,578	159,009
Total	2,054,037	2,777,395
Average per team	256,754	347,174
Average per game	3,661	5,446
Pacific Coast League (AAA)		
Highest	306,640	324,046
Lowest	84,134	150,054
Total	2,039,641	2,608,026
Average per team	203,964	260,803
Average per game	2,869	3,684
Eastern League (AA)		
Highest	316,034	223,503
Lowest	37,267	76,921
Total	792,215	1,369,589
Average per team	99,026	171,199
Average per game	1,433	2,466
Southern League (AA)		
Highest	263,198	271,302
Lowest	75,728	82,676
Total	1,604,758	1,859,367
Average per team	160,476	185,937
Average per game	2,248	2,582
Texas League (AA)		
Highest	222,163	256,074
Lowest	101,060	124,142
Total	1,248,886	1,580,399
Average per team	156,111	197,550
Average per game	2,326	2,926

Table I.2 (Continued)

League	1986	1990
California League (A)		
Highest	100,348	190,890
Lowest	38,818	33,465
Total	683,595	946,780
Average per team	68,360	9,468
Average per game	964	1,341
Carolina League (A)		
Highest	197,125	300,499
Lowest	48,845	70,647
Total	894,877	1,286,715
Average per team	111,860	160,839
Average per game	1,621	2,327
Florida State League (A)		
Highest	126,242	190,146
Lowest	21,486	18,884
Total	693,208	989,575
Average per team	57,767	70,683
Average per game	851	1,042
Midwest League (A)		
Highest	179,189	212,485
Lowest	57,495	53,373
Total	1,244,068	1,648,095
Average per team	103,672	117,721
Average per game	1,486	1,731
South Atlantic League (A)		
Highest	180,715	153,232
Lowest	16,833	37,412
Total	781,541	1,100,014
Average per team	78,154	91,667
Average per game	1,159	1,288
New York–Penn League (A-Short)		
Highest	71,463	101,110
Lowest	17,199	29,742
Total	457,399	744,830
Average per team	38,117	53,202
Average per game	1,001	1,384

entertainment—"good clean fun." This is exemplified by the variety of promotions used to attract fans. Virtually every club uses promotions of some sort. These include performances by the San Diego Chicken and

Table I.2 (Continued)

League	1986	1990
Northwest League (A-Short)		
Highest	116,286	129,999
Lowest	14,916	40,849
Total	453,394	692,126
Average per team	56,674	86,516
Average per game	1,532	2,276
Appalachian League (Rookie)		
Highest	62,701	69,182
Lowest	10,338	17,013
Total	208,411	383,766
Average per team	26,051	38,376
Average per game	772	1,103
Pioneer League (Rookie)		
Highest	108,721	192,366
Lowest	22,566	13,350
Total	379,720	542,078
Average per team	63,287	67,759
Average per game	1,817	2,008

Note: *Highest* = highest average attendance for a team in the league; *lowest* = lowest average attendance for a team in the league; *total* = total league attendance; *average per team* = the league's average attendance per team; *average per game* = the league's average attendance per game played.

Max Patkin, who is known as baseball's clown prince, appearances by Morganna the Kissing Bandit, fireworks displays, cow milking contests, concerts after the games, and innumerable giveaways (e.g., bats, balls, batting gloves, helmets, seat cushions, and coffee mugs).

Attendance at minor league games, especially in the lower-level leagues, is not necessarily related to the quality of team play. Most team representatives agreed that if a team is not competitive, attendance will be hurt, but a winning team is not necessary to attract large crowds. One owner estimated that fewer than half the fans attended a game for the contest itself.[3]

Team representatives identified their competition not solely as other sports activities, but as any opportunity that competes for the individual's leisure time, whether it be major league games on television; participant sports, such as softball or hiking; or more passive entertainment, such as movies and concerts.

In the 1940s and 1950s, the major league teams were the principal owners of minor league teams, especially at the AAA, AA and A level.

For example, major league teams owned or controlled through working agreements 79 percent of the AAA teams, 88 percent of the AA teams and 80 percent of the A teams in 1952 (U.S. Congress, 1952: 765). Overall, "independent" owners owned 46 percent of the minor league teams, concentrated mainly in the lower-level leagues, which were then classified B, C, and D.

There is evidence that the financial success of minor league teams helped subsidize the major league owners before the 1950s (Sullivan, 1990: 237). This changed in the 1950s, and by the 1970s, tired of losing money, the major league clubs were selling their minor league teams. Combined income statements of the major league clubs show that the major league teams sustained annual operating losses ranging from $459,746 to $954,050 per team, beyond other player development expenses, during the period of 1974–79 (Markham and Teplitz, 1981: appendix D).

Franchises, which were virtually given away or sold for no more than a few thousand dollars only a few years ago, are in the 1990s attracting offers of hundreds of thousands of dollars for A-level teams and several million dollars for AA-level and AAA-level teams. The Buffalo franchise, for example, was bought for approximately $800,000 in 1986 and was estimated to be worth as much as $8 million in 1990. The A-level South Bend White Sox were purchased in 1990 for a reported price of approximately $4 million. That franchise was bought as an expansion franchise in 1985 for $40,000 and sold in 1987 for $465,000 before it ever played a game (see the South Bend case study). Other recent franchise sales include Omaha (AAA) for approximately $5.0 million in 1991, Williamsport (AA) for approximately $3.0 million in 1991, Peninsula (Newport News-A) for $1.7 million in 1991, Birmingham (AA) for $3.6 million in 1990, Oklahoma City (AAA) for $4.5 million in 1989, Tucson (AAA) for $3.3 million in 1989, Memphis (AA) for $3.0 million in 1989, and Louisville (AAA) for $4.2 million in 1986.

Fees for AAA expansion franchises were set in the summer of 1990 at approximately $5.0 million dollars. Expansion franchise fees at the AA level were set at $3.0 million in 1991 for 1994. Expansion franchise fees for the 1991 season in the A-level South Atlantic League were $1.3 million. Expansion franchise fees in the short-season A New York–Penn League cost $150,000 in 1989.

Communities are pursuing franchises just as eagerly as team owners are seeking communities to host their teams. Thirty-five franchise relocations occurred in minor league baseball between 1987 and 1992. Cities that have lost teams remain interested in hosting a franchise.

A minimum of four new minor league franchises (one each at the AAA and AA levels and at least two at the A level) must be created for each major league expansion franchise. The National League is scheduled to expand by two teams in 1993, and there has been speculation that the American League will expand by two teams later in the decade. This portends a significant restructuring of the minor leagues and offers the potential for cities without a franchise to obtain one and for cities with an A-level or AA-level franchise to host a team at the AAA level. In 1990, nearly twenty owners from as many communities formally expressed interest in obtaining AAA expansion franchises. Of these, fourteen represented communities with teams in lower-level leagues. At the end of 1991, communities reportedly interested in hosting a team included Binghamton, New York; Wilmington, Delaware; Wilmington, North Carolina; Charlottesville, Virginia; Wilson, North Carolina; Hickory, North Carolina; Mobile, Alabama; Montgomery, Alabama; Pensacola, Florida; Oceanside, California; Sacramento, California; Fresno, California; Atlantic City, New Jersey; Lehigh County, Pennsylvania; Springfield, Missouri; Rome, Georgia; Missoulo, Montana; Round Rock, Texas; Baton Rouge, Louisiana; Suffolk County, New York; Nassau County, New York; and Prince George's County, Maryland. By the 1992 season, Binghamton and Ottawa had secured commitments for teams in the future.

Sports entrepreneurs periodically propose the creation of new minor leagues. Investors and communities express interest, even though these leagues would lack affiliation with the National Association and would be without any major league team affiliation.

Franchise Ownership

A team owner must be awarded a franchise from a league for a team to operate and compete as a minor league team. The franchise prevents another team from operating within the team's "home territory." Under the rules before 1991, a team's home territory was defined as a circle within a thirty-five-mile radius from the team's stadium. The 1991 Professional Baseball Agreement maintains the home territories in existence at the time of its approval; however, representatives of the National Association and the major leagues continued to negotiate the definition of home territory in 1992.

If an owner of a franchise in a higher-level league wants to operate within another team's home territory, that encroaching owner's league can "draft" the territory for its use. This effectively forces the original lower-level franchise from the territory, but with "just and reasonable" compensation.

Minor league teams are owned by private individuals, major league teams, nonprofit organizations, community residents organized as stock-holders, and local governments. As interest in minor league baseball has increased, new owners have appeared, ranging from such celebrities as Mark Harmon, Bill Murray, and Jimmy Buffett to small investment groups and Japanese corporate interests. Several individuals and owner-ship groups own and operate more than one team. Minor league teams owned by major league teams tend to be at the lower levels. For example, major league teams own eleven of the fourteen A-level Florida State League teams and several of the Rookie-level Appalachian League teams.

To ensure financial stability of franchises, the Professional Baseball Agreement imposes formal requirements on new owners. It requires that they demonstrate "financial viability" by possessing, and having the ability to maintain, an equity-to-liabilities ratio of at least 55 to 45 and "a ratio of current assets to current liabilities of at least 1.0 after any injection of new capital by the new owner." New owners also are required to submit to the league a three-year operating budget and business plan for the franchise.

The PBA also requires that the franchise "be owned and/or managed by individuals with strong ties to the local community" and that new owners have "a strong interest in maintaining the stability of the fran-chise in its existing location." Any intent to relocate a franchise after a purchase must be revealed to the league.

The Player Development Contract

A standard Player Development Contract (PDC) is negotiated between the National Association and the major leagues as part of the Profes-sional Baseball Agreement. The PDC details the relationship (or "working agreement") between the major league teams and their minor league affiliates. Although there are slight variations between league levels, the PDC applies uniformly to all minor league teams. No PDC can be negotiated individually by a team owner or modified by a major league team or minor league team. The 1991 PBA limits PDCs to either a two- or four-year term. No PDC is permitted to extend beyond 1997, the year the PBA is scheduled to expire.

In nearly all cases, major league teams provide their minor league affiliates with players. It is possible, however, for a minor league fran-chise owner to operate without a PDC. This occurs only in A-level and Rookie-level leagues. In such instances, owners will stock their team with players from a number of major league teams or sign their own players, including foreign players (e.g., Japanese). These teams are referred to as cooperatives in the former case and independent clubs in the latter case. It is difficult to operate profitably as a cooperative club or as an independent club because the owner must cover a significantly higher percentage of the team's expenses and because the quality of the team's players is not likely to be as high as that of the teams with which it competes. In 1991, Salinas (California) and Salt Lake City (Utah) operated as independent clubs; Bend (Oregon), Erie (Pennsylvania), Miami (Florida), Pocatello (Idaho), and Reno (Nevada) operated as cooperative clubs.

The PDC that expired in 1990 obligated the major league team to supply the minor league team with a minimum number of players, coaches, and a manager; a certain amount of equipment, including bats (twenty-five dozen), balls (a hundred dozen), and one set of uniforms per year; the players' salaries (AAA teams paid $200 of each player's salary); and a portion (ranging from $3.25 to $8.00 daily per player, depending on the league level) of the players' meal money when they play away games.[4] In other words, the PDC covered a significant portion of the minor league organization's labor expenses as well as a good percentage of its operating expenses. Minor league teams also were compensated for telecasts of major league games into their territory. Compensation ranged from $5,500 at the short-season A level to $25,000 at the AAA level.

The agreement negotiated for 1991–97 significantly changes this financial arrangement. It requires the National Association to pay to Major League Baseball a fee of $750,000 in 1991 and a minimum of $1.50 million in 1992, $1.75 million in 1993, and $2.00 million in 1994. Each minor league team will contribute to these payments on the basis of its net ticket revenue (exclusive of sales and admissions taxes). A percentage formula begins at 5 percent of net ticket revenues and declines to 1 percent as a team's net ticket revenue increases. The base upon which the percentage is determined varies according to league level.[5]

Also lost to the National Association is the $35 fee for each player transaction it had been receiving from Major League Baseball as compensation for maintaining player transaction records. That payment amounted to between $300,000 and $400,000 annually. The fee paid by major league teams for telecasting games into the minor league teams' territories also was eliminated. As a result, the new PBA forces minor league teams and their leagues to assume greater financial responsibility for the National Association's operating expenses.

The new PBA increases the number of people for whom minor league teams must pay travel expenses for away games. Under the previous PDC, AAA teams paid the travel expenses for 20 players, AA teams paid for 19, and lower classifications paid for 18. Under the new agreement, for 1991 and 1992 the respective numbers are 29, 27, and 26 individuals. Teams at all levels will pay for a maximum of 30 people (including the manager, two coaches, and a trainer) beginning in 1993.

The major league clubs, however, are obligated by the new PBA to pay all players' salaries (including those of AAA players) and players' meal money for away games. The major league clubs also must purchase all equipment for the minor league teams. The National Association and its members will also receive nearly $3 million guaranteed over four years from a joint licencing program with Major League Baseball Properties (MLBP), which controls trading card and logo rights. Since this is the estimated value of trading card revenue that minor league teams are capable of generating, some thought it represented no new income. Others believed that MLBP's access to national and international markets would produce much more revenue than individual clubs could produce by themselves.

Minor league team representatives projected that these changes in the PDC would cost minor league teams an estimated $25,000 to $100,000 per season, depending on the league level, how much each club previously invested in equipment, and how the National Association distributes its financial obligations. Whatever the amount, the new PBA and PDC have imposed greater costs on minor league teams.

Team Finances

A minor league team depends on several sources for its revenues. Table I.3 provides a summary of the financial statements of three AAA teams for the 1987 and 1988 seasons. In general, it is difficult to assess the profitability of minor league teams, but it is fair to conclude that although not all teams are profitable, it is possible to make a significant profit operating a minor league franchise.[6]

Revenue sources include the sale of season tickets and luxury boxes (if a stadium has such), outfield fence signs advertising a product or business, advertisements in a team program, and a broadcasting package (and telecasting, in a few cases). These sales take place before the season begins and provide the owner with a pool of cash with which to begin the season's operations. Fence signs can be sold for as much as $5,000. Typically, two dozen or more signs will be on a stadium's outfield fence. Parking revenues also can be appreciable, if a stadium has parking facilities and if a team retains the parking fees.

Another source of revenues is ticket sales during the season. Ticket prices for minor league games in 1989, when the field research for this

Table I.3: Revenues and Expenses for Three AAA Franchises

Columbus Clippers		
Revenue	1988	1987
Ticket sales		
Home games	$ 966,255.00	$ 967,699.00
Play-offs	—	—
Concessions (net income)	526,407.00	596,310.00
Advertising	229,306.00	230,419.00
Investment	53,231.00	97,282.00
Other income	89,200.00	62,572.00
Radio network (net income)	—	—
Parking	125,231.00	129,500.00
Total revenue	1,989,630.00	2,083,782.00
Expenses		
General and administrative	1,254,279.00	1,109,737.00
Team operating	238,468.00	221,213.00
Advertising	26,673.00	20,177.00
Other	116,432.00	67,426.00
Total expenses	1,635,852.00	1,418,553.00
Net income (before taxes)	353,778.00	665,229.00
State and federal taxes[a]	0.00	0.00
Net income	353,778.00	665,229.00

Indianapolis Indians		
Revenue	1988	1987
Ticket Sales		
Home games	$ 759,589.00	$ 627,236.00
Play-offs	51,344.00	33,007.00
Concessions (net income)	389,205.00	356,053.00
Advertising	63,998.00	60,738.00
Investment	74,111.00	35,606.00
Other income	8,883.00	49,288.00
Radio network (net income)	26,376.00	21,751.00
Parking	—	—
Total revenue	1,403,506.00	1,183,679.00
Expenses		
General and administrative	287,513.00	247,070.00
Team operating	142,394.00	128,269.00
Advertising	146,286.00	120,192.00
Other	469,437.00	402,744.00
Total expenses	1,045,630.00	898,275.00

Table I.3 (Continued)

Indianapolis Indians (Continued)		
Net income (before taxes)	356,876.00	285,404.00
State and federal taxes	12,857.00	111,844.00
Net income	228,019.00	173,560.00

Toledo Mud Hens		
Revenue	1988	1987
Net admissions (after league share deduction)	$ 367,858	$ 366,216
Scorebook sales	18,959	20,075
Scorebook advertising	120,300	109,800
Fence advertising	39,200	39,350
Radio and television	93,010	108,035
Concessions	83,989	91,903
Souvenirs	71,137	71,121
Selection rights	24,250	24,250
Miscellaneous	20,372	4,043
Interest and other	29,294	22,477
Total revenue	868,369	875,270
Expenses		
General & administrative	$ 230,530	$ 215,919
Park[b]	134,649	120,280
Stadium rent	36,000	31,000
Team	111,884	96,072
Players' salaries	19,334	18,800
Spring training	4,867	4,161
Publicity and advertising	66,986	60,652
Ticket and advertising Sales commissions	66,247	68,370
Radio broadcast costs	61,851	71,853
Total expenses	732,348	687,107
Excess of revenue over operating expenses	136,021	170,163
Distribution to county	81,613	102,097

[a]The Clippers are a not-for-profit organization, not subject to state and federal corporate income taxes.
[b]Includes depreciation expense of $17,326 (1988) and $12,855 (1987).

study was conducted, ranged from less than $1 to $5. For the 1991 season, ticket prices for some teams had risen to $6 and above. Ticket price increases continued to be announced in 1992, which the team owners attributed to the new PBA.

A park will frequently be "bought out" for a night by a community organization or business, and tickets will be given at no charge or minimal charge to customers, clients, employees, or community residents. This occurs more frequently at the lower-league levels than at the AAA or AA levels. There is a difference of opinion among team operators as to whether giving tickets away in this manner or in other ways devalues the product and hurts attendance in the long run. Some are afraid that if "buy outs" are too frequent, fans will not buy tickets but will wait for the free ones.

High attendance is desirable not only for the ticket revenue, but also for the revenue from the sale of concessions and novelties. The size of concession revenues greatly influences whether a team is profitable. In many cases, concessions account for more than 25 percent of a team's revenues. In some circumstances, tickets can therefore be given away, and a profit will still be realized.

As noted, much of a minor league team's operation is subsidized by its major league affiliate. Estimates are that a major league team expends approximately $600,000 on a PDC (Gammons, 1990: 42). A minor league team's labor expenses are principally for office staff and part-time stadium help (e.g., vendors, ticket takers, and clean-up crews). Many team employees work on a commission basis, earning income from advertising and ticket sales. Travel expenses are a significant portion of a team's operating expenses, as are advertising and promotion expenditures.

The ownership or lease of a stadium is a critical factor in a team's financial equation because many of a team's expenditures, other than rent, are mandated by the PDC. To the extent that the new PBA threatens the profitability of minor league teams, team owners will look to their local government–landlords to improve stadium rental terms, because rent is one of the few expense factors that can be reduced without undermining revenue potential.

Arrangements for a playing facility, therefore, are the crux of the relationship between a local government and a minor league team and are a critical factor in determining a team's profitability. The results of a 1989 International City Management Association (ICMA) survey of communities that hosted minor league teams during the 1988 baseball season provides insight into this relationship (see appendix A).

Stadiums, Leases, and Community-Team Relations

More than 95 percent of the respondents to the 1989 ICMA survey described their stadiums as being publicly owned. In a small number of cases, a team's owner owns the stadium or, more often, in some way has made an investment in the playing facility.

A majority (60.9 percent) of stadiums were built before 1960, but 18.4 percent of the stadiums in the reporting communities were built in the 1980s. In the reporting communities, more stadiums (thirteen) were built between 1983 and 1988 than in any other previous six-year period, with the exception of the 1946–51 period, when sixteen stadiums were constructed, and the 1935–40 period, when thirteen were built. In fact, a total of nine new stadiums opened across the country in 1988, four new stadiums were completed in 1989 (Artiaga, 1989), and three were completed in 1990.

The cost of each of the reporting communities' stadiums built in the 1980s, with one exception, was in excess of $1 million. A majority of the new stadiums cost more than $4 million. If the cost of Buffalo's Pilot Field ($42 million) is excluded, the average cost of these stadiums was $2,987,715.

The stadiums built in the 1980s appear to have been built for teams that were new to the community. Half of the stadiums built between 1980 and 1984 house teams that located in their host communities during that time period. Similarly, 70 percent of the stadiums constructed in the reporting communities since 1984 house teams that located in their communities since then.

Minor league stadium leases tend to be short-term. Of the eighty-eight reporting communities, 72.4 percent had stadium leases of five years or less. Communities that host AAA and AA teams tend to negotiate longer-term leases than do communities with A and Rookie league teams. More than half (55.5 percent) of the former have leases of more than five years compared with 17.5 percent of the latter.

There is no typical minor league stadium lease. Some communities subsidize the cost of operating a stadium for the team (e.g., utilities, water, field maintenance). Other communities seek to recover the stadium's operating costs and impose a rental fee, which is often a flat fee or a percentage of revenues derived from ticket sales.

Communities tend not to share directly in revenues that are produced by minor league teams at the stadiums. Only 19.1 percent (89) reported sharing stadium advertising receipts; 33.0 percent (88) reported sharing concession revenues; and 46.0 percent (37) of those communities whose teams generated parking revenues shared parking fees.

Very few communities, regardless of the league level of their team, reported generating sufficient revenues from professional baseball to cover the operational costs of the stadium. Of those communities that reported operating costs in support of and revenues derived from minor league baseball for the years 1986, 1987, and 1988, the majority reported expenditures in excess of revenues in each year. In 1986, 75.9 percent of the reporting communities experienced a shortfall, as did 74.6 percent in 1987 and 76.1 percent in 1988.

Lease negotiations offer the opportune time for a team to make demands on its host community. Given the short-term leases most cities have, it is not surprising that 75.3 percent of the responding communities reported that their teams had made demands on them within the three years prior to the survey (1986–88). The most frequent demands centered on improved lease terms (49.3 percent) and stadium improvements or stadium expansion (84.5 percent). Increased parking was demanded by 18.9 percent of the teams, and a new stadium was demanded by 15.9 percent of the teams. Operating subsidies were sought by 11.4 percent of the teams.

Sixty-one communities (66.3 percent) reported making stadium renovations since 1980. More than half (54 percent) of these were made between 1987 and 1989. Twenty-three communities (25 percent) reported expanding their stadiums. Of these, 60.9 percent completed expansions between 1987 and 1989.

There is evidence that team demands for stadium improvements are both justified and effective. Communities that reported renovating their stadiums most frequently cited facility deterioration (73 percent) and team demands (68.3 percent) as the reasons renovation was undertaken. Almost 13 percent undertook renovations in an attempt to lure a team at a higher league level. Of those that reported expanding their stadiums, team demands (68.2 percent) and increased attendance (50 percent) were the most frequently cited reasons for expansion, while 31.8 percent enlarged their ball parks as part of their pursuit of a team at a higher league level.

Although team demands were not always accompanied by a threat to relocate, 40 percent of seventy communities that reported being the target of team demands said they were threatened with relocation. Of these communities, 39.3 percent stated that the threat of relocation actually developed into a community issue.

Franchise relocation is a reality in minor league baseball; no league level is immune. Thirty-five franchise relocations (i.e., changes in home territories) occurred between 1987 and 1992 (see Table I.4). A small number of other teams relocated to stadiums in a different jurisdiction but within their home territories (as in the cases of Birmingham and Charlotte). Des Moines, Iowa (AAA); Jackson, Mississippi (AA); Myrtle Beach, South Carolina (A); and Winter Haven, Florida (A) were among cities that have faced relocation threats since 1990. Those franchises remained in place, however. Franchises did relocate from Columbus, Georgia; Riverside, California; Wausau, Wisconsin; and Sumter, South Carolina before the 1991 season. (Sumter, however, was able to obtain an expansion franchise for the 1991 season, which it lost the next year.)

Table I.4: Minor League Franchise Relocations, 1987–92

League Level	1987	1988	1989	1990	1991	1992	Total
AAA	0	1	1	0	0	0	2
AA	2	1	4	0	1	1	9
A	4	6	5	1	3	2	21
Rookie	1	0	0	1	0	1	3
Total	7	8	10	2	4	4	35

The responding communities overwhelmingly asserted that maintaining professional baseball is a priority (86.2 percent) in spite of the financial costs of hosting a minor league team and team demands for additional public expenditures. Respondents reported a general agreement among local government officials that the presence of minor league baseball in their communities is important (83.7 percent). (Several of the communities hosting major league spring training camps volunteered that their minor league team's importance was secondary to that of spring training activities. See the Fort Lauderdale case study.)

A majority (58.9 percent) of the reporting communities were without other professional or college sports activities (i.e., no major league sports, no other minor league sports, no training facilities for major league teams, and no college or university sports). Nearly a third (31.6 percent) of the communities reported being without a community theater, a symphony orchestra, and a zoo. Altogether, 22.1 percent of the reporting communities lacked professional or collegiate sports alternatives and these cultural options. Of these communities, 63.2 percent have a population of less than 50,000. Minor league baseball, therefore, offers many communities, especially smaller communities, a significant entertainment opportunity.

Sullivan (1990) maintains the principal purpose of minor league baseball is to bring the game of organized baseball to small towns. Historically, the minor leagues made baseball the *national* pastime. The place of minor league baseball in the nation's small communities, however, became threatened when the minor leagues declined and local economies weakened. Sullivan (1990) argues that the goal of serving the economic and player development interests of the major leagues has been imposed on the minor leagues and has taken priority over the goal of regional entertainment.

In the 1990s, the ability of small communities to retain their teams continues to be threatened by the economics of minor league baseball. Of the smallest communities in each of the fifteen minor leagues in 1986, five (Old Orchard Beach, Maine—AAA; Glens Falls, New York—AA; Sumter, South Carolina—A; Little Falls, New York—short-season A; and Wytheville, Virginia—Rookie) had lost franchises by 1990. Nearly two-thirds of the franchise relocations between 1987 and 1991 occurred from communities with a population of less than 100,000. The new PBA requires that new and existing facilities meet enhanced facility standards. Existing facilities have until April 1, 1994, to comply with these standards, and any plans for renovations to meet those standards must be reviewed by the Commissioner's Office. This promises to confront communities, especially those in the lower-level leagues, with significant costs that local officials either will not be able to meet or will not be willing to incur.

The Major League–Minor League Nexus

The ability of local officials to determine the degree of risk entailed in investing in a minor league baseball facility is complicated by the fact that minor league baseball's financial health is dependent on major league baseball and by the fact that minor league baseball does not have independent decision-making authority for many issues.

As previously noted, the major league affiliate heavily subsidizes a minor league team's operations. This subsidy was reduced by the new PBA because major league team owners believed that minor league teams had become very profitable businesses at their expense and minor league team owners no longer needed subsidies. Although major league baseball teams appeared to be able to afford such subsidies in 1990 (estimated to be approximately $4 million for each major league team), it is not certain that major league baseball will be so profitable throughout the 1990s. When the 1991 season opened, the major league clubs faced a bill in excess of $270 million as a result of a 1989 arbitration decision concerning collusion, rapidly escalating players' salaries, and unknown expenses for expansion. CBS, the broadcast corporation that signed a $1 billion television contract with Major League Baseball, was seeking to reduce its payments as a result of lower than expected ratings for baseball in 1990. Baseball Commissioner Fay Vincent announced in February 1991 that between eight and ten major league teams lost money in 1990.[7]

If the economic health of major league baseball suffers, the consequences will be felt at the minor league level. A consolidation of a major league team's minor league system would be an obvious way to reduce costs. Each major league team in 1991 was affiliated with at least six minor league teams. The new PBA, however, guarantees only 119 PDCs, or an average of less than five per major league team. Whether a minor league team can be financially viable over the long term without a PDC is debatable.

Another issue is one of control. The new PBA recognizes the right of the commissioner of Major League Baseball to intervene in decisions of the National Association and to reverse a decision if it is deemed to be not in "the best interests of baseball." All proposed franchise sales and transfers must be registered with the commissioner, who in certain instances can reject a sale or transfer. Minor league clubs must submit an audited financial statement to the commissioner upon request. Eighteen months notice must be given to the commissioner if a minor league intends to expand or reduce the number of its teams. The commissioner can overturn the National Association's approval of such expansion or reduction, as he can any approval of a proposed franchise relocation. The commissioner also must approve any grant of protected territory (i.e., home territory) to a minor league club.

It is unclear how this power will be used by the major leagues in the 1990s, but history does not provide reasons to be optimistic. Sullivan (1990) describes the history of the minor leagues as being scarred by the major leagues' successful efforts to keep the minor leagues subordinate. He writes, "The majors have continually made decisions about personnel policies, franchise relocation, expansion and broadcasting that were indifferent or damaging to the minors" (Sullivan, 1990: viii).

Many minor league owners saw the 1990 PBA negotiations as another example of the "greed and animosity" that characterize the attitudes of major league owners toward the minor leagues. One owner suggested in a February 1991 interview that one result of the negotiations is that it will become more difficult for owners to take a long-range view of their operations. Implicit in his analysis is greater instability in franchise ownership and, consequently, in franchise location.

Approvals of franchise relocations will not be withheld at the major league level if such relocations promise improved playing facilities, better player accommodations, or more fans in front of whom to play. In fact, major league clubs are likely to pressure their minor league teams to relocate if they are unable to acquire modern facilities from their host communities. For example, in 1990, the New York Mets gave Norfolk, Virginia, officials an ultimatum to build a $15 million stadium or lose their AAA team, despite a twenty-one-year association between the community, its minor league team, and the Mets; and, a year later, the Mets announced plans to move their Williamsport (AA) franchise to a new stadium in Binghamton, New York, in 1992.

Finally, local officials should be aware that the increased number of televised major league baseball games has an impact on minor league baseball. Minor league baseball's popularity declined after World War II, partly because major league games were televised in the minor leagues' territories (Horowitz, 1974). In 1990, the number of games televised on cable and local stations exceeded 2,700 ("Baseball 1990," 1990: 36). This number will expand in the 1990s as major league clubs further exploit cable television opportunities and other developing broadcast technologies. Local telecasts of major league games decreased by fourteen games from 1989 to 1990, but regional cable telecasts of games increased by seventy-six games to 1,137. This compares with 820 such telecasts in 1985 ("Baseball 1990," 1990: 36).

Conclusion

This analysis makes clear that the governance structure and the economics of minor league baseball are responsible for making stadiums, and the arrangements through which minor league teams occupy them, the essence of the relationship between a team and its host community. The conditions that influence franchises' financial viability and the supply and stability of franchises not only fix attention on stadiums and the terms of their rental but also warn against long-term assumptions about such arrangements.

Limited revenue sources and expenditures mandated by the new PBA focus team owners' attention on stadiums and negotiated lease terms as an obvious means to increase revenues and decrease operating costs.[8] Team owners identify their options as the reduction or elimination of rent, acquisition of a new stadium that will attract more fans and permit more revenue streams, or relocation to a larger market within the region where the league operates. As current owners sell their franchises either to take advantage of inflated value or to avoid the less favorable economics introduced by the new PBA, new owners must seek ways to recoup their investment. These owners justify their stadium demands by citing their large investments in their teams.

The history of the minor leagues is not one of stability. Local officials who understand the history, structure, and economics of minor league baseball, especially of its lower-level leagues, will view skeptically stadium proposals based on assumptions about the long term. The relatively large number of minor league teams does not imply greater franchise availability for cities without teams because minor league teams relocate within specific regions, not nationally as major league teams do. At the same time, the short term of minor league leases suggests the potential for greater franchise instability.

This analysis also suggests why minor league teams are not significant economic forces within communities. In nearly all cases, the economic impact of a minor league team will be minimal, given attendance levels, payroll size, number of employees, media interest, and other factors. The fact is minor league teams have relatively small operating budgets (see Table I.3), especially in the lower-level leagues, and best fit the analogy of a small business. Also, it is reasonable to assume that smaller communities may not be able to capture all of the potential economic benefits that a sports operation produces; leakage (i.e., expending or investing money earned or generated within a local economy beyond local boundaries) is probably greater in communities with minor league teams than in those with major league teams.

This is not to deny that minor league teams contribute to local economies, but it is to warn against expecting them to have the same impact that major league teams have. As the Fort Wayne case study and other case studies in this book demonstrate, local officials must pay careful attention to locational decisions and alternative uses in order to maximize the economic return on minor league stadiums. In essence, a development strategy is necessary to maximize the likelihood that a minor league stadium will play a positive role in local economic development.

NOTES

1. These attendance figures include the Mexican League, which drew 2,743,955 fans in 1990 and 2,419,567 in 1991.

2. Only two of the team representatives who were interviewed disagreed with this description of their business. These team officials, both of whom operate at the AAA level, identified their business as baseball.

3. Many managerial decisions are not made in minor league games for the purpose of winning the contest. From the perspective of the major

league affiliates, who employ and direct the manager, the primary goal of
minor league teams is to develop players for the major leagues. A pitcher
may therefore be left in the game when he is in trouble to give him the
experience of working out of a jam or to test his nerve and composure.

4. Salaries for minor league players are as low as $700 a month for the
playing season. Salaries will be higher for the player progressing through the
development cycle at the AA and AAA levels. The maximum amount paid
to players for meal money for days the club played away from home was
$14.00 (at the AAA level), $6.50 of which the major league club reimbursed
the minor league team. Players at the A level received $11.00 per day for
meals.

5. The percentages of ticket revenue owed to Major League Baseball are
indicated in Table I.5.

Table I.5: Percentage of Team's Ticket Revenue
to Be Paid to Major League Baseball

League Classification	Percentage of Net per Club Ticket Revenue[a]				
	5 Percent	4 Percent	3 Percent	2 Percent	1 Percent
AAA	$0–600,000	6–700,000	7–800,000	8–900,000	900,000+
AA	0–400,000	4–500,000	5–600,000	6–700,000	700,000+
A	0–200,000	2–300,000	3–400,000	4–500,000	500,000+
Short A and Rookie	0–75,000	75–150,000	150–200,000	2–250,000	250,000+

[a]Net ticket revenue paid to clubs (i.e., less sales and admissions taxes and after
reduction for payments based on percentage of ticket sales under leases existing on
November 17, 1990).

6. Rudolph (1988: 39) reported that 75 percent of minor league teams are
profitable operations.

7. Such claims are made periodically, usually in the wake of escalating
salaries. Commissioner Vincent acknowledged that his report lacked credibility for this reason (Hyman, 1991).

8. If a team owner can obtain a modern stadium, the value of that
franchise increases since its revenue potential will be increased. This makes
the sale of the team more likely. The sale of the Birmingham and South
Bend franchises shortly after new stadiums were built provide support for
this hypothesis.

Fort Wayne, Indiana 1

Mark Rosentraub
David Swindell

The justification for bringing any team to a city, including a minor league team to a smaller community, is the anticipated economic impact and benefits of the team. Smaller communities seemingly are mesmerized by the idea "Build it and they will come." In this instance, the "it" is the stadium, and the "they" are fans, businesses, major league glamour, and economic development. Sports, after all, means money for cities, and minor league sports means money and benefits for smaller cities. Or does it?

An Offer Refused

In 1989, a group of investors from the city of Fort Wayne, Indiana, bought a Class A minor league team, the Wausau (Wisconsin) Timbers. They intended to relocate the team to Fort Wayne; however, to do so, they needed a stadium, and they wanted the community to help pay for it. In considering whether to invest in a playing facility, the city of Fort Wayne and community groups in that area had to address a basic question: Would the city of Fort Wayne or the Fort Wayne economy sufficiently benefit from the Timbers' relocation?

The city did not have an appropriate facility for a minor league team when the Fort Wayne owners acquired the Timbers. A long-term solution appeared to be the construction of a new stadium, but the owners wanted to move the team to Fort Wayne within fifteen months. To meet this deadline, the owners and city officials proposed renovating an existing city park and stadium. This facility was located in the midst of Fort Wayne's busiest retail/commercial area, 1.5 miles east of Indiana's largest enclosed mall (with approximately 130 stores) and 4.5 miles south of Indiana's largest outdoor mall (with approximately 75 stores). In addition, the facility was across from the regional campus of Indiana University and Purdue University (which had an enrollment 10,000) and adjacent to Allen County's coliseum (home of a minor league hockey team) and convention center. Although this location would provide the necessary parking, traffic control and congestion in the area were already a major concern to the city and business community.

Plans were developed to renovate the existing facility. The total cost of the project was estimated to be $1,950,201. After considerable discussion, the city of Fort Wayne offered to give the Timbers owners a fifteen-year loan for $1,200,000 (at an interest rate of 6.48 percent). The team would be responsible for repaying the loan and providing the additional $750,201 needed for reconstruction. The team would pay no rent for use of the facility, and the city would assume responsibility for maintaining the stadium.

The mayor of Fort Wayne and the Timbers owners tried to find private groups that would either guarantee the loan or provide the needed $750,201. At least two foundations in Fort Wayne could have provided the funds, guaranteed the loan, or given financial assistance. Several large financial institutions were also approached to help finance the stadium for the Timbers. In the end, however, no financial guarantees could be found from the private sector or from the foundations, and the Timbers owners elected not to move the team to Fort Wayne. Less than twelve months later, the Fort Wayne owners of the Timbers sold the franchise and ended their interest in bringing minor league baseball to Fort Wayne.

Did the city of Fort Wayne make the right decision in offering to provide a loan for a portion of the stadium's total cost and requiring a substantial investment from the team's owners or some other actors in the city? Did the private sector, community groups, and businesses make the right decision in refusing to support construction of the stadium? This study examines the anticipated economic impact of the team and the conditions under which an investment in minor league baseball is feasible for a city similar to Fort Wayne. It then briefly reports developments in 1991–92.

Conceptualizing the Impact of Sports on Local Economies

Determining the economic impact of a baseball team is no different from assessing the influence of any business on a community. The economic impact of baseball can be analyzed or segregated into several different tiers (see Figure 1.1). Any assessment of economic growth resulting from a baseball team's location in a city must consider each tier.

The primary tier involves *new* spending by consumers that results from the team's presence in the community. New spending is not equal to the total spending or economic impact related to the presence of a team. Prior to the existence of a baseball team in any community, people attend concerts and movies, dine out at restaurants, buy books, go to skating rinks, and engage in other leisure activities. Recreational spending occurs whether or not a baseball team exists.

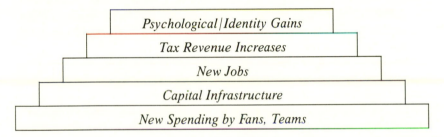

Figure 1.1: The Tiers of the Economic Impact of Minor League Baseball Teams

If a baseball team moves to a community and consumers simply shift their spending patterns from other recreational activities to baseball, there is no *real economic growth;* the presence of the baseball team would merely represent a shift in recreational spending. Estimating the impact of a team without subtracting the transfer of recreational spending from other activities is equivalent to assuming that no recreational activity occurs without the presence of sports in a community.

Similarly, if the presence of a baseball team transfers spending patterns from other activities (e.g., education, food, transportation) to recreational spending, no real growth occurs. Transfers of spending within a community as a result of the presence of a baseball team do represent an impact, but economic impacts do not necessarily imply economic growth.

If transfers within the recreational sector and between the sectors of an economy in a community do not represent economic growth, how does a baseball team increase economic activity? There are four possible ways. First, there is a positive impact if the team attracts recreational spending away from other geographical areas. For example, the host city registers an important economic impact if baseball fans from communities outside of the city that hosts a team come to games instead of attending movies in their communities or elsewhere. This impact is not limited to simple attendance at the game. If fans come from outside of a community to attend a game, they also make ancillary purchases (e.g., food, overnight lodging, souvenirs, and other goods and services). Second, the host city again gains from direct and ancillary spending activities if the presence of a baseball team in a city discourages residents from going elsewhere for baseball games or recreation. Third, visiting teams also bring new economic activity to a community. The economic actions of these teams represent economic growth since the teams would not come to the city if it did not have a baseball team. There is also some small impact from scouts from major league teams who come to games to recruit and evaluate minor league players. Fourth, real economic growth occurs if the presence of a baseball team in a city actually increases overall aggregate spending. This can result from a decrease in consumers' savings or an increase in income through higher levels of productivity.

The second tier of economic growth results from the construction of the playing facility and related transportation improvements. These activities add to the demand for construction workers and create jobs, if only for a short period. There also can be a negative impact from this growth, however. If there is a shortage of construction workers and materials, the construction of the playing facility could increase costs for other businesses seeking these workers.

The third tier of economic benefits includes the creation of permanent and seasonal jobs. Baseball teams, directly and indirectly, employ both full-time workers (e.g., office staff) and part-time or seasonal workers (e.g., players and stadium personnel). These new jobs represent a positive impact on the community, assuming no jobs are eliminated elsewhere in the community because of shifting patterns of recreational consumption.

The fourth tier, which could be subsumed within each of the existing tiers, involves the changes in tax revenues resulting from the team's presence in a community. Spending by fans, players, and others can produce increased sales- and property-tax revenues, increased user fees, and increased income-tax revenues where local income taxes exist. The last tier of benefits involves any psychological gains the community might derive from the presence of a team.

To produce an estimate of the economic growth associated with each tier, a set of standardized procedures can be used. The area served by the baseball team is defined as the "Basic Trade Area (BTA)," which is somewhat larger than the standard metropolitan statistical area (SMSA) defined by the Bureau of the Census. Since the BTA recognizes the dependence of rural or smaller communities on larger urban centers for recreation, transportation, and other services, it is common to use the BTA, not the SMSA, as the geographical area of reference in calculating attendance at games and spending.

After accurate attendance figures are discerned, the next step in calculating economic impact is to apply the attendance figures to project sales figures for in-park and out-of-park spending (primary and secondary-direct, respectively). Secondary spending is further refined into direct and indirect categories. The secondary-direct spending is the money spent directly related to the team's presence in a city (e.g., the money spent for a meal before or after the game). The secondary-indirect spending is inferred from the secondary-direct spending. This indirect spending is the money from direct spending, spent and respent, as it circulates through the local economy before "leaking" out of the community.

This respending can be calculated by applying an appropriate multiplier to the direct spending value. Some studies of minor league baseball have used multipliers of 3.0 or higher (Peck, 1985); other studies of recreational spending have used multipliers of approximately 1.5 (Stough, 1987). A review of regional input-output literature and current practices suggests a multiplier effect of 2.0 is reasonable for this analysis (U.S. Department of Commerce, 1986).

The Economic Impact of Minor League Baseball in Fort Wayne

TIER I BENEFITS: NEW SPENDING

Expenditures by fans, the Timbers baseball team itself, and visiting teams represent potential new economic activity for Fort Wayne. To assess the expenditures by fans, it is first necessary to estimate the number of fans likely to attend games and the proportion of their spending that is likely to be new economic activity for Fort Wayne. These expenditures can then be added to the expenditures of the Timbers and the visiting teams to estimate the impact of the team on the local economy.

ATTENDANCE LEVELS   Estimating attendance levels is important but difficult. The importance of this task lies in its connection to overall spending levels. If attendance levels are inflated, or deflated, the impact on spending or economic change is substantial. Supporters of a team usually prefer larger estimates, while opponents seek lower estimates. Three different techniques were used to establish a valid estimate of the number of fans likely to attend games in Fort Wayne. The initial measure was derived from data provided by the Midwest League (the league in which the Timbers play). The league office provided a complete tabulation of the 1988 attendance for each team in the league, as well as the 1988 win-loss percentage of each team, stadium capacities, and the number of years each team had been in the league.

These data were supplemented with interviews of team owners or general managers to understand each team's operating costs better. Seven of the teams' owners or general managers agreed to be interviewed. Among the data collected during the interviews were the number of persons employed in part-time and full-time positions, the number of season tickets sold in the 1988 season, and current ticket prices. When necessary, the averages for the seven teams were used to estimate league figures.

The data supplied by the Midwest League were used to calculate average game attendance (see Table 1.1). Average per game attendance levels ranged from a high of 2,961 (Peoria) to a low of 789 (Wausau), and a mean of 1,691 for the league. Using the BTA for each team, an average attendance figure per 1,000 population was calculated. This figure was then used to predict that annual attendance in Fort Wayne would be 262,430, the highest in the league. In part, this higher average is a function of the larger BTA that would be served by the Fort Wayne team.

Projecting attendance levels from league averages is sometimes not the best method to use because attendance is affected by many factors. For example, attendance is clearly related to market size, which accounted for 38 percent of the variance in league attendance. Other factors affecting attendance include income, proximity to alternate entertainment outlets, and the performance of the team.

Two other estimates of attendance at the Fort Wayne Timbers games were made. First, an analysis was made of the attendance of two other professional sports teams in Fort Wayne, the Fort Wayne Komets and the Fort Wayne Flames. The Komets are a hockey team with a long history in the International Hockey League. The Flames are a charter member of the American Indoor Soccer Association. In 1988, the Komets average attendance per 1,000 residents of the BTA was 5.23; the corresponding figure for the Flames was 5.06. Given the popularity of baseball, the Timbers might be expected to draw as well as the Komets. Using 5.23 as the average attendance per 1,000 residents of the BTA would yield a

Table 1.1: Projected Attendance for
a Fort Wayne Baseball Team

	Total Attendance	Average per Game	BTA Population (in 000s)	Average Attendance per 1,000
Team				
Appleton Foxes	85,310	1,219	390.6	3.12
Beloit Brewers	96,616	1,380	211.5	6.53
Burlington Braves	78,308	1,119	147.2	7.60
Cedar Rapids Reds	166,121	2,373	246.2	9.64
Clinton Giants	127,251	1,818	158.4	11.48
Kenosha Twins	64,285	918	292.3	3.14
Madison Muskies	88,343	1,262	578.2	2.18
Peoria Chiefs	207,294	2,961	477.8	6.20
Quad City Angels	115,459	1,649	446.9	3.69
Rockford Expos	158,674	2,267	415.7	5.45
South Bend White Sox	171,144	2,449	325.1	7.53
Springfield Cardinals	155,413	2,220	262.8	8.45
Waterloo Diamonds	87,819	1,254	272.1	4.61
Wausau Timbers	55,255	789	222.6	3.55
Midwest League	1,657,595	1,691	317.7	5.79
Fort Wayne Projection	262,430	3,749	647.5	5.79

projected attendance of 3,386 per game, or 237,020 people for a seventy-game season.

Second, a survey was conducted of randomly selected households in Fort Wayne to determine how many people would attend games if baseball tickets were priced at $2.50. Based on survey responses, the projected attendance was 191,000 from Allen County, which includes Fort Wayne and is about half of the BTA. Although that figure cannot be projected across the counties in the region because of differential costs of attendance (travel) and lower incomes in the areas surrounding Fort Wayne, the survey data indicate that an attendance level of 225,000 to 240,000 people could be expected.

An estimate of an annual attendance of 235,000 will be used for the balance of this analysis. Since it is reasonable to expect that attendance in the first year will be higher than subsequent years because residents of Fort Wayne and the region will be attracted to the "newness" of minor league baseball, an adjustment for this "honeymoon" period will be made in the assessment of the team's economic impact for one year.

EXPENDITURES BY FANS Calculating revenue from ticket sales must account for variations in prices at the gate and promotions. The owners of the Timbers were planning to charge $2.50 as an average ticket price, but clearly that average was not sustained anywhere else in the league because of the number of promotions. The league's adjusted price per ticket (including promotions) was estimated to be $0.81 (Peck, 1985). For this analysis (see Table 1.2), an average of $1.00 to $1.25 was used, meaning ticket revenue would be anywhere from $235,000 to $293,750. It seems prudent to expect ticket revenues to produce approximately $265,000.

Spending at the stadium on such items as food, beverages, and souvenirs was estimated to be $1.58 per fan by the consulting firm retained by the city of Fort Wayne. This figure also was accepted as valid by the Timbers owners (William L. Haralson and Associates, 1988). If 235,000 fans came to games, $371,300 would be spent within the stadium. Total revenues at the stadium, then, could be expected to be $636,300 each season.

Two central questions need to be addressed in considering this figure. First, how much of this money is likely to originate from outside the city of Fort Wayne and therefore represent potential real growth? Second, how much of the money from Fort Wayne residents is simply a reallocation of funds from existing recreational spending, and how much represents new economic growth?

Some measure of the extent to which Fort Wayne already attracts recreational dollars from residents of surrounding counties is necessary to answer the first question. Fort Wayne, as the central service city in a BTA of 647,000 people, already expects to receive a great deal of revenue from residents outside of the city. Virtually all movie theaters, plays, shows, and concerts in the region are staged or located in Fort Wayne.

A survey of cars was performed at one of Fort Wayne's movie theater complexes to estimate the proportion of recreational consumption in Fort Wayne that comes from residents who do not live in the county. It is relatively easy to ascertain where consumers live because Indiana license plates designate the county of residence. A survey of more than five hundred cars at the theater complex indicated that 55.6 percent were from inside the county in which Fort Wayne is located, and 44.6 percent were from other counties. In other words, Fort Wayne's recreational economy is already based on extensive participation by nonresidents of the area.

Using this ratio, it is estimated that $283,790 of the $636,000 projected in-stadium spending would come from nonresidents. For baseball to

Table 1.2: Economic Impact of the Fort Wayne Timbers
(excluding construction of new stadium)

Revenue Source	Total Impact	New Revenue Estimate		Local Gov't Income	
		11.9%	27.3%	11.9%	27.3%
Fans' Spending					
Ticket sales	$ 265,000	$ 31,535	$ 72,345	$ 315	$ 726
In stadium[a]	371,300	44,185	101,365	442	1,017
Outside stadium[b]	1,880,000	223,720	513,240	4,027[c]	9,273
"1st year"	315,230	37,512	86,058	771	1,976
	2,831,530	336,952	773,008	5,555	12,992
Timbers' Spending					
Players' salaries	316,000[d]	158,000	158,000	316	316
Jobs created	200,000	200,000	200,000	400	400
Operations	100,000	11,900	27,300	71	164
	616,000	369,900	385,300	787	880
Visiting Teams	178,500	178,500	178,500	4,356[e]	4,356
Parking Revenues				100,000	100,000
Total Spending	3,626,030	885,352	1,336,808	110,698	118,228
Total Spending with Multiplier of 2	$7,252,060	$1,770,704	$2,673,616	$121,396[f]	$136,456[f]

[a]Includes advertising revenues.
[b]Includes parking fees.
[c]Assumes 20 percent of expenses subject to 5 percent hotel tax; 80 percent of expenditures subject to 1 percent food and beverage tax.
[d]Players' salaries, while paid by the Major League Affiliate, do have a direct impact on the Fort Wayne economy.
[e]Assumes half of the expenditures subject to 5 percent hotel tax; half of the expenditures subject to 1 percent food and beverage tax.
[f]Multiplier not applied to direct local government income from parking, but is included in calculation of additional income and sales tax dollars through the new revenue columns.

bring additional revenue to the city, the proportion of nonresidents attending games would have to exceed 44.6 percent since that is what Fort Wayne's economy already experiences. Could the Timbers exceed this ratio?

South Bend's minor league team's officials believe only 20 percent of their attendees are from outside the region. The Indianapolis Indians, a

AAA team, have found that 60 percent of the fans at their games are not from Indianapolis. If Fort Wayne replicated Indianapolis's success, 15.4 percent of the fans' expenditures in the stadium and for tickets would be new income for the city's economy. If Fort Wayne's experience approximated South Bend's, the city's economy would realize no new economic gain from increased recreational spending by people outside the county.

To address the second point—how much of the funds spent by Fort Wayne residents is a reallocation of existing recreational dollars—one assumption was made, and a survey was performed of baseball fans' attendance patterns. The assumption involves households' marginal propensity to consume and their demand for recreation. With savings' rates no higher in Fort Wayne than in other parts of the country, it was assumed that consumer spending is unlikely to increase simply for another recreational activity. People will certainly go to games, but with spending levels in excess of 95 percent of income, it is unreasonable to expect reduced savings or the assumption of debt simply to attend minor league baseball games.

This assumption does allow for a redirection of recreational dollars as a result of the presence of the team. Baseball fans in Fort Wayne might travel to Indianapolis, South Bend, Chicago, or Cincinnati to see baseball games in the absence of a team in Fort Wayne. A survey of 786 randomly selected households found that 39.9 percent (314) of the households had made a trip to another city to attend a sporting event. This attendance represents a loss for Fort Wayne's economy. If these people elected to stay in Fort Wayne to see baseball games instead of making a trip, new economic growth would be generated.

The respondents who indicated they did make trips to other cities for sporting events were asked if they would reduce their trips if a team were in Fort Wayne. A total of forty respondents, 12.7 percent of the group who went to out-of-town games, indicated they would cancel some of their trips if a team were located in Fort Wayne. These forty respondents represent 5.1 percent of the total sample.

If this group actually cancelled 50 percent of their out-of-town trips and attended seven games in Fort Wayne with at least two people at each game, and if the patterns of their spending were projected to all households in the county, then this group would account for 28,000 of the tickets purchased. In terms of economic activity generated by the team, this analysis suggests 11.9 percent would be deflected from losses to other counties and, at a maximum, 15.4 percent of the revenues generated would be from new spending from outside the community.

At a maximum, therefore, 27.3 percent of the revenues resulting from the baseball team represent new growth for the Fort Wayne economy.

Put another way, at least 72.7 percent of the recreational spending by fans attending baseball games would be a simple redistribution of recreational dollars within the Fort Wayne economy.

In terms of the first tier of benefits, therefore, it is estimated that a total of $636,300 would be spent by fans at the stadium. To these expenditures is added an estimate of $8.00 per fan for expenditures outside of the playing facility. This estimate was taken from surveys of fans attending minor league games in Illinois and Denver (Peck, 1985) and adjusted for inflation. Total fan expenditures are estimated to be $2,831,530, of which no more than $773,008 would be new growth for the Fort Wayne economy. The real gain, however, would be less than $336,952 if Fort Wayne was only as successful as South Bend in attracting out-of-town fans, since that city reported less out-of-town attendance than Fort Wayne's recreational sector already enjoys.

EXPENDITURES BY THE FORT WAYNE TIMBERS The expenditures by the team itself also add to the local economy. In addition to the creation of jobs, there are income payments to the players. A portion of this money would be spent in the city, but some would be spent elsewhere, because the players probably would not live in Fort Wayne for the entire year. Based on the league average, player salaries were estimated to be $316,000. Of this money, it seems reasonable to assume that approximately 50 percent would be spent in the city for living expenses. In addition, teams receive income from their major league affiliates. The average amount received from major league teams was $69,500. These funds were included as income for the team, $100,000 of which would be spent in the city of Fort Wayne for operating expenses.

EXPENDITURES BY VISITING TEAMS Studies by the El Paso Diablos, Sumter Braves, Riverside Red Wave, and the Springfield (Illinois) Economic Development Council were reviewed to estimate the new spending generated by the visiting baseball teams. From these studies, an estimate of $85 per player and team official for each visit was derived to project new spending in Fort Wayne. This produces a total of $178,500 for seventy home games.

TIER II BENEFITS: CAPITAL INFRASTRUCTURE

The Fort Wayne Timbers were to play in an existing field that would be improved to meet the needs of a minor league team. The cost of the improvements, as agreed to by the city and the owners of the Timbers, was $1,950,201. No other construction plans were involved since the existing street and road system was deemed adequate and parking facilities at an adjacent facility (the coliseum) would be used for fans attending the Timbers games.

TIER III BENEFITS: JOBS CREATED

Each team in the Midwest League was surveyed to learn how many full-time-equivalent positions were created. The reports received listed both annual and seasonal employees, and the average number of jobs created by the fourteen teams was reported to be 21.53. These jobs were classified as service industry positions, and in Indiana the average pay for this job classification was $18,500 (U.S. Department of Commerce, 1986). The net impact of the team in terms of job creation was therefore $398,305; however, since most of the jobs with minor league teams are only seasonal or part-time, the dollar impact of the jobs created was valued at only $200,000.

TIER IV BENEFITS: TAX DOLLARS RECEIVED

The ability of any local government to capture the benefits of professional sports is partially a function of the taxing instruments available. The city of Fort Wayne has a property tax, and it also shares in the revenue from a countywide income tax. The city does not have an add-on to the state's sales tax — no city in Indiana is authorized to levy such a tax — but the county does have a 5 percent hotel tax and a 1 percent tax on food and beverages consumed in restaurants. The latter tax is to support the county's coliseum.

With the income and expenditure patterns identified in the previous tiers, the total revenue local governments could expect from the Timbers operation in Fort Wayne is between $21,254 and $42,128. This is based on the .002 percent income tax levied against all new incomes (50 percent for players, because they would not be full year residents), and the 5 percent hotel tax and 1 percent food and beverage tax on expenditures by fans and visiting teams.

There are other sources of income that could accrue to local governments. If the stadium was rented to the team, the city could earn as much as $100,000. The city (or county) could also expect to net an additional $100,000 in parking revenues.

TIER V BENEFITS: PSYCHOLOGICAL/IDENTITY GAINS

The economic impact of sports may pale in comparison with the psychological importance of sports in American society. Indeed, the mayor of Fort Wayne believed a baseball team could help market the city and enhance the city's identity in that people would know the city exists, would know where it is located, and would identify more closely with it.

Noll (1974) and others have argued that investments to attract teams should not be defined in economic terms, but rather in terms of psychological and social gains and losses (DeBare, 1989a, 1989b).

Different actors in Fort Wayne clearly had different perceptions of the value of a Class A minor league baseball team. Surveys of business leaders indicate that major league franchises have little impact on locational decisions (Nunn, 1977). It would not be surprising, then, that decision makers in Fort Wayne were not very attracted to the Timbers. In addition, Fort Wayne leaders, seeing the city as the largest city in the Midwest League, may have believed a Class A team would have underscored the image of Fort Wayne as a minor league community. The city may have believed its long-term image would be better served by trying to attract a AAA team or having no team at all. Because these sentiments are difficult to measure and quantify, they were not included in the fiscal impact analysis.

The Fiscal Realities of the Fort Wayne Timbers

Since the economic impact of the team has been identified for each of the tiers, with the exception of the construction of the stadium, it is now possible to assess elements of the fiscal viability of the team. The total economic impact of the team, without the cost of the stadium, is summarized in Table 1.2. Although the total annual economic impact of the team would have been more than $7 million, the new economic activity generated by the team, using a multiplier of 2, would have been between $1.77 million and $2.67 million. At first blush, then, it might appear that building the stadium as the price of getting the Timbers to move to Fort Wayne would have been a worthwhile investment. But who should have made the investment?

The original proposal to develop an adequate playing field for the Timbers in Fort Wayne required an investment of $1,950,201. The city proposed loaning the team $1,200,000 at 6.48 percent interest and requiring a $750,000 investment from the owners or some other group in the community. At the proposed interest rate, the annual payments to retire the loan in fifteen years would have been $125,282. These costs would have been borne by the owners, assumed by the public sector, or supplied by other actors in the area's economy.

If the owners of the Timbers had assumed the cost of the loan, the $125,282 in loan payments would have had to be added to their other fixed costs. The data in Table 1.2 estimate the Timbers would have spent $300,000 for jobs and operations in Fort Wayne. Other operating costs of the team incurred beyond Fort Wayne's boundaries (e.g., travel and lodging for away games) would have had to be added to this figure. These are estimated conservatively at $50,000. The cost of the stadium and other operating costs would thus have been $475,282. The projected income of the team was approximately $636,000. Although there also was the possibility of income from radio broadcasts, that amount would have been relatively small (Rosentraub, 1977). The estimated profit of the team was therefore $160,718.

The renovations of the stadium would have still required a down payment of $750,000. Without a subsidy from local foundations, local businesses, or government, the Timbers would have had to invest all profits for five years to cover this cost. Because these first-year estimates include a substantial honeymoon impact, it is unlikely that the team could have produced comparable profits in subsequent years. In short, the owners of the Timbers might not have been able to afford to build the stadium.

Notice also that revenues returned to the local government would not have been sufficient to pay for the stadium. As noted, the city of Fort Wayne does not have a local-option sales tax. As a result, its only source of revenue from the team would have come from a local income tax, .002 percent of gross income in 1989, and increases in the property tax. It is very unlikely that the team would have made any changes in property-tax revenues, since the area of town proposed for the stadium was already well developed as Fort Wayne's prime commercial district. An income tax at two-tenths of 1 percent would not have produced enough revenue for a stadium. Parking and rent revenues would, at the very best, have covered capital and renovation costs.

Allen County government does administer a 1 percent food and beverage tax for its sports coliseum and also levies a 5 percent hotel tax. Adding the revenues from these taxes to the income-tax revenues means the most optimistic estimate of new revenue for city and county government would have been slightly more than $100,000. A stadium for the Fort Wayne Timbers would not have been self-sufficient.

Conclusion

Fort Wayne made the right decision in declining to finance the stadium through the public sector. Indeed, the final loan proposal to the team was the very most the city should have offered to the owners of the team. Publicly financing a baseball stadium would have resulted in a very large fiscal loss.

It is difficult to envision the circumstances under which the owners of the Timbers could have accepted the loan from the city to renovate the existing facility. Even optimistic measures of their income suggest they could not afford the costs of operating the team and renovating the stadium. Since the community would not finance the stadium, the owners made a prudent decision in electing not to move to Fort Wayne.

Is minor league baseball for Fort Wayne and similar cities a "tragedy of the commons" issue? In other words, the owners of the Timbers and local government did what was in their own self-interest—neither could afford to build the stadium—and the Fort Wayne economy lost between $4.1 million and $2.7 million. Is this an instance where both acted in their own self-interest and the community lost? The answer to this question is no.

The most favorable projection of the economic gain for the local economy was $4.1 million. While this is a large sum of money, it is not a very substantial portion of the income of the Fort Wayne BTA. The Indiana Business Research Center reported that the total income in the eight counties within the Fort Wayne BTA was $7,299,167,000 in 1985 (Creeth, 1989). If the economic impact of the Fort Wayne Timbers were $2,673,616, this would mean an increase of less than one-half of 1 percent in total income for the area. If the new growth were $1,770,704, the increase in income would be less than one-fourth of 1 percent.

Minor league baseball, at least as represented by the Fort Wayne Timbers, has too small an impact to warrant a substantial level of risk and investment by the public sector. Indeed, the private sector, in refusing to make the needed investments without public sector involvement, implicitly verified what has been spelled out here. Minor league baseball does not make enough money to warrant the investment.

A contrary position could be argued, since new growth would occur if the team located in Fort Wayne. Like other investments, expenditures for minor league baseball in Fort Wayne would generate returns that spread or spill over through the entire economy. The problem is that the benefits diffuse quickly and without any perceptible concentration. No natural constituency develops to support the needed investments.

There is no economic constituency in the public sector because neither the city nor the county would earn a sufficient return to warrant participation. Other actors in the private sector (i.e., business leaders, leaders of the recreation industry, and restaurant and hotel operators) also cannot realize a sufficient enough return to galvanize their political and economic support for an investment in sports.

There are circumstances, however, under which it might have made economic and political sense and might have been possible to galvanize support for the team. As noted, the stadium where the team was to have played was located in Fort Wayne's most intensively developed commer-

cial region. Given existing street traffic patterns, many business leaders
might have opposed locating another activity in such a congested area.
From a traffic perspective, there was no worse place to locate a team.
There was, however, another alternative.

Like other cities, Fort Wayne is striving to keep its downtown center
vibrant. Developing a facility for a team in the downtown area could
have meant that more than a quarter of a million people would have
come to that part of the city each year. This would have represented
very real growth for that part of Fort Wayne. As a result, Fort Wayne
could have had an economic stake in bringing a team to downtown Fort
Wayne.

Locating the team downtown could have enhanced the image of that
part of the city and convinced other businesses to locate in the area or
stay in downtown Fort Wayne. Locating the team in the downtown area
would have concentrated benefits sufficiently to galvanize support for
the team and its needs.

The case of the Fort Wayne Timbers highlights an important point.
Minor league teams in smaller cities may well bring real growth to the
community, but the overall impact of the team is usually so small that an
economic constituency to support the team is difficult to find. Owners
of minor league teams and public officials must appreciate the relatively
small economic impact of minor league sports on local economies and
the difficulty in containing these benefits.

Compared with major cities, Fort Wayne is not a large market. With
an annual income in excess of $7 billion, however, business and local
government leaders could hardly be expected to invest substantial sums
of money in an enterprise that would increase incomes by less than
one-half of 1 percent. Economically and politically, their support would
have to be contingent on a sufficient concentration of the benefits to
make investments economically and politically viable.

Should Fort Wayne and similar cities "just say no" to minor league
teams? If the decision is made on purely economic grounds, they should.
There are, however, circumstances under which the investment would
make sense for a local government, even with the tax structure of cities
and counties in Indiana. First, if team owners are willing to locate where
cities need to increase development and recreation, then minor league
baseball would be a good investment. A second scenario under which
investment in sports would be economically viable is if enough corporate support exists to finance the stadium. Sufficient time is needed to
develop this constituency, but Fort Wayne could not meet a deadline
imposed by the Timbers owners.

Finally, it must be remembered that some have argued economic analyses are not the most important element in considering whether to invest in sports (DeBare, 1989b). If a city or its leadership decides that participation in SportsWorld and the larger fabric of American society is necessary for the city's identity, then perhaps the investment should be made and considered a marketing or development expense. Although the economic impact of a minor league team will never be as large as the impact of numerous other activities, none of those other activities offers the escapism and publicity of sports. If a city hosts a team, it receives some level of publicity in the media each day the team plays.

Given the level of economic data regarding labor, land, capital, and utilities that companies can access (Warren and Rosentraub, 1986), however, it seems difficult to argue that one needs a baseball team to supplement the economic image available from Standard and Poor's, Moody's, and similar sources. It is this actual economic identity, not the sports image of a city, that drives locational decision making by private firms (Schmenner, 1982).

Epilogue

The economic impact analysis for this case was performed in 1989, at the time of the negotiations between the city of Fort Wayne and the owners of the Timbers. Since then, there has been renewed interest in attracting a minor league baseball team to Fort Wayne.

As noted earlier, Fort Wayne is host to an International Hockey League team, the Komets. This team has prospered over the last three years, and in 1992 showed its highest level of attendance. Furthermore, the city became host to a Continental Basketball Association (CBA) basketball team that led the CBA in attendance. An increased interest in professional sports in the area convinced both citizens and governmental officials that the time was right to obtain a baseball team. This sentiment was mirrored in the private sector by the establishment of the Fort Wayne Sports Corporation, a not-for-profit corporation dedicated to bringing more spectator sporting events to Fort Wayne. During the first encounter with a minor league team, the private sector gave lukewarm support to augmenting the city's proposed investment. The new sports corporation worked to increase this support. In early 1992, it appeared the Kenosha Twins would relocate to the Fort Wayne area for the 1993 season. At the time this was written, the only official action impeding the move was final approval by the league's commissioner. To obtain the team, Fort Wayne and Allen County agreed to build a stadium.

As noted in Part I, the new PBA governs the construction of new minor league stadiums. The specifications of the PBA forced the discarding of the original proposal; the new stadium's projected cost increased to between $5.0 and $5.5 million. This large increase in projected costs forced the interested parties to pursue alternative financing sources. Allen County became the lead public institution instead of the city of Fort Wayne. Specifically, responsibility was given to the county's Coliseum Authority. To use the Coliseum Authority as the lead agent in this endeavor, the county agreed to move forward with the renovation of the ball field next to the coliseum. This facility was on land originally owned by the city but now belonging to the county as a result of a land exchange deal. This new county land was then transferred to the coliseum's control.

The first $1.5 million of the facility's renovation is expected to come from the coliseum's unappropriated general funds. The reason behind the land exchanges is that the coliseum would then be able to use its food and beverage tax from activities at the coliseum to finance the stadium. At the time that the initial deal fell through, the county had issued bonds to pay for the expansion of the existing coliseum. Indiana state law provides for a 1 percent food and beverage tax to finance this bond, which will last until two years after the retirement of that debt (approximately 2017). Furthermore, revenues from this tax can be used for renovating additional coliseum facilities. Given that the ballpark is adjacent to the coliseum, proponents planned on using these revenues for approximately $2.5 million of the total costs of renovation. A lawsuit was promptly filed challenging this arrangement.

Finally, the city of Fort Wayne and the county have entered into an intergovernmental agreement. Under this agreement, the city has pledged $2.2 million for the renovation effort. This money is to come from the same source as the original offer by the city to the Timbers. Under this agreement, the county will repay this loan through the Fort Wayne Sports Corporation. The corporation is soliciting local businesses and other private interests for contributions.

In summary, the city's role has been scaled back, though it is supporting a loan to the county. The economic benefits will still be very small. There will be no tax increases, but public money is being spent on a private endeavor.

Is this decision right? On the economic side, the answer remains no, for all of the original reasons. Moreover, the county is now in the position of having no choice except to locate the stadium in an overdeveloped area, which promises to strain the local infrastructure and ignores area-wide development plans. There will be an increase in the number of jobs at the coliseum, however. The coliseum does have a staff already trained and experienced in dealing with professional sports. Locating the stadium next to the coliseum may allow the county to tap its food and beverage tax revenues while not interfering with repayment of the bonds for the coliseum's earlier renovations. The city has acknowledged there will be no significant economic benefit from the stadium and the team on the local economy. Instead, the local governments are focusing on the nonquantifiable character of the analysis we performed: the psychological benefits.

In conclusion, to get A-level minor league baseball, which the city acknowledges will have no significant economic impact, a plan has been developed to permit the coliseum to annex land and use existing taxes to improve the stadium. This has the effect of ensuring no public referendum or hearing to learn if citizens want to use public funds for the team. In addition, while thwarting public participation, the city also forfeits its ability to locate the stadium where it is needed (downtown) and requires its placement exactly where it is not needed. In the end, it remains for city councils and voters to decide if the "boys of summer" really define a community's image, culture, quality of life, and place in the fabric of American society, or if a minor league baseball team is simply an example of "big boys wanting big toys" at someone else's expense.

NOTE

This case study was adapted from Mark Rosentraub and David Swindell, "Just Say No? The Economic and Political Realities of a Small City's Investment in Minor League Baseball," *Economic Development Quarterly* 5 (May 1991). Used by permission of Sage Publications, Inc.

PART II

Development Planning, Sports Strategies, and Minor League Baseball

In recent years, scholars and practitioners have written a great deal about urban decline and public management within the context of limited resources. These commentators insist that local officials must have well-defined goals and a preconceived strategy for achieving those goals if they are to engage in successful economic development activities (Blakely, 1989; Fosler, 1988).

There are many obstacles that can sabotage the planning process, and many requirements must be fulfilled to successfully implement the adopted plans. The capacity for undertaking planning and the political will to implement a plan are necessary to develop a plan that will guide successful economic development. The planning effort must have the support of the city's top officials and key community leaders. One or more of these individuals must serve as the champion or policy entrepreneur of the plan.

At the same time, consideration must be given to the role the public will be expected to play in the policy formulation and implementation stages. Those in charge of the planning process often view public participation as an obstacle to efficiency and clarity, but public participation provides the necessary legitimacy for the plan.

Large as well as small communities find it difficult to tap the necessary resources for successful planning in the face of other pressing needs. Small communities, in particular, may lack the expertise to develop and implement a strategic plan. In fact, Bryson and Roering (1988: 995) assert that "normal expectations have to be that most efforts to produce fundamental decisions and actions in government through strategic planning will not succeed."

The political reality of local government favors incremental decision making and short-term solutions as opposed to rational, comprehensive decision making and long-range thinking (Yates, 1977). Levy (1990) found, for example, that local economic development practitioners devote most of their time to sales activities as opposed to planning activities implied by the "rational model" and that local economic development activity is divorced from the community planning process.

Nevertheless, commentators are insistent that development efforts have greater likelihood of success if they are products of a planning process. The analysis of Blakely (1989) is typical and can serve as the foundation for this discussion of planning and local economic development.

Blakely begins with the assumption that a community's economic destiny is a major component of its political agenda. Development is desirable to stabilize local economies and to provide civic services for local residents. Communities, especially those that have experienced a loss of jobs and general economic decline, increasingly are insecure about their economic future. Economic decline is a result of many factors, several of which are beyond the control of local governments.

Blakely insists, however, that in response to pressures fostering decline, cities must take the initiative to build economies that are competitive. Cities must take control; they cannot be passive. The failure to adopt some type of policy is either wildly optimistic or foolish. The question is not whether to act but what action should be taken.

A strategic plan is a step toward a specific set of goals; it is not the end in itself. Strategic planning forecasts the emerging nature of a jurisdiction's environment, identifies future jurisdictional goals, assesses available resources, and produces a plan whereby identified goals can be met within a changing environment with available resources (Olsen and Eadie, 1982: 14). Actions based on the plan are steps taken that will determine whether or not the plan's goals are achieved. They are not the strategy. Although in reality it is difficult to distinguish between strategies and tactics, conceptually the former are concerned with broad, long-range issues, and the latter are narrower and more concerned with short-term, programmatic operations. Strategies link programs and projects to goals.

Constructing a stadium to acquire or retain a sports team will be highly visible and may appear to be a bold action that constitutes a community's attempt to launch an economic development effort. If such action is taken apart from an overall strategy or a specific development logic, however, it is not in keeping with the precepts noted above.

Instead, if an overall plan exists, a stadium project should be conceptualized as one part of that plan and designed to achieve one or more specific goals of the plan. If it is acknowledged that minor league baseball has relatively little economic impact, the acquisition or retention of a minor league team will not be significant in and of itself. It will be significant strategically only when conceptualized as a means to a specific goal. This is true in larger communities, where a team's impact will be little recognized, as well as in smaller communities, where a minor league team may attract attention but will not be able to bring about significant economic growth or change solely by its presence.

The three cases in this section address the issue of thinking strategically about sports. They illustrate different approaches to developing a "sports strategy," the different goals that communities may select for minor league baseball franchises, and the different organizational arrangements and processes that are employed to pursue sports franchises.

Developing a "Sports Strategy"

When the Baltimore Colts of the National Football League relocated to Indianapolis in 1984, much credit was given to the fact that Indianapolis had implemented a "sports strategy." It was emphasized in Maryland that no strategic considerations had been given to sports as an economic development tool. In fact, following the logic of the preceding discussion, it is more accurate to state that Indianapolis had identified specific goals and had in place a strategy that gave a role to sports in pursuing those goals.

Indianapolis provides an excellent example of a strategic planning process carried out successfully. James Owen's analysis in this section reminds us that although community leaders recognized sports' potential as a tool of economic development, it was only one of several used to achieve agreed upon development goals. In fact, the "sports strategy" of Indianapolis emphasized amateur sports, not professional team sports. The relocation of the Colts was a bonus, but it was not a critical element in the success of the Hoosier Dome (indeed, a nonsports rationale had been developed for its expansion) or in achieving the city's goals. Indianapolis's planning paid virtually no attention to minor league baseball, which was a long-standing institution in the city.

Few other communities have been able to imitate Indianapolis's approach to strategic planning and the incorporation of sports into a strategic plan. Columbus, Ohio, and Colorado Springs, Colorado, have not-for-profit corporations working to pursue sports opportunities, but they lack a comprehensive sports strategy. Most jurisdictions mobilize in response to opportunities to attract sports teams and events or to threats to those teams and events as they arise. This reactive mode proves to be costly to communities, as the case studies in this book demonstrate.

For example, the city of Buffalo, which has a colorful history of pursuing major league sports franchises over the past four decades (Foschio, 1976), has no comprehensive strategy for using sports as a development tool. Major league franchises are pursued for the sake of having major league franchises. The city has been and is being whipsawed by its major league franchise owners, as James Milroy describes later in this section. The influence and energy of Mayor Griffin and Bob Rich, a local businessman and sports entrepreneur, brought minor league baseball to the city's agenda as a means for obtaining a major league franchise.

Buffalo invested heavily in a stadium for its minor league team as its primary means of pursuing a major league franchise. Milroy's analysis, however, suggests that Buffalo is in less control of its sports agenda than Indianapolis is. Buffalo's major league football and hockey team owners demand that the same process and a similar state-local partnership that made the minor league stadium a reality be implemented to provide them with new facilities.

Both cities, using different criteria, claim to have used sports successfully. Indianapolis's strategy generally is viewed as having stimulated economic activity and having created a positive image for the city. Buffalo's baseball stadium is a model minor league stadium that can be converted into a stadium for a major league baseball team. It is located downtown, poised to assist downtown revitalization. Milroy also suggests that the city and the team have the common goal of luring Canadians to Buffalo. The team has proven remarkably successful, leading all minor league teams in attendance and topping several major league teams' attendance figures as well.

There have been political costs in each city, however. Owen notes Indianapolis Mayor William Hudnut's wariness about future investment in sports facilities (i.e., a reluctance to build a baseball stadium without a major league commitment), thereby leaving the city's minor league team in limbo. Owen and Milroy note there are increasing demands that public investment be directed to the cities' neighborhoods rather than to the downtowns. Buffalo's stadium saga was fraught with political controversy and failed to win a major league expansion franchise for the city. Will the community continue to support minor league baseball if there is no hope of attracting a major league franchise? If the community does not, will the stadium's costs (more than $800,000 in annual debt service) be tolerated by the taxpayers?

The case of Frederick, Maryland, provides an example of a smaller community's desire for minor league baseball apart from any major league aspirations. Local officials viewed acquisition of a team as a means to develop Frederick into a destination city. The city's success in obtaining a franchise was partly a result of a fortuitous set of circumstances—an aggressive mayor willing to act as entrepreneur, an ideal fit and perfect timing with a major league team's marketing and organizational plans, and the availability of a stadium site.

More important, the city's success was made possible by the state government's acceptance of sports as an economic asset. The state of Maryland has an agency to help local governments attract sports events and franchises, but it is heavily dependent on the incumbent governor and his control of funds. Maryland's governor, William Donald Schaefer, learned much about professional sports and the perfidy of team owners during his four terms as mayor of Baltimore. During his tenure as mayor, he came to believe in the value of sports franchises to local economies. The case of Frederick demonstrates the importance of having a state government prepared and willing to assist a local government with the "sports issue."

No other state in the sample of case study communities is as focused on sports as Maryland is. Generally, states have adopted the attitude that sport is a local issue. Nevertheless, communities were successful in obtaining state aid in a majority of the case studies in this book. The means by which they did so raise serious political, budgetary, and ethical questions. For example, in their bid for state assistance, Indianapolis officials claimed the Hoosier Dome would accommodate professional baseball, but in fact, professional baseball will never be played in that facility. In states where more than one community hosts a franchise, state subsidy of one city can create future demands from others and can prove to be divisive, as has been the case in California, Missouri, New York, Ohio, and Pennsylvania regarding major league sports.

In sum, Indianapolis has pursued a "sports strategy" as part of a larger economic development strategy, but it has virtually ignored minor league baseball. This suggests the minimal economic importance of minor league baseball in a large community. However, the city of Buffalo, another large community, has attempted to exploit minor league baseball and a new stadium for the primary goal of obtaining a major league franchise. Promoting downtown redevelopment is a secondary goal. In the case of Frederick, a small community built a stadium and acquired a minor league team as part of a plan to become a destination city and as a result of the willingness of the state government to invest in sport as a development tool.

These three cases, in addition to providing contrasting approaches to sport and planning, serve to introduce other themes as well. The need for partners—especially intergovernmental partners—is one that recurs throughout the book. The importance of policy entrepreneurs, especially aggressive mayors, is seen in these cases and those that follow. Also, each of the three cases reflects the value of having local citizens own and operate the minor league franchises, but the role of the general public is less clear. Finally, they remind us that cities of all sizes, large and small, make public investments in minor league teams and their stadiums.

Indianapolis, Indiana 2

C. James Owen

Contemporary Indianapolis watchers immediately are attracted to the changing downtown skyline that features, among other developments of the 1980s, a new thirty-eight-story American United Life office tower, a 300,000-square-foot convention center, four modern hotels, and a 60,000-seat, domed athletic facility (home of the National Football League Colts). These physical amenities provide dramatic evidence of Indianapolis's emergence as a major midwestern city, earning it the *Wall Street Journal*'s designation as "Star of the Snowbelt" in 1982.[1]

After a long period of conservatism and a declining "frostbelt" economy, Indianapolis is widely recognized as a host city for international athletic competitions, a hub for national conventions and tourism, and a regional center for commerce, finance, entertainment, and culture. Indianapolis's emergence as a major American city can be attributed partly to community leaders' success in incorporating the sports industry as an integral element in the city's economic revitalization effort.

The Indianapolis experience contains a number of unusual characteristics that make it questionable as a model to be replicated elsewhere, however. Few cities have developed a more deliberate and ambitious strategy to incorporate athletic enterprise into their community development plans. Indianapolis also has an unusual system of consolidated city and county government that was very instrumental in the success achieved. Unigov, as the unified government arrangement in Indianapolis is called, combines city and county jurisdictions and places strong mayoral authority in the combined city-county executive office of the mayor. Additionally, the city has been the beneficiary of unrivaled financial support from one of the nation's largest endowment foundations.

Nevertheless, Indianapolis has more in common with other cities, especially the Midwest's "frostbelt" cities, than it has differences. What it shares most with other cities is a declining industrial-based economy, corresponding unemployment problems, a diminished revenue base, and a downtown in need of revitalization.

This case study is organized into four parts, beginning with an examination of the process of developing community goals and incorporating sports activities as a major strategy for goal attainment. A second section deals with the formal adoption of the community goals into the city's general plan and the role that private-public partnership played in implementing the goals. The third section focuses on the role of professional baseball in the overall sports strategy. A fourth section examines the policy dilemma that has emerged as a consequence of the city's commitment to subsidize sports development as an economic development tool.

Developing an Urban Policy

The new economic development plan for Indianapolis was developed in two general stages: first, a formulation stage, wherein community leadership in the private sector developed an informal agenda of five basic community goals; and second, a more formalized adoption and implementation stage, where the public sector took the lead in setting the goals and choosing the strategy for their attainment. The development of an athletic infrastructure and the promotion of sports activities (especially amateur sports) was a deliberate strategy pursued throughout these deliberations.

FORMULATING COMMUNITY GOALS

Indianapolis, as a major manufacturing city located near the center of the American Midwest, experienced many of the same plant closings, depressing conditions of unemployment, and general economic decline that imperiled most "rustbelt" cities in the 1970s. A group of civic notables (Policy Group[2]), realizing that the city would not survive its economic malaise and recover with its previous manufacturing base intact, began meeting to discuss a new economic development agenda for the 1980s.

The new urban strategy was formulated in a series of informal meetings of key community leaders conducted over a period of two years— 1976–78. The meetings, which involved approximately twenty-five people, varied in attendance as some participants dropped out and new members were added. The group had no formal legal standing. There was no set agenda, and no minutes were kept. Some funding was provided by the Lilly Endowment Foundation, Inc., and staff support was provided by the mayor's office when requested.

The most obvious characteristic of the Policy Group was its blue-ribbon composition. While different participants were involved over time and with changing issues, membership was representative of top government officials, the city's largest business and manufacturing firms, real estate developers, the Chamber of Commerce, and the major foundations and trusts. In effect, most of the community leaders who could make things happen, once plans were agreed to, were involved in the early deliberations.

The most perplexing challenge facing the community leaders had to do with establishing a community image. It was not that Indianapolis had a negative image; it had no reputation at all. Thousands of travelers daily crossed through or over Indianapolis because of its central geographic location, but few found reason to stop. There was wide agreement that the city needed to develop a focus to exploit its air, highway, and rail transportation advantages. As Mayor Hudnut described it, "Indianapolis needed a plan that would make it a destination city instead of a pass through city" (Hudnut and Keene, 1987: 174).

The goals that emerged were a distillation of a number of ideas that were designed to make the downtown area a regional center for commerce, finance, government, and convention-tourism activity. Five goals eventually emerged from the Policy Group as the strategic goals for the coming decades. Three members of the Policy Group later recalled that the areas most consistently targeted for development were (1) amateur sports, (2) convention and tourism, (3) culture and arts, (4) education research, and (5) health and medical science technology (Frensen, 1989).

A similar statement of goals, which substantiate the memories of the Policy Group interviewees, appeared in the president's address at the 1982 annual meeting of the Lilly Endowment Foundation, Inc. That address outlined five areas of the foundation's commitment: cultural achievement, educational resources, health sciences, agriculture, and athletics (Lake, 1982: 12–15).

Three of these community goals evolved as consensus issues of highest priority for government: amateur sports, convention and tourism, and culture and arts. Projects relating to these objectives were to be established in the square-mile area delineating the city's central business district, which was already a center for government, finance, and insurance services. The remaining topics continued to be pursued, but, as nonmunicipal functions,[3] they were sought outside of the city government framework.

SECURING GOALS: A PUBLIC–PRIVATE PARTNERSHIP

The city proceeded to develop a formal plan to incorporate the Policy Group's goals into its development focus for the downtown square-mile area shortly after the Policy Group concluded its work. Although the ideas incorporated into the city's plan for the 1980s were formulated by a select group of community leaders, the plan was adopted on a far broader base. The plan, published in 1981, was the product of a private-public partnership, and it incorporated a unique citizen participation process.

The *Regional Center General Plan: Indianapolis—1980-2000* was prepared by a 150-member planning committee of the Greater Indianapolis Progress Committee (GIPC). Founded by then-Mayor John Barton in 1965 as a citizen planning advisory committee, GIPC has advised the city in most major policy decisions, including Unigov's adoption in 1969. GIPC's Regional Center Planning Committee formulated the basic goals and strategies, and the city Department of Metropolitan Development's Division of Planning and Zoning provided professional staff assistance and drew up the published plan for approval by the Metropolitan Development Commission.

The planning committee had a considerably broader-based constituency and adopted a more open discussion process than did the Policy Group, even though many prominent citizens served on the Regional Center Planning Committee and it was cochaired by two distinguished businessmen. The planning committee consisted of 150 mayoral appointees, who served on nine subcommittees over a period of eighteen months. Subcommittee responsibility was to solicit and incorporate broadly based community views into proposals, which were submitted to an executive committee for final revisions and approval.

Indianapolis initiated a (as of then unheard of) citizen involvement process to further broaden community input. A city center was established on Monument Circle as a public meeting place where citizens could visit and learn about what was going on and voice their dreams and concerns for downtown. The city center attracted over 25,000 visitors in its first year, approximately 2,000 of which took time to answer an extensive computer terminal questionnaire.

The stated overall Regional Center goal was to "implement projects and programs which continue the development of the Indianapolis regional center as the physical, social, and economic heart of the city and the state" (*Regional Center General Plan,* 1982: 14). The objective of the recreation and tourism element of the plan was to increase annual attendance at events from the 1981 figure of 2.7 million to 7.5 million by

1990, which was achieved in 1989. Infrastructure developments that were cited as vital to the achievement of these objectives included the completion of the Hoosier Dome (a convention center/multi-purpose sports facility), Union Station (rehabilitated as a festive market place and hotel), and Indiana University's natatorium and Olympic-class track and field facility (*Regional Center General Plan,* 1982: 16). A district designated for amateur sports was strategically placed immediately adjacent to the Indiana University Medical Center, which was in the process of developing one of the nation's foremost sports medicine programs.

Amateur sports, convention and tourism, and cultural activities were adopted formally as part of the Regional Center Plan and were featured as a part of the city's overall strategy to develop Indianapolis as a major regional city (*Regional Center General Plan,* 1982: 16). Capital investments for downtown development focused on the Convention Center and Hoosier Dome complex and expanded to encompass physical development in most of the southwest quadrant of the downtown. Most of this investment was linked to the Convention Center complex, White River State Park, the Amateur Sports district, and the Union Station project to create a critical mass of people and activities. Indianapolis, with the completion of these elements of the Regional Center Plan in 1989, fulfilled a determined strategy to create an "opportunity for recreation, entertainment, and tourism that makes the Regional Center an attraction to 7.5 million people a year" (*Regional Center General Plan,* 1982: v).

Implementation of the Sports Element

The implementation of the sports element of the Regional Center Plan consists of three related dimensions: facilities, sports organizations, and athletic activities. The sports facilities constructed since 1979 are the most visible of these.

From 1974 to 1989, the community of Indianapolis invested $142.8 million in its sports infrastructure (see Table 2.1). All but $16.4 million of this amount was invested between 1979 and 1989. Of the total investment, all but $4.5 million was invested in the downtown square-mile area.

The $16.4 million Market Square Arena (home of the National Basketball Association Pacers and the Indianapolis International Hockey League team) is included in Table 2.1 for two reasons, even though it predates the planning period of the Regional Center Plan. First, it was the first sports facility used to fill a part of the downtown development plan, and it denotes the role that professional sports has played in the city's development. Second, it is strong evidence of the power of the mayor's

Table 2.1: Indianapolis's World-class Sports Facilities

Facility	Year of Completion	Cost in Millions
Market Square Arena	1974	16.4
Indianapolis Sports Center	1979	7.0
Indiana University Natatorium	1982	21.5
Indiana University Track and Field Stadium	1982	5.9
Major Taylor Velodrome	1982	2.5
Hoosier Dome	1984	77.5
William Kuntz Soccer Complex	1987	1.3
Rowing Course at Eagle Creek Park	1987	0.7
Indiana/World Skating Academy	1987	7.0
Renovation of Indianapolis Sports Center (tennis)	1988	3.0
Total		142.8

office to direct the location of a development project. This latter point requires further examination because of its relevance to the subsequent success of the present effort.

In 1973, developers approached then-Mayor Richard Lugar with plans to locate a new basketball arena in an open field on the city's north suburban fringe. The mayor and his planning advisers thought the arena could be better situated as an anchor to development on the east side of the downtown. Mayor Lugar, as the chief executive officer under the unified government arrangement of both the city and the county who had executive authority over countywide planning and redevelopment functions, was able to persuade the developers to build on the downtown redevelopment site. Mayor Lugar's successor, William Hudnut III, also was very successful in using the executive authority of the mayor's office and the countywide jurisdiction of the Department of Metropolitan Development in directing and stimulating growth in the downtown regional center.

The most imposing physical structure and financial investment in the downtown sports infrastructure is the Hoosier Dome—a multipurpose stadium that seats 60,000 football fans and adds 300,000 square feet to the adjacent convention center facility. The multipurpose dimension of

the Hoosier Dome dramatizes the point that the community's investment in sports infrastructure is just one symbiotic element of a complex
matrix of cultural, entertainment, business, and government projects
operating in concert to attract people to the downtown area. The
multipurpose dimension of the Hoosier Dome proved to be politically
expedient in getting legislative approval and an important revenue
generator.

When Indianapolis first approached the state's general assembly to
request a 1 percent food and beverage tax on restaurant and hotel sales
to fund a proposed football stadium bond issue, the request was turned
down. Indianapolis did not yet have an NFL franchise, and Indiana
legislators were hesitant to invest in a speculative venture. When
Indianapolis returned with a revised proposal showing that the stadium
could be configured for baseball and would add 300,000 square feet to
the existing convention center, the new tax was passed.

The Hoosier Dome, in fact, has not been configured for baseball. The
Convention Authority, however, has capitalized on the stadium's multipurpose features to attract a variety of events, including NCAA football
and basketball contests, auto races, tractor pulls, and conventions
(especially religious conventions) to generate more revenue than originally was projected.

The Hoosier Dome benefited from a contribution of $30 million from
local foundations. *Washington Post* writer Neal Peirce described the
Lilly Endowment Foundation's gift of $25 million as "virtually unprece-
dented in the history of philanthropy" (Peirce, 1981). Lilly's contribution
of nearly one-third of the cost of the Hoosier Dome is the preeminent
indicator of the overall contribution that the Lilly and other foundations
and trusts have made to the fulfillment of the Regional Center Plan.
Other notable Lilly contributions include $25.0 million for a new down-
town zoo, $4.7 million toward the renovation of City Market, $1.5
million to build a tennis center, and $5.0 million pledged for the develop-
ment of White River State Park. Other foundations, such as the Krannert
Trust, which contributed $5.0 million to the Hoosier Dome, also have
been involved in numerous projects, many of them promoting cultural
activities and the arts.

PROFESSIONAL VERSUS AMATEUR SPORTS?

There was no detailed strategy specifically delineated for the attraction
of designated sports teams in the Regional Center Plan. The plan exists
as a conceptual framework within which plans to attract professional
and amateur teams are pursued as each opportunity unfolds. This planning flexibility creates some confusion among citizens over which the

city is committed to supporting, amateur sports or professional sports. This question has contemporary relevance for potential investors in any proposed major league baseball franchise. Investors will want to know if Indianapolis will support professional sports or if amateur sports will consume the lion's share of city resources.

Where does the city's commitment lie? The answer is, in effect, in both areas. Amateur and professional sports are pursued with equal excitement and energy, and the city claims to benefit from both enterprises. As then-Mayor Hudnut explained in an interview:

> You can not say that we are exclusively an amateur sports town. We have the Pacers and we have the Colts. And a great deal of the economic development success that we have experienced here in the past five years can be traced indirectly to the Colts. People hear about us and read about us. Friends like to kid me that Eric Dickerson [a popular Colts player] did more to advertise Indianapolis in his first news conference than I did in twelve years as mayor! And, the estimate is that the Colts generate about $30 million in business per year. They estimated at the time of the Pan Am Games that there was an $1.75 million impact. So amateur sports are important too.

Obviously, the former mayor appreciated what professional and amateur sports did for his city. The difference in policy priority given to one or the other is a function of time and politics. Amateur sports is more clearly identified as a long-term and continuous policy commitment for the city. Professional sports franchising is more of an episodic event, where an opportunity for a new team may occur once a decade. It also is politically more expedient to gather community support for a nonprofit amateur sport than to generate support for a profit-oriented professional team. Some of Mayor Hudnut's most vexing political opposition came from opponents who questioned the city's investment in professional sports. This has contributed to a policy dilemma that is considered below.

ATHLETIC ORGANIZATIONS

Public perception of Indianapolis's promotion of amateur athletics tends to focus on such events as the Pan American Games or the Olympic qualifying trials. These are important, but the city's involvement is considerably larger than playing host to athletic events.

There were a number of former "Big Ten" Athletic Conference and Amateur Athletic Union (AAU) athletes on the Policy Group who perceived that no other U.S. city had come forward to claim amateur athletics as its major sports focus and that Indianapolis was in a good position to fill this niche. To provide land-use accommodations and to establish policy procedures to target this market, the city, as previously noted, set aside a prescribed area in its Regional Center Plan for amateur sports and invested nearly $30.0 million in an amateur sports infrastructure. These investments included $5.9 million for a world-class track facility, $0.7 million for an ice skating rink and instructional academy, and $21.5 million for an indoor Olympic-scale swimming and diving facility.

As a result, Indianapolis was, in 1992, the headquarters for nineteen amateur sports organizations, including the AAU, the U.S. Diving Association, and the U.S. Gymnastics Federation (see Table 2.2 for a complete list of amateur sports offices located in Indianapolis as of 1992).

The lead organization in attracting and organizing national and international amateur sports events and coordinating the efforts of the amateur athletic organizations in Indianapolis is the Indiana Sports Corporation (ISC). The ISC, established with seed money from the Lilly Foundation, is a not-for-profit corporation funded from donations and revenues generated by sponsored events.

Sports events dominated Indianapolis's entertainment agenda in the 1980s and were a major factor in advancing the city's image as a major urban center. The challenge for the city is to make its investment a profitable enterprise. This has required an extensive organizational effort on the part of the ISC.

The ISC's success in hosting the 1982 National Sports Festival, the 1986 National Collegiate Athletic Association (NCAA) basketball tournament games, and the 1987 Pan American Games has established a solid foundation for hosting other national and international games. This became especially evident when Indianapolis agreed to host the Pan American Games after Ecuador stepped down as the designated host a scant three years before the games were scheduled to begin.

In addition to establishing an infrastructure and an organizational structure for conducting world-class sports activities, the ISC has demonstrated that the community can mobilize thousands of volunteers to assist in making local arrangements. Over 7,000 volunteers were recruited to help host the National Games, and 37,000 were involved in hosting the Pan American Games. Indianapolis was selected to host the 1992 NCAA Division 1 basketball finals based on the city's investment in sports facilities and this recent evidence of sports enthusiasm. In 1989, the ISC assisted in preparing bids to attract a future NFL Super Bowl and the Olympic games in the year 2004.

Apart from its internal organization and staff capabilities, the ISC's

Table 2.2: Amateur Sports and Fitness Headquarters in Indianapolis, 1992

Organization
Amateur Athletic Union
American College of Sports Medicine
The Athletics Congress (Track and Field)
U.S. Diving Association
U.S. Rowing Association
U.S. Gymnastics Federation
American College of Sports Medicine
World Skating Academy and Research Center
International Baseball Association
International Institute of Sports Science and Medicine
Midwestern Collegiate Conference
National Association of Governors' Councils on Physical Fitness and Sports
National Institute for Fitness and Sport
National Track and Field Hall of Fame
U.S. Army Soldier Physical Fitness School
U.S. Canoe and Kayak Team
U.S. Synchronized Swimming Team
U.S. Water Polo
Little League Baseball Central Regional Headquarters

Source: Indiana Sports Corporation Brochure, 1989, and interviews.

success can be traced to the fact that it has no competition in filling a niche as the umbrella organization for sports enterprise in Indianapolis. The ISC has had little opposition in taking the lead in coordinating amateur sports activities for the entire community.

The Indianapolis Indians: Pride and Ambivalence

The Indianapolis Indians were one of the most successful AAA baseball team in the 1980s. From 1980 to their 1989 championship season, the

Indians won five division pennants and five league titles. For the first time in its 102-year existence (the Indians franchise was originally founded as the Hoosier baseball team in 1887), the Indians operated for an entire decade without threat of financial bankruptcy, which was a perennial condition in previous decades. In fact, the 1991 season was the team's nineteenth straight profitable year.

While the community takes certain pride in the Indians' accomplishments, it has not demonstrated the level of support for baseball that is evident in the public campaigns organized for other sports activities, such as the Colts and the Pan American Games. The Indians seem to be caught up in a curious predicament. In some ways they are taken for granted. Casual baseball supporters seem to think that the Indians always have been and always will be in Indianapolis, so they can put off enjoying them until later. For the 1987–90 period, attendance averaged approximately 4,092 fans per game, or 286,457 fans per season. This ranked the team sixth in attendance in the eight-team American Association, ahead of only Des Moines and Oklahoma City.

There seems to be an increasing sentiment among avid baseball fans to bide their time until Indianapolis gets a major league team. A strong and visible contingent of private sector investors is actively seeking an expansion team. Officially organized as the Indianapolis Arrows, this group is a perennial contender in seeking an expansion franchise at the major league team owners' annual meetings. The attention devoted to these overtures tends to focus baseball interest away from the Indians.

Another factor contributing to fan ambivalence toward the Indians is increased competition for media space and entertainment dollars. The opening of the Colts training camp in midsummer quickly relegates media coverage of a hot minor league pennant race to the back pages of the daily sports section. Competition for sports entertainment dollars was particularly notable during the 1989 AAA world series play-offs, when the Indians were playing before a half-empty, 12,500-seat Bush Stadium while the Colts were playing preseason exhibition games before capacity crowds of over 60,000 people in the Hoosier Dome.

These factors give rise to the question, How does professional baseball fit into the city's overall plans for sports as an economic development strategy?

ORGANIZATION AND OWNERSHIP OF THE FRANCHISE

The Indianapolis Indians baseball franchise is locally owned by individual stockholders and is governed by an elected board of directors. Most of the stockholders and board members reside in Indianapolis. This arrangement was born out of necessity in the fall of 1955, when the

Cleveland Indians, Indianapolis's major league parent team and franchise owner at the time, announced that they intended to end their working agreement with Indianapolis by the end of the year.

Threatened by the prospect of losing the baseball team, two Indianapolis community leaders, Frank E. McKinney, Jr., a bank president, and Robert Kirby, a funeral parlor director and chairman of the Chamber of Commerce Sports Committee, organized a ninety-day community campaign committed to raising $160,000. Stock sold at $10 per share. The campaign raised $205,000 in time to buy out the franchise in January 1956. The Indians have remained a community-owned franchise to the present.

Stockholders have not exhibited the close interest or involvement in running the team that one might expect, given its locally based ownership. Policy decisions have been made by a few interested owners and, most important, the team's general manager, Max Schumacher.[4] The principal reason for this is that the original stock sale was presented more as a community assistance campaign than as a financial investment. Accordingly, many buyers failed to keep track of their stock.

The fact that many stockholders forgot about, or lost, their shares of stock led to a management problem in later years in arranging a quorum of members for the conduct of business. This problem was rectified in 1985 through a reverse stock split, wherein original shareholders were invited to redeem their old certificates for comparable value shares of a new issue. The number of stockholders was reduced considerably, and franchise operations have become more stable and profitable under this restructuring. The board of directors declared the franchise's first dividend of $10 per share in 1987 and followed this with another $10 dividend in 1988, a $12 dividend in 1989, $15 in 1990, $20 in 1991, and $30 in 1992. The team earned profits of $246,670 in 1990 and $351,908 in 1991, which was the team's nineteenth straight profitable year.

Despite management's recent success in establishing financial stability for the Indians, maximizing profits is not the driving force behind team operations that it is for general managers elsewhere. Schumacher is not pressured to generate annual dividends. Nor is he distracted by demands to sell the franchise for the capital gains it would likely bring on the currently competitive intercity market.

The Stadium Issue

Another reason for the Indians' financial situation is the stadium lease arrangement they hold with the Indianapolis Department of Parks and

Recreation. The city's stadium ownership goes back twenty-two years, when the private owner died and the Indians owners convinced the city to buy it. Max Schumacher, the business manager at the time, recalls the terms of the purchase: "When the man died who owned the stadium we convinced the city to buy it. And they bought it right with a $300,000 ten year bond at 3.5 percent interest. The stadium was paid off in 1977." The Indians under Schumacher were the most obvious beneficiary of this deal, since they became the primary tenant on very favorable terms: "They gave us a sweetheart deal when they first bought it in 1967. I think our yearly lease rent was 25 or 30 thousand dollars during those early years. As things got better we were willing to pay more. Last year we paid $106,000 rent. In return the city put about $50,000 into capital improvements."

According to the five-year lease agreement, which expires in 1992, the team assumes nearly all operational and maintenance costs, while the city is responsible for major structural repairs. According to the city's response to the International City Management Association's 1989 survey, the city's operating revenues versus costs for 1985, 1986, and 1987 produced a positive balance of $6,760 for the three years. This, however, does not include debt retirement or indirect costs for maintenance and administrative overhead.

Although the original mortgage has been amortized, new debt for major structural repairs constitutes a continued obligation on the Department of Parks and Recreation. There is not sufficient money generated to pay for such projects as the $1.8 million bond let for Bush Stadium renovations in 1979. City officials estimate that Bush Stadium costs the Department of Parks and Recreation approximately $200,000 annually. The age and generally run-down appearance of the stadium indicates that, unless a new stadium is built, the city will be required to subsidize the Indians through stadium renovations in years to come. Moreover, costs are likely to go up, and in the end the city will still own a vintage 1931 stadium.

Although the dollar cost of the city's subsidy does not present an immediate budgetary problem, the city leadership is faced with a twin dilemma over its future commitment to baseball in Indianapolis. First, there is some question about the prudence of continuing to subsidize a AAA league team instead of investing in a new stadium to attract a major league franchise. Second, the issue of a new stadium has become the focus of a larger community debate over whether more public investment should be placed in sports activities and infrastructure while neighborhood and social assistance programs are underfunded.

BUSH STADIUM OR THE MAJOR LEAGUES?

Continued investment in Bush Stadium is a persistent and perplexing policy issue for the city. Either a new investment has to be made to incorporate the Indians into the community's overall sports strategy, or the city needs to invest in a strategy to attract a major league franchise. It cannot prudently do both.

Bush Stadium is located outside the downtown area that has been targeted for revitalization in the Regional Center Plan. The Indians neither contribute to nor benefit from the people generating activities in the regional center. Thus, if new investment is to be made in a stadium, it will likely not be at the Bush Stadium site. If the city invests in a downtown site, why not develop it for major league baseball? While the community deliberates this issue, plans for the Indians' future remain on hold. Schumacher provides a concise assessment of the dilemma: "For several years the conventional wisdom was don't put money into Bush Stadium [renovations] because the Indians might be playing in the Hoosier Dome, or we might have a major league baseball team here."

There is little question that the city would like to get Bush Stadium off of its books. The difficulty lies in offering a viable alternative. Mayor Hudnut issued a trial balloon that illustrates part of the problem: "We suggested selling the ballpark a few months ago [summer 1989]. And the fur flew because people thought we were trying to get rid of the Indians."

Although, getting "rid of the Indians" was not the stated objective (the city offered the Indians the option to buy and operate the stadium themselves), it could be speculated that once relieved of its Bush Stadium obligation, the city might feel free to move forward on the construction of a major league stadium. This could, in turn, put the old one out of business.

Whatever happens to Bush Stadium, it is clear that Indianapolis has developed plans to construct a stadium to house major league baseball, but only after it has a major league franchise in hand. Mayor Hudnut addressed this issue at some length in his biography, *Hudnut Minister-/Mayor,* and contrasted the construction of a baseball stadium with that of the Hoosier Dome:

> Our city, like a dozen others, has been interested in the possibility of securing a major league baseball franchise. We have made a presentation to the expansion committee, but we have no idea when and if a franchise might be awarded to Indianapolis. Consequently, it would be imprudent of us to proceed with the construction of a new $30- to $40-million open-air, grass-turf, 40,000-seat stadium built to Major League specifications, and we have decided not to do it until we are sure we would have a franchise. In the case of the Hoosier Dome, we expanded the Convention

Center and were able to justify the decision irrespective of whether or not an NFL team played in it. But in this case, a free-standing facility would have no other use than baseball. Some of our most avid baseball fans want us to build it anyway and provide a new home for the Indianapolis Indians, our triple A team. But we have decided not to proceed. The risk would be too great. The decision was relatively easy to make. (Hudnut and Keene, 1987: 135)

The city clearly wants to build a new stadium as a part of its downtown revitalization strategy. If city officials choose to wait until after they have a team, however, they will be at a competitive disadvantage with other cities, such as Buffalo, New York, and St. Petersburg, Florida, where stadiums are already built.

On the other hand, if Indianapolis opts to proceed with construction, it then faces the question of selecting a construction funding mechanism. The conventional process for such a capital expenditure in Indiana is to issue a capital improvement bond—a procedure that must secure passage in a public referendum. The prospect of facing the public on a baseball stadium bond subjects the proponents to criticism on the larger issue of whether it is prudent to invest additional resources on sports infrastructure while neighborhood and social assistance programs remain underfunded.

CHANGING PUBLIC SENTIMENT

Bond referendum approvals can be difficult to secure and are fraught with political danger. In former Mayor Hudnut's view, this is certainly an issue in Indianapolis: "All you have to do in this state to defeat a bond issue is to obtain one more signature on a petition than those that have been raised for it. That is easy to do.... And sports have been the lightning rod for that protest movement."

Mayor Hudnut's political memory goes back to the 1985 preparations for the Pan American Games when former city firefighter Carl Moldthan led a successful petition drive to defeat a $40 million bond issue for the games. The bond issue was later a major plank in Moldthan's 1987 mayoral campaign against Hudnut. Although Moldthan lost the election, the issue he raised is still an important factor in the city's downtown development plans. As Hudnut stated during a 1989 interview, "Politically, who knows? It [opposition] has been growing over the years. One of the people who is the focal point of this ran against me in 1987. He did not win, but his voice of opposition is still very much heard. As a result of the defeat of the Pan American [Games] bond issue we have become much more skittish about floating bond issues for very legitimate purposes—like streets and sewers."

The failure of the Pan American bond issue may have signaled the end of the honeymoon period in Indianapolis for large public investments in athletic infrastructure. The Pan American Games bond issue included $18 million for athletes' dormitories that were designed to be converted into low- and moderate-income housing after the games. Nevertheless, the issue seemed to be perceived as exclusively a sports enterprise and was defeated.

This general sense of disenchantment with the amount of community resources committed to the regional center sports strategy is fueled by a much deeper sentiment that more money should be spent in the neighborhoods or on social service programs. Although the Department of Metropolitan Development increased investments in the neighborhoods in the 1980s, and its planning division incorporated neighborhood residents' housing and employment needs in its downtown development projects, the visual magnitude of the Hoosier Dome tends to dwarf more individualized, personal, and scattered-site investments in social services and neighborhood improvements. Moreover, continued downtown investment is perceived in the neighborhoods as favoring a select group of businesses, real estate developers, and investors (Mack, 1980). Neighborhood resentment grew even more pointed in 1988, when a national survey on infant mortality rated Indianapolis as one of the nation's ten worst cities.

There has been a general shift in the city's expressed commitment to invest in the neighborhoods as a result of this shifting political sentiment at the grass roots. Former Mayor Hudnut made neighborhood and social service programs the central theme in his 1989 state of the city addresses, and he created a third deputy mayor position in his administration that had specific responsibilities in the social services area.

The general shift in community attitude toward neighborhood needs has been accompanied by a more cautious approach toward new sports ventures. This is noticeable in the city's quest for a major league baseball team. The city government's official policy is to maintain the status quo on its commitment to preserve Bush Stadium and not openly and aggressively to pursue a major league team by building a new stadium. It has marketed plans to build a stadium if a baseball franchise does materialize.

In the meantime, the campaign to land a team in Indianapolis is left to private sector entrepreneurs. This partnership, which has worked well in Indianapolis before, appeared as if it would be successful once again. In the summer of 1989, two Indianapolis businessmen purchased the Seattle Mariners baseball franchise, raising speculation in Seattle and Indianapolis that the team would be moved to the Midwest. In early

1992, however, the new owners sold the team to a local investment group pledged to keep the Mariners in Seattle.

NOTES

1. Literature describing Indianapolis's downtown revitalization abounds. See, for example, Bamberger and Parham (1984), Levathes (1987), and Policinski (1978).

2. The term *Policy Group* is the author's usage to provide a consistent identity for the group of civic leaders that had no designated formal title.

3. The school corporation is structured as an independent entity in Indiana and operates outside the aegis of city government. The provision of public health services is a function of the Health and Hospital Corporation, an independent special service board.

4. Max Schumacher, a native of Indianapolis, has been with the Indians for nearly forty years. He has held every important administrative position in the franchise and currently serves as general manager of the team and as president and chairman of the board of directors. He also is the principal owner of the franchise's stock.

Buffalo, New York 3

James Milroy

Buffalo reached its peak population and employment in the 1950s and since that time has experienced a drastic decline in both. Between 1970 and 1984, the Buffalo SMSA (Standard Metropolitan Statistical Area) had a job loss rate of 5.4 percent (or 20,000 jobs), while the nation had a job increase rate of 36.0 percent (Center for Regional Studies, 1987: 4). During the same period, the Buffalo area suffered a manufacturing job loss rate of 40.6 percent (over 70,000 manufacturing jobs), whereas the nation's rate of decline was only 2.2 percent (Center for Regional Studies, 1987: 3–4). From March 1984 to March 1987, the number of manufacturing jobs dropped from 103,800 to 99,100, representing an additional 4.5 percent manufacturing job loss.

While these employment contractions were not unique to the Buffalo area, "the proportional impact on Buffalo was greater because of the region's historical dependency on basic manufacturing and the fact that these jobs were not being replaced at the same rate as elsewhere in the state or nation as a whole" (Greater Buffalo Development Foundation, 1988: 2). The area's unemployment rate stood at 9.5 percent in 1980 and 7.2 percent in 1986.

A decline in the population accompanied this job loss. "The eight county region experienced one of the most dramatic losses of population between 1970 and 1980 of any major industrial region in the country, dropping 5.3 percent," with the core counties of the SMSA suffering most of this decline (Center for Regional Studies, 1987: 8–9). The Buffalo CMSA (Central Metropolitan Statistical Area, consisting of Erie and Niagara counties) experienced an 8.3 percent decline in population between 1980 and 1990, dropping from 357,870 to 328,123. Buffalo ranked as the nation's twenty-eighth largest city in 1970; in 1990, it ranked fiftieth.

An analysis conducted by Coopers and Lybrand (1988: i) concerning the renovation of Buffalo's Memorial Auditorium, the home of the city's National Hockey League franchise, put these figures in a "sports policy" context. The analysis concluded, "In comparison to other NHL franchise cities, Buffalo has one of the smallest economic markets in terms of retail sales, effective buying power, and population."

Buffalo's economy stabilized in the late 1980s, however. In 1988, Buffalo's economic growth rate exceeded the state average, and by 1990, the CMSA's unemployment rate had fallen to 5.0 percent. Forecasters believed the trends that stabilized the economy—a strong service sector, a stabilized manufacturing base, and increased Canadian trade—would continue and therefore enable the local economy to grow.

Buffalo's Baseball History

Buffalo has a rich baseball history that began on August 3, 1877. Since then, the city's teams have occupied fourteen home ballparks, the latest being Pilot Field, which opened on April 14, 1988, and signaled the beginning of a new era for professional baseball in Buffalo.

In 1961, the Buffalo Bisons moved into War Memorial Stadium, which had been built in 1937. The Bisons' move to War Memorial began a period of decline for Buffalo baseball. In the season before moving to War Memorial Stadium, the Bisons drew a then-record 413,263 people. The team had trouble attracting 150,000 people to War Memorial, even though the stadium was three times as large as the team's previous ball park. A combination of bad teams and racial unrest in the neighborhood surrounding the stadium accounted for much of this decline. The neighborhood was the site of rioting during the 1960s, and perceptions of the neighborhood were such that from 1967 to 1969 the team decided to play some of its weekday night games in Niagara Falls.

The Bisons attracted only 9,260 people to the team's thirteen home games in 1970. The team owners' lack of financial resources forced the AAA International League to forfeit the Buffalo franchise. The franchise was purchased by a Montreal-based group and moved to Winnepeg.[1]

For the next eight seasons Buffalo was without a professional baseball franchise. Efforts to regain professional baseball received a new impetus when Mayor James D. Griffin took office in January 1978. In 1979, a group of ninety investors, headed by Mayor Griffin, paid $1,000 each to purchase the AA Jersey City Eastern League franchise and move it to War Memorial Stadium. Mayor Griffin viewed this move as the first step in returning major league baseball to Buffalo, reflecting his strong belief that Buffalo is a town that wants strong professional sports and that it will support them.

These community-based owners, however, did not possess sufficient resources to rekindle and maintain fan interest. In its first season, the team attracted 133,148 fans, but the next season attendance declined to 130,674 (Fink, 1988: 22). By the 1982 season, attendance had dropped to a low of 77,077, barely 1,000 fans per game (DiCesare, 1988: 34).

The city was close to losing its second minor league franchise in thirteen years when, at the end of the 1982 season, Robert E. Rich, Jr., president of Buffalo-based Rich Products Corporation, offered to buy the team. Bob Rich bought the AA Eastern League franchise from its discouraged and financially troubled community-based stockholders for an amount reported to be slightly more than $100,000. According to reports in the *Buffalo News,* the Bisons stockholders could have held out for more money if they had not insisted on maintaining local ownership (DiCesare, 1988: 34). The owners wanted to maintain local ownership so the city's chances of landing a major league expansion franchise, which was their principal motivation for purchasing the team, would not be jeopardized.

Under Rich's leadership the Bisons organization flourished. The Bisons instituted outstanding promotional activities, giving away as many tickets as they sold. Buffalo sported the best attendance figure in the Eastern League in 1983, drawing 200,531 fans and demonstrating that with proper management and adequate resources baseball could be a successful enterprise in Buffalo.

With Bob Rich's success with the Bisons, the mayor achieved exactly what he wanted—a viable minor league franchise that he could use to further his goal of attracting a major league expansion franchise. The enhanced credibility that Rich's success brought to the Bisons organization encouraged the Griffin administration to approach the New York State legislature for help in financing a new baseball stadium.

Griffin had two principal objectives in advancing the stadium idea: to develop a professional sports facility designed to attract a major league baseball franchise, and to create a catalyst for the redevelopment of Buffalo. However, according to Chuck Rosenow, president of Downtown Development Inc., an ancillary agency of city government, and a key advisor to the mayor on the Pilot Field project, the state did not support the idea of building a new stadium for a AA minor league tenant.

Attendance increased to 223,433 in 1984, and Rich, saying that fan support warranted it, paid $1 million to move the AAA-level American Association franchise from Wichita, Kansas, to Buffalo. Joining the American Association, according to Rich, would enhance Buffalo's chances of landing a major league expansion franchise because it would allow the Bisons to showcase their team nationally, playing head-to-head against other expansion candidates (DiCesare, 1988: 37).

The idea of a new ballpark was once again resurrected when Rich purchased the AAA American Association franchise in 1984. The next year Governor Mario Cuomo, supported by the local delegation to the state legislature, recommended a budget that included $22.5 million in state Urban Development Corporation funds for a Buffalo stadium.

With hopes growing that Buffalo would someday return to the major leagues, the Bisons drew an all-time team season attendance record of 425,113 in 1986. By 1987, the Bisons' last season in old War Memorial Stadium, attendance reached 495,760.

In 1988, the Bisons moved into a new $40 million stadium—Pilot Field. In 1988, 1989, 1990, and 1991, the team drew record numbers of minor league fans of 1,147,651, 1,116,441, 1,140,437, and 1,188,972, respectively. The city and the Bisons ownership appeared to be ideally situated to achieve their goal of winning a major league expansion franchise.

The History of Public Investment in Sports Facilities

THE CITY OF BUFFALO

Given Buffalo's economic decline, it is not surprising that the city's investment in its two major sports facilities prior to the construction of Pilot Field—War Memorial Stadium and War Memorial Auditorium— has been minimal, relative to the cost of new facilities or even modernized facilities. War Memorial Stadium and War Memorial Auditorium were both built during the depression. The stadium served as home to the football Buffalo Bills until 1973, when they moved into Rich Stadium in Orchard Park, a suburb of Buffalo located in Erie County. The auditorium houses the Buffalo Sabres of the National Hockey League. The city lost its National Basketball Association Buffalo Braves to San Diego in 1979. Prior to that time, the Braves also occupied War Memorial Auditorium.

In recent decades the city has sold bonds to renovate each of these structures. In 1971, the city floated bonds in the amount of $8,955,000 to raise the roof on the auditorium to accommodate additional seating. The annual debt service on these bonds was $450,000. The debt's twenty-year term expired in 1990.

War Memorial Stadium sat vacant from 1973, when the Bills went to Rich Stadium, to 1979, when the city refurbished the stadium in preparation for the move of the AA Jersey City Eastern League franchise to

Buffalo. When Bob Rich bought the team, the city and the Bisons again refurbished the stadium for a nominal sum. Except for the 1971 bond sale for raising the auditorium roof, the city has maintained both facilities through its operating budget.

Pilot Field, therefore, is the city's first major expenditure for a sports facility since 1971, when it rehabilitated the auditorium. In 1989, the city had planned to invest another $38.3 million to rehabilitate War Memorial Auditorium into a modern facility, but these plans were scaled back by 1990 because Seymour H. Knox III, chairman and president of the Buffalo Sabres, demanded a new facility.

The city also planned to invest in an amateur sports facility to be constructed on the site of War Memorial Stadium. Demolition of the stadium was under way at the time of this writing. The cost of the new facility was estimated at between $7.0 million and $17.5 million, depending on which plan was adopted.[2]

ERIE COUNTY

Erie County's history of sports facility financing is checkered by a twenty-year legal dispute with the would-be developers of a domed stadium in Lancaster, New York. The domed-stadium saga began in June 1967, when Ralph Wilson, owner of the Buffalo Bills, the city's National Football League franchise, called on the community to build a new stadium because War Memorial Stadium was too small and dilapidated. The Buffalo Area Chamber of Commerce took up Wilson's charge and undertook a feasibility study, which concluded that two stadiums should be built—one for football and one for baseball. The plan went nowhere, however, since neither the city nor the county was in a position to finance such a large undertaking.

At this point, the city of Buffalo offered to provide land at the foot of Main Street in downtown Buffalo for the stadium if Erie County would pay for its construction. County legislators, representing mostly suburban constituencies, complained that the city was run-down and that their constituents were afraid to travel downtown at night, igniting a city versus suburbs debate. Eventually the plan collapsed under heavy criticism.

In August 1969, developers signed a contract with Erie County executive B. John Tutuska to build a 60,000-seat, domed stadium in the quiet suburb of Lancaster, New York. The Erie County legislature supported the contract by a twelve-to-seven vote, authorizing $50 million for the project. In July 1970, bids for the project came in at $72 million. That same month the legislature failed by two votes to get the eleven votes needed to approve a lease agreement with the developers. As a result, the domed-stadium idea was declared dead in Erie County.

Eventually, two legislators were convicted for "conspiracy to extort" bribes for their votes on various funding aspects of the project. They were each sentenced to three years in jail. Subsequently, the developers sued the county for $90 million for breach of contract. Almost twenty years and many rounds of litigation later, the county settled with the developers for $10,159,000.

In the interim, the county built Rich Stadium in Orchard Park, which opened in August of 1973 at a construction cost of $23 million. The county pays in excess of $1 million per year on the Rich Stadium debt. The city of Buffalo was not involved in the financing of the project.

As the foregoing illustrates, neither the city nor the county has had great success dealing with major league sports issues. The county lost a $10 million lawsuit, and the city lost an NBA franchise to another city and an NFL franchise to a suburban community.

The processes by which the area's sports facilities have been constructed and maintained are marked by a lack of coordinated strategic planning between county and city governments. No institutionalized mechanisms exist between the two governments for financing or planning sports facilities. In fact, all major capital sports projects to date have been financed by either the county or city government, without the participation of the other level of government.

Decision making in this area is best described as reactive. This is true of the decisions that led to the domed-stadium lawsuit and the construction of Rich Stadium, as well as more recent decisions regarding the future of War Memorial Auditorium. Every major capital sports project, except Pilot Field, directly resulted from a demand by a team owner or league official for a new or improved facility.

How Pilot Field Came to Be

Pilot Field, not unlike many projects in Buffalo, is a stadium born of controversy. Stadium proposals surfaced before Bob Rich ever took over the Bisons organization. In 1979, the Erie County Sports Board, an advisory committee established by Erie County executive Edward Rutkowski, a political ally of Mayor Griffin, recommended that a stadium feasibility study be conducted. The study concluded in 1981 that Buffalo had a reasonable chance of attracting a major league expansion franchise, but it left unanswered the question of whether a stadium should be built before or after a franchise was secured. The board also concluded that any stadium built in Buffalo should be domed.

In November 1983, consultants hired by the city recommended the construction of an $89 million, 40,000-seat, domed stadium that included a field house for Erie Community College City Campus.[3] Almost immediately, Mayor Griffin passed the recommendations on to the state legislature, along with an appeal for $40 million in state assistance. Shortly afterward, the mayor went to Nashville, Tennessee, for the winter major league baseball meetings to present the project and to lobby for Buffalo as an expansion candidate.

Despite the fact that this proposal eventually died in Albany, the mayor's efforts were important because in the early stages of the project many doubted that a new baseball stadium could be built in downtown Buffalo. For one thing, Erie County was embroiled in the domed-stadium lawsuit. In fact, the entire domed-stadium controversy left most people leery of efforts to build another stadium, especially in downtown. According to James Keane, a city councilman at the time and an early supporter of the project, stadium supporters faced a very negative attitude throughout the community.

Attitudes began to change, however, through the efforts of Griffin and Bob Rich. Mayor Griffin is credited with developing an early consensus that any stadium built should be built downtown. As noted earlier, Griffin viewed the construction of a new ballpark downtown as a catalyst for the redevelopment of the city, and he effectively used this argument in selling the project. According to David Rutecki, chairman of the city council's Stadium Task Force, "The successful, first-class operation Bob Rich established made it possible to sell the idea that a stadium would bring people downtown" (Heaney, 1988: 14). Of course, Griffin was aided in his efforts to "sell" the idea that the stadium should be built downtown by the fact that Erie County was refusing to participate in the funding of the project unless it contained a field house for Erie Community College City Campus, which is located in the heart of downtown.

Despite the best efforts of Bob Rich and Mayor Griffin and an early consensus on a downtown site, the debate dragged on while three alternative downtown sites were considered. Also, questions of who should pay for the stadium and whether it should be domed continued to be debated.

In 1984, two other cities in New York State were seeking state aid to build sports facilities—New York City for a domed stadium and Albany for an auditorium. Governor Cuomo consequently established an advisory committee known as Sportsplex to study the three proposed projects. In June 1984, Sportsplex recommended state funding in the amount of $22.5 million for a 20,000-seat, open-air stadium in Buffalo that had the capability of being expanded. The Sportsplex recommendations did not provide for the inclusion of a field house for Erie Community College.

According to Buffalo's representative on the Sportsplex board, three factors made an expandable stadium "a reasonable investment" (Heaney, 1988: 14). These factors were Bob Rich's success with the Bisons, the prospect of a major league expansion franchise for Buffalo, and Major League Baseball's cooling attitude toward domed stadiums.

In January 1985, Governor Cuomo adopted the Sportsplex recommendations, and in April 1985, the state legislature appropriated $22.5 million in state Urban Development Corporation funds for the project. Actual authorization for releasing the funds was still contingent on the approval of tripartite agreements by the state Public Authorities Control Board (PACB). The PACB was created in the 1970s to oversee the state Urban Development Corporation and other public corporations that had overcommitted themselves financially. The tripartite agreements spelled out the responsibilities of the state, the city, and the Erie County Industrial Development Agency (ECIDA),[4] which was the developer of the project.

Under these agreements, the state must be repaid from any profits that may be realized after a maintenance reserve fund of up to $75,000 annually is established and after the debt service is paid on the bonds issued by the ECIDA and the city. This particular provision caused the PACB to table the tripartite agreements until it had an opportunity to review the lease between the Bisons and the city. The board said that before it would give its approval to the agreements it wanted to approve any "prime leases" for use of the stadium, including the city's planned lease with the Bisons, to ensure that the state's interests were protected. The PACB wanted to make sure that the lease had the potential of generating sufficient revenue to at least hold out the possibility that the state might be repaid.

At this stage the project faced some of its most serious challenges. Mayor Griffin, with the backing of the state, wanted to proceed quickly but the council wanted answers to a number of questions before giving its approval. What would the final design look like? How would the project be financed? What effect would a stadium bond sale have on the city's bond rating?[5] How much would the Bisons pay to lease it? What was going to happen to old War Memorial Stadium?

The mayor's political opposition on the council pressed for answers while keeping the heat on the mayor to ensure that city taxpayers, as well as specific constituencies, got the best possible deal. The debate over the stadium involved at least one political issue that was central in the mayoral campaign of 1985, which pitted council president George K. Arthur against Mayor Griffin. Arthur campaigned on a platform that emphasized neighborhood revitalization, an area he accused the mayor

of ignoring in his efforts to redevelop downtown. Arthur and his majority coalition on the council, which consisted of African-American representatives as well as several white representatives who were not supportive
of Mayor Griffin, wanted guarantees that the city would not abandon
old War Memorial Stadium and the neighborhood that had endured its
presence for so long.

Their support for Pilot Field was made contingent on a redevelopment plan for War Memorial. War Memorial is located on Buffalo's East
Side, an area that houses a majority of the city's African-American
population, which was Arthur's political support base. According to
council member David Collins, representative of the Masten District
where War Memorial is located, the feeling was that the Bills and the
Bisons received new stadiums while the neighborhood that had suffered
years of inconvenience was getting nothing but an imposing old stadium
that dwarfed the neighborhood and presented health and safety problems.
Griffin eventually agreed to a plan that called for developing an amateur
sports complex on the site, and money was set aside in the budget to
begin planning for the project, though other hurdles remained.

Several members of Arthur's coalition were also concerned about the
affirmative action provisions of the tripartite agreements. Several council members, especially majority leader James Pitts, feared the affirmative action provisions of the tripartite agreements were not strong enough
to guarantee that minority- and women-owned business enterprises would
benefit from the project.

The council amended the tripartite agreements by adopting the state
affirmative action set-aside of 15 percent to correct this shortcoming.
Under the terms of the agreement, 15 percent of the project, defined in
terms of total contracts and labor time, was to go to minority-owned
businesses.

The issues of stadium design and location also concerned the council.
Resolving these issues was time-consuming, involving lengthy discussions with architects, planners, and local historic preservation groups,
who were worried about the effect of the stadium project on the character of the Joseph Ellicott Preservation District.

With every issue came additional delays, annoying Griffin and provok-
ing him to refer to council members as "obstructionists" and "goofs"
who displayed little leadership. According to James Keane, these dia-
tribes were counterproductive: "He let his feelings toward the Council
get in the way and it damn near cost us the project" (Heaney, 1988: 61).

Although all these issues were important to the council's various
constituencies, the most important concerns to the council were the
cost of the project and its impact on the city's ability to finance other

projects of importance to council members. Cost was of particular concern to the council because the tripartite agreements required the local government to pay for all cost overruns.

Under the terms of the tripartite agreements, the city was also responsible for the operation and maintenance of the facility. Its major source of revenue was a contract with the Buffalo Bisons, the principal tenant. Lease negotiations were therefore seen as critical by some members of the council in order to guarantee that the city could operate and maintain the stadium without having to subsidize the operation with additional tax dollars.

The importance of the cost overrun issue was not lost on the council. Requests for additional funding to cover costs incurred from unforeseen problems, or "change orders" as they are known to council members, are a daily part of council business. Despite the fact that the city is required by charter to accept the bid of the lowest responsible bidder, bid specifications are seldom expansive enough to anticipate all possible contingencies. Frequently, unforeseen difficulties lead to change orders, which increase project costs beyond expectations. The council was afraid that if it committed the city to developing the project, it would be caught holding the bag in the likely event that project costs exceeded projections.

This problem was overcome by the participation of the ECIDA as the project's developer. According to council member David Rutecki, whom Arthur appointed as chairman of the council's Stadium Task Force to study the issue, the most important benefit derived from the ECIDA's participation as project developer involved the agency's ability to establish a construction price ceiling for the entire project. The construction contract awarded by the ECIDA established a construction price ceiling that the contractor was required to meet. If the city had served as the developer, it would have been compelled by the city charter to bid each of the various aspects of the project and face the inevitable change orders.

Comfortable with the cost overrun issue, the council turned its attention to the effect a bond sale would have on the city's ability to fund future projects. Related to this issue was the question of how fair it was for the city to fund the stadium without county participation, when the project had been justified in terms of regional benefits.

In May 1985, city comptroller Robert Whelan prepared a report for the council setting out the city's ability to pay for Pilot Field. The document concluded that the county and the private sector should be involved in financing the project to ease the financial burden on city taxpayers. As justification for seeking county support, Whelan pointed out that county sales-tax revenue would increase from the project, that the city had given up its share of a percentage point hike in the county sales tax,[6] and that the stadium would be a regional attraction.

Whelan proposed that the ECIDA issue the bonds and that they be backed by stadium revenues and by city and county property taxes on a one-eighth to seven-eighths ratio. Planners' projections showed that approximately one-eighth of the potential customers for Pilot Field would be city residents. Whelan estimated that the city would still be responsible for approximately 40 percent of the local contribution under his plan, when the value of city land and other city contributions were taken into account.

Soon after Whelan released his report, council president Arthur sponsored a resolution, which passed the council unanimously, calling on the county to participate in financing Pilot Field. Whelan's and Arthur's appeals to the county were rejected outright by county executive Edward J. Rutkowski. There was little sentiment among county officials for county participation in the project because the county already was spending more than $1 million per year to finance Rich Stadium, it was facing the lawsuit over the failed Lancaster dome, and the Pilot Field project did not contain a field house for Erie Community College.

The project slowly came together, in spite of these problems. The council approved the Swan and Washington streets site, so the stadium would serve to anchor, along with War Memorial Auditorium, the downtown end of the city's newly constructed subway and pedestrian mall. Arthur's coalition was satisfied that the War Memorial site would be redeveloped and that the affirmative action provisions of the tripartite agreements were strong enough to hold out the prospect that MBEs (Minority Business Enterprises) and WBEs (Women Business Enterprises) would benefit from the project. The cost issue was not resolved completely, but a majority of council members thought the project was important enough to the revitalization of downtown to go ahead without county participation.

In July 1985, the council approved the tripartite agreements and authorized the sale of city bonds in the amount of $5.32 million to cover part of the city's share of the project. Under the terms of the tripartite agreement, the ECIDA is the owner of Pilot Field, and the city has a noncancelable, fifteen-year agreement with the agency. At the end of the lease, title to the stadium passes to the city. Lease negotiations between the Bisons and the council's Auditorium Task Force were still under way at this point, but a majority of council members thought that negotiations had progressed sufficiently to approve the project. Table 3.1

details the contributions made by the major parties to the tripartite agreements as well as those made by other parties.

Table 3.1: Financial Participation in
the Construction of Pilot Field

Contributions	Amount (in millions)
City of Buffalo	
General improvement serial bonds	5.32
Down payment on bonds	.28
Three-year operation and maintenance budget	2.10
	7.70
New York State	
State Urban Development Corporation funds	22.50
ECIDA	
Revenue bonds	4.20
Other Contributions	
Buffalo Development Companies	4.00
Buffalo Bisons	3.00
Buffalo Urban Renewal Agency (land credit)	2.00
Erie County Legislature	.75
	9.75
Total Cost of Pilot Field	44.15

As Table 3.1 reports, other groups contributed to the project as well. The Buffalo Development Companies, a consortium of local development agencies, contributed $4 million, including $150,000 in Urban Development Corporation handicapped-access funds. The Buffalo Urban Renewal Agency, an ancillary agency of city government, contributed the land. The Bisons contributed $3 million dollars toward the purchase of the scoreboard and the construction of the concession areas, the restaurant, and team offices. The project also was aided by federal involvement when Senator Daniel Patrick Moynihan added language to the federal tax reform act which extended a sunset provision of the tax code that allowed stadium developers to finance the project with tax-exempt bonds. This amendment saved project developers an estimated $17 million.

One council member, Alfred T. Coppola, a representative of the city's most affluent district, still was not ready to commit the city to spending $7.7 million for the development of the facility, nor was he ready to obligate the city to operate and maintain the facility before there was a lease in place with the Bisons. Coppola, a member of Arthur's coalition and himself a mayoral candidate in 1981, was particularly upset over the fact that the council had approved the tripartite agreements and had voted to sell bonds in support of the project before the council had completed lease negotiations with the Bisons.

Coppola, working in conjunction with the New York Public Interest Research Group, a not-for-profit organization whose goals are to increase citizen power and improve the quality of life in New York State, attempted to put the bond issue to a public referendum. Coppola managed to collect over 26,000 signatures requesting repeal of the bond resolution. This was several thousand signatures more than required to force a vote; however, the petitions were disallowed by the Erie County Board of Elections because the witness statement that is required by law to appear at the bottom of each page of signatures was judged to be inadequate.

With this hurdle overcome, the final item the council had to approve was the lease with the Bisons. This time the council moved quickly to finalize a lease for presentation to the PACB. The lease, as finally approved by the council, added approximately $200,000 annually to the revenues the city could have expected to receive from the proposed lease originally submitted by Mayor Griffin. According to Pitts, the council's Stadium Task Force reviewed dozens of leases before formulating the Bisons' lease. He said that since the project involved the construction of an expandable stadium, the council wanted to create an expandable lease to make sure the city would benefit in the event of growth. As Rutecki succinctly put it, "The basic principle behind the lease with the Bisons is that we would be partners. If the Bisons made money, we would make money. In harder times, we would share the loss" (Warner, 1988: A-8).

To forge this partnership the council added a clause to the lease that linked the rent to paid admissions. That is, the percentage of ticket revenues that the Bisons pay to the city increases as gross receipts increase. Any profit the city realizes from the operation of Pilot Field is to be applied toward the $800,135 it pays annually for principal and interest on the bonds issued by the ECIDA and the city for stadium construction. The term of these bonds is fifteen years, corresponding to the term of the lease agreement the city has with the ECIDA. In 1988–89, the city enjoyed $158,405 in excess revenues over expenditures from stadium operations, if depreciation expenses are excluded.

After all was said and done, the result was a downtown baseball stadium that has been called "a minor league stadium with all the major league amenities," "the best ballpark in the minor leagues," and "the city's ticket to Glory Days."

Has the Pilot Field Project Been Worth It?

From the Bisons' perspective, the Pilot Field project has certainly been worth it. Pilot Field not only greatly enhanced the Bisons' chances of landing a major league expansion franchise, but also increased the Bisons' earning potential. Although calculating the Bisons' profit is complicated, experts estimate the figure at anywhere from several hundred thousand dollars to $2 million, and total revenues from stadium operations at $9 to $10 million.

Bob Rich says these are "realistic projections." He cautions against accepting the higher projections, however, because he says that "it's very apparent that Bison baseball is reinvesting a lot of money for a long-range goal." The Bisons spend money on a major league level to guarantee that everything about their operation is major league. Top Bisons officials travel the country spreading the word about Buffalo and Pilot Field, and no expense is spared entertaining top baseball officials when they are in town for such events as the Old-Timers Classic and the AAA All-Star Game. The Bisons also have a very large staff. Fellow AAA executives reportedly chide Bob Rich by telling him, "You're the only team that will have to cut its staff when you go to the major leagues" (Warner, 1988: A8).

Judging whether the project has been worth it from the city's perspective involves several considerations. First among them is whether the project has realized its initial goals as espoused by Mayor Griffin. Recall that the principal objectives of the project were to develop a professional sports facility designed to attract a major league baseball franchise and to act as a catalyst for downtown redevelopment.

The city's chances of realizing the goal of attracting a major league expansion franchise certainly were enhanced by the project and by the Bisons' subsequent actions and the city's promotion of the project. In December 1990, Buffalo was named one of six final contenders for two National League expansion franchises that were scheduled to begin play in 1993.

Just before Major League Baseball announced the expansion franchise finalists, however, Rich wrote a letter to the editor of the *Buffalo News,* in which he questioned whether the changing "economics of baseball" made sense for his family, the city, the county, and the fans. He cited the high expansion franchise fee ($95 million), a threatening recession, declining television ratings for baseball, and escalating player salaries. It was uncertain whether this was a sincere questioning of the logic of bringing major league baseball to Buffalo or the first step in lease negotiations with the city. Whatever the case, the National League awarded its expansion franchises to Miami and Denver.

As for the second goal, there is evidence, albeit largely anecdotal, that the project has contributed to the revitalization of the city. Chuck Rosenow, president of Development Downtown, Inc., estimates Pilot Field's direct and indirect benefit to the community is at least $20.6 million annually.[7] Others note that the location of the stadium allows the city to "concentrate these benefits" downtown. In addition, the stadium project has enhanced the potential for future investment. Rosenow has claimed that "the atmosphere for further investment downtown has been greatly affected by the sheer size of the project and its visibility" (Fairbanks, 1989).

There also is a complementary relationship between the city's and the Bisons' long-range goals. The city has been trying to persuade investors from Canada to locate in Buffalo as part of the city's effort to realize benefits from the Free Trade Act. The Bisons also have an eye on Canada, and they have been pushing group ticket sales to organizations there. According to the Bisons vice president and general manager, Michael Billoni, the Bisons' marketing efforts in Canada are designed to demonstrate to the "Lords of Baseball" that the team can draw from a population base of several million people in Canada, Pennsylvania, and western New York. Robert McDermott, the Bisons representative in Canada, said the Bisons just want to get Canadian baseball fans over to Buffalo to see a game so their thinking about Buffalo can be turned around. The city also would like to turn around the attitude of Canadians toward Buffalo.

Under Rich, the Bisons have been Buffalo-boosters, working hard to attract a number of highly visible baseball promotional events. These promotions include the hosting of the "Battle of the Great Lakes," an exhibition game between the Cleveland Indians and the Toronto Blue Jays, the first game of its kind in Buffalo; the inaugural AAA All-Star Game; and the National Old-Timers Classic, the premier game of its type. These promotions are credited with bringing Buffalo national and international recognition, thereby enhancing the city's image and its chances of landing not only a major league franchise but other business enterprises and sports events as well. For example, Buffalo has been selected to host the 1993 World University Games.

From the city's perspective, the potential for future economic development generated by the construction of Pilot Field justifies the annual expenditure of the $1 million the city pays in debt service. The benefits to Buffalo associated with the construction of Pilot Field go far beyond economic considerations. Pilot Field has done more to rejuvenate civic pride in Buffalo than anything else in recent history, except perhaps for the recent success of the Buffalo Bills football franchise. Pilot Field, in conjunction with other redevelopment projects in the downtown, including the new pedestrian mall and subway, is thought to have changed people's negative thinking about downtown.

Still, there remains another consideration in judging whether the project will prove to be "worth it" to the city in the long run. This consideration, which was identified by the Common Council during lease negotiations with the Bisons, involves whether the city will continue to realize its goal of making the operation of Pilot Field self-supporting. This goal was achieved in the first three years of the stadium's operation (discounting depreciation and debt service), but whether it will continue to be achieved without hope of major league baseball is uncertain.

What Will the Future Bring?

The Pilot Field project resulted from a unique partnership between the city, the state, and a regional industrial development agency. Although the project bogged down from time to time as it traversed the various bureaucracies, and although it embroiled the county and the city in a funding controversy characteristic of previous major capital sports projects, it did appear to have the potential for serving as a model for future projects of this type.

The importance of the project as a model for future large-scale capital projects should not be underestimated. In 1989, the community faced demands from its two major league sports teams for new facilities. Neither the county nor the city was in a financial position to respond to these requests without first developing a regional or a statewide approach to funding these projects.

Seymour Knox, president of the Buffalo Sabres, announced in 1989 that the Sabres concluded that

> renewal of a long-term lease in the Aud is an unacceptable strategy on which to build the franchise's economic future. Based upon the Sabres' internal forecast of financial operations, the franchise has concluded that the only reasonable basis for future financial stability entails the development of a new and modern sports arena in Buffalo. . . . The creation of

Pilot Field, hopefully the future home of a major league baseball franchise, is tangible evidence of the renaissance of Buffalo. Regional planning for the 1990s and beyond should also include provision for a modern indoor arena to serve the City and the citizens of the Niagara Frontier. (Buffalo Sabres, 1989)

This demand for a new auditorium caught many in the community by surprise. One particularly disturbing aspect of this demand from the city's perspective involved the lost opportunity costs associated with moving the city's major indoor arena away from its present location at the foot of Main Street, where it serves to anchor, along with Pilot Field, the city's newly constructed pedestrian mall and subway. It is feared that Memorial Auditorium will become a white elephant, costing more to maintain than it can generate in revenue.

Another disturbing aspect of this demand was that it closely followed a similar demand by Ralph Wilson, owner of the Buffalo Bills, the city's National Football League franchise. Wilson says that despite the fact that the Bills almost consistently sell out the 80,000-seat Rich Stadium, he is losing money because maintenance costs for the sixteen-year-old facility are simply too high. The team pays approximately $1 million per year for maintenance and cleaning, and it spent $500,000 in 1990 to replace the dated scoreboard. In August 1989, Wilson, reacting to a transformer problem at the stadium, stated that after the team's lease expires in 1998, the Bills would no longer be playing in Rich Stadium, a stadium its developers believed had a fifty-year life span.[8] Wilson suggested that he may move the team unless he receives a new domed stadium on the city's waterfront (in close proximity to Pilot Field) when his current lease expires.

As a result of these demands for new facilities, city and county governments made pronouncements supporting the area's sports franchises. The city began preliminary discussions with the Sabres over the idea of a new facility, which the Sabres estimate will cost between $65 and $90 million. The Sabres indicated a willingness to participate in financing the project, and many council members, including Arthur and Pitts, supported the Sabres' request for a new arena.

The county legislature, for its part, passed a resolution creating a special ad hoc committee on sports to work with city administrators, state representatives, and private entities to define further what role the county can play in securing the future of the Buffalo Bills and the Sabres in Erie County and in attracting new franchises to the area.

In addition, Mayor Griffin and county executive Dennis Gorski petitioned Albany for $500,000 to conduct a feasibility study on the new indoor arena. Also, Arthur undertook preliminary discussions with members of the county legislature urging more cooperation between the two governments in planning and financing the project.

It is not possible to predict the outcome of these events. It is a wonder these discussions even occurred, given the history of city-county relations in the area of sports facility financing. However, as the demands for new facilities mount and as the state's budget becomes increasingly tight, it is clear to most officials that a regional approach to financing major sports projects must be developed, or the community will face the prospect of losing its major league sports teams. This is a prospect that the community and its leaders are not prepared to accept.

NOTES

1. Interview with Joseph Overfield, team historian for the Bisons, January 8, 1989. See also Fink, 1988.

2. The debate over the nature and extent of the new facility was divided along the same lines that divided the debate surrounding Pilot Field, pitting the Griffin administration against a coalition of council members, headed by council president George K. Arthur. In 1989, the city had bonding authorization for $4.5 million, but council member David Collins, who represents the Masten District, where the stadium is located, was asking for an additional $13.0 million for plans that include the construction of a field house and an indoor swimming facility. The administration, while willing to add to the $4.5 million, was asking that Collins scale back his plans.

3. Erie Community College (ECC) could lose its accreditation because it lacks recreational facilities for its students. For this reason, the county has sought to tie the development of a field house for ECC to other developments in the Joseph Ellicott Preservation District, where the campus is located. Other proposals have involved adding a field house to a parking garage, which was proposed to replace parking that was lost as a result of the construction of Pilot Field. From the city's perspective, the inclusion of the field-house component in the project was a hook to attract county participation in the funding of Pilot Field. These proposals have always run into trouble in the state capital because of a general lack of funds at the state level.

4. The Erie County Industrial Development Agency is a public benefit corporation created in 1970 by an act of the New York State legislature to foster economic prosperity in Buffalo and Erie County through the retention, attraction, and expansion of commerce and industry. Serving as a stadium developer is arguably outside of the organization's purview, but it does possess the technical expertise for the task since it was involved in earlier feasibility studies and project planning.

5. The fear was that Wall Street might lower the city's bond rating,

making it more expensive for the city to sell bonds for other capital projects. The unique financing mechanism employed in the project, along with an extension of a provision in the Federal Tax Code that allowed municipalities to finance stadium projects with tax-exempt bonds, left the city's financial condition unharmed.

6. In 1977, the city and the county entered into a sales-tax revenue distribution agreement, which provided that 35.3055 percent of sales-tax revenue would be allocated to the county and the rest would go to the cities of Buffalo, Lackawanna, and Tonawanda. The intent of this provision was to enable the county to appropriate 11.4 percent of its annual yield from sales-tax revenues for the support of various cultural and public benefit organizations, such as the zoo and the philharmonic orchestra.

When the state legislature authorized the county to raise the sale tax from 7 percent to 8 percent, the city gave up its share of the additional 1 percent. At the time of its passage, this tax rate increase was to last only two years but it has been extended several times and appears to be institutionalized.

7. The estimate is based on a study conducted by Coopers and Lybrand, a national accounting firm, that concluded Pilot Field would generate $10.3 million if it attracted 272,000 paid admissions. Attendance has far surpassed this early estimate.

Not everyone is entirely thrilled with Pilot Field, however. Some restauranteurs in the area around the stadium are disappointed by the negative impact the stadium's restaurant has had on their lunch trade. Not all restaurant owners agree, however. Some say their lunch business is down, but their business overall is up. There also is a dispute involving parking spaces that were lost or displaced as a result of the construction of Pilot Field. Office building owners in the area surrounding Pilot Field were promised by the city and the ECIDA in bond documents that the 1,530 parking spaces lost when the field was built would be replaced. As of 1990, 530 spaces still needed to be constructed to meet this target. Building owners complain that the lack of parking in close proximity to their buildings adversely affects their ability to rent office space, causing many of their tenants to flee to the suburbs, where parking is not only more plentiful, but free.

8. Under the terms of the lease, the Bills and Erie County divide revenues from ticket sales, parking, and concessions at Rich Stadium. A provision in the lease guarantees that the team will pay at least $17.5 million in rent over twenty-five years, the term of the lease. According to James L. Magavern, county attorney at the time the lease was negotiated, "The lease is very much to the county's advantage. It was at the time it was negotiated, and as municipalities have given more and more to teams to keep them, it's become less palatable to Mr. Wilson." The Bills claimed to be losing money even though the team set an NFL attendance record of 622,793 in 1988, the team's season ticket sales were the highest since 1974, and ticket prices increased by a third with no loss in attendance. See Beebe, 1989.

Frederick, Maryland 4

For a community to obtain a minor league baseball franchise, several conditions must be fulfilled. Individuals owning a franchise must be willing to locate it in the community; a community must be willing and able to provide a stadium or permit the owners to obtain use of an acceptable privately owned facility; and the league that controls the franchise must approve the owner and the location of the franchise. Ideally, a franchise will have a Player Development Contract (PDC), and the relationship between the franchise and its major league affiliate will be a cooperative one.

The case of Frederick, Maryland, illustrates how each of these factors must fall into place for a community to obtain a team (refer to Part V for other cases of relocation). The case especially highlights the role that state government can play in assisting a local government in its pursuit of a minor league franchise. Maryland is led by a governor who is committed to the use of sport as an economic development tool and had in place a structure for promoting sports operations in Maryland, until the state suffered severe fiscal crises in 1991 and 1992.

The Governor and
the Maryland Office of Sports Promotion

William Donald Schaefer served fifteen years as mayor of Baltimore, Maryland, before being elected governor of the state in 1986. Throughout the early and mid-1980s, the mayor was annually faced with speculation that one or both of the city's major league teams—the National Football League's Colts and Major League Baseball's Orioles—would move from Baltimore.

In 1984, the actions of the Colts owner, Robert Irsay, brought the issues of a new stadium and franchise relocation threats to a crisis point. Despite a number of face-to-face meetings with the mayor and a financial package from the state offering millions of dollars in benefits, the Colts moved to Indianapolis in March 1984. A month later, then-Governor Harry Hughes signed legislation creating the Advisory Commission on Professional Sports and the Economy.

The legislation mandated the Advisory Commission to collect information "that relates to the economic, fiscal, and social effects of professional sports franchises in the state" and to "encourage the retention expansion and location of professional sports franchises in the state." The state's Department of Economic and Community Development was to staff the Advisory Commission.

The Advisory Commission's first product was a study of the economic impact of professional sports in Maryland. That study, which was published in January 1985, identified eleven professional sports active in the state, ranging from horse racing and breeding to wrestling. The analysis attributed an economic impact of $1,155,660,000 to professional sports in Maryland. The Orioles, according to the study, contributed $93.70 million to local economic activity, and the A-level Hagerstown Suns, the state's only minor league team, contributed $3.37 million.

The second product, published in September 1985, was the *Professional Sports Action Plan,* which was produced for the commission by the consulting firm of Touche Ross. This action plan identified "strategic action steps for securing and enhancing the professional sports industry in Maryland and outline[d] a legislative framework to implement the strategic action steps." The report's recommendation to build either a new baseball-only stadium or a new multiuse stadium attracted much attention. Acquiring a franchise in minor league baseball's Carolina League for the state's Eastern Shore, which is a popular summer vacation area, was among its twenty-two recommended action steps. This recommendation was tied to an expectation that Major League Baseball would expand before 1990.

Discussion of a new stadium for the Orioles and the pursuit of a National Football League franchise intensified in 1986. After much debate, the Maryland Stadium Authority was created by the 1986 General Assembly for the purpose of constructing and managing a baseball-only stadium for the Orioles and a football stadium once an NFL franchise was secured. The site to be selected for the new stadiums was one of the few issues of the 1986 Democratic gubernatorial primary. The Advisory Commission and its consultants recommended a suburban site, which Schaefer's opponent in the Democratic primary endorsed. Schaefer favored a site within Baltimore to enhance the city's major tourist area—the inner harbor (also known as Harborplace). Schaefer easily won the primary and the November election. One month after Schaefer's election, the Stadium Authority selected Camden Yards— eighty-five acres near Harborplace—as the site for both stadiums.

Schaefer took office in 1987 and reorganized the Department of Economic and Community Development into the Department of Economic and Employment Development (DEED). Within DEED, the Division of Tourism and Promotion was created, and one person was assigned to concentrate on promoting sports.

The governor also supported a proposal to replace the Advisory Commission on Professional Sports and the Economy with the Advisory Commission on Sports. The new commission's primary mission was to "encourage the promotion and development of amateur and professional sports in the state," according to the proposed legislation. It was to be advisory to the newly reorganized Department of Economic and Employment Development, rather than to the governor and the general assembly, as its predecessor had been. The legislation was adopted and went into effect July 1, 1988.

The Office of Sports Promotion was also created within DEED in 1988 and began work with the Advisory Commission.[1] The newly appointed director of the office did not include acquisition of a second minor league team for Maryland among his goals for the office when he made a presentation to Governor Schaefer. The governor directed him to include that as an additional goal.

The creation of the Office for Sports Promotion was the logical outcome of the governor's experience as mayor of Baltimore and several years of intense debate over professional sports franchises at the level of state government. The Office of Sports Promotion, however, is concerned with amateur as well as professional sports and acts on the belief that both rural and urban areas can benefit from sports.

In 1989, the Office of Sports Promotion played a critical role in securing and hosting the World Championships in White Water Kayak and Canoeing in rural western Maryland and an Audi Race Week (yachting) in rural Solomons in southern Maryland. It helped persuade the Thoroughbred Racing Authority and the Steeplechase and Hunt Association to locate in Fair Hill (in rural Calvert County). It worked to develop an adventure sports program and facilities (backpacking, hiking, mountain biking) for rural western Maryland in conjunction with the Department of Natural Resources and Frostburg State University. In western Maryland, the state is also supporting the construction of a Jack Nicklaus signature golf course, for which the Office of Sports Promotion is seeking a PGA tour event. The 1990 Veterans World Table Tennis, the U.S. Open, and the Junior International Championships took place in

Baltimore, and the 1992 Junior Maccabiah Games were secured for the Baltimore area.

During its first years, the Office of Sports Promotion worked on an event-by-event basis and had no overall strategy. Developing such a strategy was a goal of the director for 1990–91. One obstacle to the development and implementation of a comprehensive strategy is the number of actors on the Maryland sports scene. For example, the Maryland Stadium Authority is responsible for securing an NFL franchise for the state, private organizations are active in getting such events as the Ladies Professional Golf Championship slated for the Bethesda Country Club, and local governments control their facilities and can be reluctant to work with the state, such as when Baltimore and Annapolis announced they would not attempt to host a World Cup (soccer) event. In addition, the Maryland State Games had been established in 1987 as a state government program in amateur sports.[2]

Cooperation was the key, however, when an opportunity developed in 1988–89 to secure a second minor league team for the state. As previously noted, this was not a new idea. A second minor league team had been recommended by the Advisory Commission on Professional Sports and the Economy in 1985 and was on Governor Schaefer's agenda. Two earlier attempts to bring a minor league team to Maryland had failed because of one local government's unwillingness to accept the financial burden of a new stadium and because of community opposition in another jurisdiction. One of the differences in 1988–89 was the attention and support the governor's office gave to the project.

The City of Frederick

Frederick, Maryland, is located approximately forty-five miles northwest of Washington, D.C., and forty miles due west of Baltimore, Maryland. Frederick is positioned at the intersections of interstate highways I-270 and I-70.

Frederick, led by Ronald Young, who served as mayor from 1973 through 1989, has pursued aggressive development policies. These policies have resulted in a successful revitalization effort and impressive growth for the city and Frederick County. The city's policies, combined with the city's ideal location, have transformed it from a quiet rural community into the eleventh fastest growing area in the nation. The city was the eleventh largest community in the state in 1970 and the fourth largest in 1980; it is projected to be second only to Baltimore in 2000.

Frederick's population and that of Frederick County have grown together. Frederick's population increased from 27,557 in 1980 to 36,325 by 1987 and to 40,148 by 1990. The county's population increased from 114,792 in 1980 to 135,960 in 1987 and was projected to reach 143,300 by 1990 and 174,200 by 2000. Most of the county's recent business growth has been in and near the city, which is where water and sewer services exist. Despite these impressive figures, city and county leaders have been concerned that the city possessed no image—negative or positive— beyond the county's borders.

The Young administration had the goal of developing Frederick into a destination center to serve a multicounty, multistate (Pennsylvania, West Virginia, Maryland, Washington, D.C.) area and to provide jobs for its own residents. Another goal was to have a majority of residents commute to jobs within the county's borders and to resist the tendency to be a bedroom community for the District of Columbia and the Washington suburbs.

The centerpiece for Young's ambitious plans for the city was the Carrol Creek project. This project was designed as a flood control project capable of managing the creek's flash floods that, in the past, have been costly to the city's downtown business area. It was also to provide economic stimulation to a one-and-a-half-mile stretch of the creek that flows through the center of the city. The project was patterned after San Antonio's Riverwalk and carried a projected cost of more than $50 million.

Growth and ambitious plans cost money. The cost of maintaining, increasing, and improving infrastructure to serve new businesses and residents forced the Young administration to borrow more money than the city had ever before borrowed. In 1989, the city floated a $45 million bond issue, which was its largest ever.

Young, an outspoken and, at times, controversial mayor, had been a part of the Frederick political scene for more than two decades. Young believed his revitalization plans for the city would be realized when the Carrol Creek project was completed during his next term, which he led some to believe would be his last. To his dismay, however, he was upset in his 1989 bid for a fifth term by a Republican challenger, Paul Gordon. Although disagreement exists as to why Young lost, most cite the mayor's personality and style, the need for better growth management that many newcomers to the city desired, and the increased borrowing by the city, especially for the Carrol Creek project.

As chair of the city's planning commission, Gordon had unsuccessfully opposed the stadium site recommended by the Young administration for the Frederick Keys, a minor league team that Mayor Young took credit for when it relocated from nearby Hagerstown. As a mayoral candidate, Gordon made an issue of the hidden costs of the stadium and characterized the stadium as a "done deal." Gordon believes that the new stadium for the relocated Keys contributed directly to his election victory.

The Relocation

In the mid-1980s, Mayor Young let it be known to several minor league presidents that he was interested in bringing a team to Frederick. The mayor, with assistance from one of the county's state legislators, secured a commitment from a team owner in the Carolina League to relocate to Frederick. The Carolina League's directors approved the relocation before the mayor took the proposal to the city's board of aldermen.

The mayor proposed that the new team play at McCurdy Field, where the local Babe Ruth League played its games. A new field, to be located in neighboring Loats Park, was promised to Babe Ruth League officials. This field was to be built with money that the Junior Chamber of Commerce promised to raise. The city itself did not have money budgeted to create a new playing field for local amateur teams.

Babe Ruth League baseball is popular in Frederick and has a broad base of support. State and regional tournaments are played in Frederick, and the national Babe Ruth Championship has been held in the city. Local Babe Ruth League officials objected to the mayor's proposal because they were doubtful that a new field would be ready in time for their next baseball season and feared that they would be without a playing field. They were able to gain the support of a majority of the board of aldermen. The board rejected the mayor's proposal to use McCurdy Field for minor league baseball by a vote of three to two, which made the acquisition of the Carolina League franchise impossible.

This effort to obtain a minor league team for Frederick motivated Terry Randall, owner of the nearby Hagerstown Suns of the Carolina League, to support a change in the National Association of Professional Baseball Leagues' rule defining the size of the territory that a franchise owner exclusively controls. When the National Association changed this rule from ten miles to thirty-five miles, Frederick, which is thirty miles east of Hagerstown, fell within Hagerstown's territory.

According to Randall, as a result of the change in the territorial rule, it now made economic sense for the Hagerstown Suns owners to operate a team in Frederick. The teams could share personnel, sell joint advertising, and take advantage of other economies of scale. In 1988, he began the process of bringing a team to Frederick.

Randall discussed the concept of placing a AA team in Frederick with the Baltimore Orioles, which was the Hagerstown Suns' major league affiliate. This discussion did not get into specifics because the

Orioles still had a working agreement with Charlotte in the AA Southern League. Signals clearly were sent by both parties, however. The fact that the Hagerstown Suns were an affiliate of the Orioles at the A level made Randall a familiar figure to the major league club and gave him access to a key actor in this case.

Randall also served on the Advisory Commission on Professional Sports and the Economy. Through his membership on the commission Randall knew about the interest in bringing a second minor league team into the state. He was able to make known his desire to become part of the group that did so.

Randall began to make informal inquiries about which franchises were for sale. He spoke with Carolina League officials about moving a AA or an A franchise into Frederick and found they were unlikely to object.

Randall identified the Williamsport franchise of the AA Eastern League as a target for his plans. When he made inquiries of the Eastern League president, he once again signaled his intentions to the Advisory Commission on Sports. There was no immediate response. In August 1988, however, an unofficial representative of the governor's office met with Randall to find out what Randall was planning and what was needed to get the project moving.

Randall posed two questions for him: Does the governor want another team in Maryland? Can the governor provide financial support for a new stadium? Randall asserted that the Carolina League, because of its previous experience in Frederick and on the Eastern Shore,[3] would approve another franchise for Maryland only if a new stadium was guaranteed in advance.

Within a brief time, a meeting was arranged for Randall, the governor, and Mayor Young. The purpose of the meeting was to have Randall's questions answered and for all the parties to assure each other that they were committed to the project of bringing a second minor league baseball team to Maryland.

Mayor Young and Randall discussed the issue only once before the meeting with the governor. In anticipation of the meeting, Young met informally with his board of aldermen. The mayor fully supported building a stadium for a minor league team, but he was wary of such a project because of his experience a few years earlier. The aldermen, especially the women members, also were wary, but within a week the mayor had three of the five votes committed to the project. It was clear that a new stadium would have to be built to avoid the opposition of Babe Ruth League officials and to meet the demands of Randall and the Carolina League. The board agreed to commit no more than a million dollars to the project.

The meeting with the governor was to the point. Randall told the governor he was in the process of purchasing the Williamsport franchise for an estimated $1.5 million and would need a new stadium to bring the team to Frederick. He estimated the cost of a new stadium suitable for AA-level baseball to be $3.0 million. The governor pledged $1.5 million of state support if local sources provided the remaining funds. The mayor made a $1 million commitment to the project, leaving $500,000 to be secured.

On the basis of these verbal commitments, Randall pledged to purchase the franchise with the intention of moving it to Maryland. No promises could be made about whether the AA team would go to Hagerstown or to Frederick. The governor and the mayor assured Randall that the remaining $500,000 would be found.

By chance, the Williamsport franchise was for sale in 1988. It had been bought a year earlier by a public body representing local governments in the Wilkes-Barre-Scranton region of Pennsylvania. Local officials there were in the process of building a minor league stadium so they could bring AAA baseball to the area. No AAA franchise was for sale at the time, however, so local officials bought the AA Williamsport franchise in anticipation of completing their stadium in 1989.

In 1988, however, the Old Orchard Beach AAA franchise was put on the market (see the case study of Old Orchard Beach), and the Pennsylvania officials were successful in purchasing it. They now had no interest in operating the Williamsport franchise, and they requested sealed bids for the franchise. Randall's first bid was rejected, as were all others. After several telephone calls, Randall and his partners were awarded the franchise in the second round of bidding. The sale price was higher than Randall's original estimate of $1.5 million and was all cash, with no contingencies. The owners now possessed a second franchise, but they did not have a PDC or any place in Maryland to relocate the team. Both issues were quickly resolved.

The owners immediately informed the Orioles of their interest in affiliating with the Orioles. It was public knowledge that the Orioles were not satisfied with the stadium situation in which their Southern League Charlotte affiliate was mired (see the case study of Charlotte). That team had been relegated to playing in a temporary facility after its old wooden stadium was destroyed by fire in 1985. The team's owner, George Shinn, had been unsuccessful in negotiating with the city of Charlotte for a new stadium. Shinn had talked about building his own stadium but had finalized no plans. The Orioles wanted to remove their players from the Charlotte situation and place them in a modern facility more conducive to AA baseball.

The Orioles dropped their affiliation with Charlotte. Shortly thereafter, they gave Randall's ownership group a positive response to its request for a PDC. Although other ownership groups approached the Orioles about affiliation, they did not receive serious consideration, even when they were willing to locate on Maryland's Eastern Shore. The Orioles knew the Hagerstown owners and were comfortable with their operation.

Perhaps even more important, the Orioles had been considering consolidating their minor league operations by bringing their affiliates closer to Baltimore. If minor league teams are located a short distance from their parent club, the parent club's cost of moving players back and forth between teams and monitoring their progress is reduced. Also, according to the Orioles assistant director of player development, the Orioles wanted their minor league players to develop an identity with the Orioles. This would be facilitated, Orioles officials believed, by locating the players within the Orioles' marketing area.

The Orioles also viewed an additional team in Maryland, especially one located less than fifty miles away, as a means of creating greater fan interest in the Orioles. The Orioles have marketed themselves as a regional team since the early 1980s (Miller, 1990: 271). Hagerstown and Frederick are within the Orioles' marketing area. The Eastern Shore is beyond a reasonable commute to Baltimore to view a game and return home the same evening.

Each of these factors made the request by Randall's ownership group an attractive one to the Orioles. The Orioles promised a five-year PDC, which is unusually long for minor league baseball, if the franchise was located either in Hagerstown or, if a new stadium was built, in Frederick. The Orioles offered only a one-year PDC if the franchise remained in Williamsport. This, in part, was because the Williamsport stadium was inferior to the Hagerstown stadium or a new stadium.

The Eastern League had to approve the relocation of the Williamsport franchise, and the Carolina League had to approve relocating the Hagerstown franchise to Frederick. The owners used the Orioles PDC as their selling point to the Eastern League. The markets of the Orioles and the Eastern League overlap. From a marketing perspective, fans in Eastern League cities were expected to be more interested in players in the Orioles organization than players from the Seattle Mariners, which was the other alternative.

The Eastern League also wanted a more southern city than Williamsport because of weather conditions. The promise of a better playing facility, whether in Hagerstown or Frederick, was another factor in Randall's favor. Randall told Eastern League officials that the Carolina League would have to decide the ultimate location of the franchise since it controlled the territory. It was believed that the Carolina League would prefer Frederick. Eastern League officials approved the new owners and the proposal to relocate the Williamsport franchise to either Hagerstown or Frederick.

Shortly thereafter, in the fall of 1988, Randall met with Carolina League officials to discuss the relocation. Carolina League officials saw the proposal to relocate the Hagerstown franchise to Frederick as a risk, since they already had a successful operation in Hagerstown. Permitting another team to operate within thirty miles posed a threat to that success. Also, Frederick was an untested market.

Randall argued that having two minor league teams within seventy miles of their major league affiliate was precedent setting and that the Carolina League could be a part of that development. He argued that the costs of operation could be reduced with common ownership of the two teams. He also pointed out that the league had the option of selecting either of the two sites.

Carolina League officials remembered their previous experience with Frederick and Charles County in Maryland. They remained skeptical but gave their preliminary approval of the relocation of the league's Hagerstown franchise to Frederick, providing the 1989 season was played at McCurdy Field and a new stadium was constructed for the 1990 playing season.

The Carolina League chose to operate in Frederick rather than in Hagerstown because it was a better fit geographically. Frederick was thirty miles closer to all other league members and allowed one team to avoid overnight stays. Frederick also promised a larger market and a new stadium.

In October 1988, representatives of the two leagues, local officials, representatives from the Orioles, and a representative from the governor's office met in Hagerstown to reassure each other of their commitments. Reassurance that a new stadium was forthcoming was critical. Financing for the stadium was still questionable, however. The remaining $500,000 still had not been found, and the state's share was not available until the 1990 fiscal year (July 1, 1989). This would undermine the construction schedule and sabotage the project. The governor's representative promised to provide a decision on the issue of the state's money within thirty-six hours. The next day he was able to give assurance that the state's money would be available when needed. Once that commitment was made, the leagues were reassured, and the project moved forward. Attention then focused on locating, financing, and designing the stadium.

The Stadium

The location of Frederick's new stadium was obvious to city officials. Loats Park was property once owned by the Loats Foundation. The foundation was created in 1879 to house and care for "destitute and deserving female orphan children," but in 1956, the foundation's board broadened its charitable activities to include other youth-oriented projects. In the early 1980s, the foundation, to satisfy Internal Revenue Service regulations, offered the city six acres of an undeveloped thirty-three-acre site for use as a youth park. The city requested and received the complete thirty-three-acre site. City planning documents called for a community baseball field and park to be built on the site.

The site appeared ideal for a minor league facility and pleased Carolina League officials and team owners. It is visible and easily accessible from the interstate highways that pass by the city, and it is within walking distance of downtown. It is bordered by a truck stop, a plumbing business, the interstate highways, and a cemetery. A small Seventh Day Adventist church is located approximately a quarter of a mile from the field, next to I-70. It appeared, therefore, that minor league baseball activities would not be disruptive and were in keeping with existing and proposed land use.

Completing the financial arrangements was a more difficult task. The city, which had capped its contribution at $1 million, planned to use part of a recently passed $45 million bond proposal. The $45 million was more than what the city actually needed for proposed projects. Thus, according to Mayor Young, the $1 million was available to the city for the stadium without sacrificing any other project—planned or ongoing.

The governor's office had pledged its share, $1.5 million. Half of this total came in the form of a grant from the Maryland Industrial and Commercial Redevelopment Fund (MICRF), which the Department of Economic and Employment Development manages. Not only are grants from MICRF rare, but this was the first support given to a sports-related project. MICRF allows the state to make loans to subdivisions at interest rates no higher than bond issue rates. According to MICRF's director, it was recognized that even with a low interest rate, stadium revenues coming back to the city could not sustain debt service on the stadium if a loan rather than a grant was selected as the method of state financing. The remainder of the state's share came from $15 million set aside annually in its capital budget for use by local governments. This money is assigned to local government projects after deliberations with local legislative delegations.

The mayor turned to the county to produce the remaining $500,000.

The county commission, which had not always had a cooperative relationship with the city, did have a positive working relationship with the mayor, especially on economic development matters. Nevertheless, the county commission refused the mayor's request. The governor's office and a state legislator from the county then communicated to the county Commissioners that they expected the county to participate in the project, implying that the county might not receive a positive response to its capital project requests if cooperation was not forthcoming. At that, the county commissioners reversed their decision and pledged half the requested amount.

The city still needed to raise $250,000. Mayor Young made a public announcement that the city would name the stadium after anyone who contributed the remaining $250,000. Within a week of his announcement, an individual stepped forward and offered the money to the city in exchange for naming the stadium after his father. The offer was quickly accepted. Although Young admits he had a small number of potential benefactors in mind when he made his announcement, this was not one of them.

By the middle of November 1988, the city had identified the site, had commitments for financing a $3 million stadium, and had negotiated a lease for the stadium using the Hagerstown lease as a model (see below). Construction of the stadium, however, could not be completed for the 1989 season.

It was agreed that McCurdy Field would be upgraded and that the team would play at McCurdy Field for one year. Team owners agreed to play games in Hagerstown if scheduling conflicts with the Babe Ruth League developed. Local Babe Ruth League officials agreed to this plan in a hastily called meeting a few days before the November 17 meeting of the board of aldermen, at which the aldermen approved the stadium lease and finalized the deal.

According to one alderman, who was the board's leading spokesperson for the stadium, a citizen called him half an hour before the board's November 17 meeting and asked him to vote against the lease because the stadium was too close to the Seventh Day Adventist church and baseball activity would disrupt the church's activities.

Controversy

The stadium proposal met relatively little opposition before November. The chairperson of the planning commission had opposed the site, suggesting instead a site near the city's airport, which would not have been as accessible from downtown or from the interstate system. This proposal received little support. The mayor and stadium advocates remained in control of the issue, despite opposition to the stadium voiced at public hearings.

One month after the board of aldermen approved the stadium lease, the Seventh Day Adventist Church filed a lawsuit seeking to block construction of the stadium. The church contended that city planners did not follow proper procedures in reviewing the stadium proposal and that the use of the site for a minor league stadium was inconsistent with its residential zoning and with restrictions placed on the deed when it was transferred to the city. The church also argued that the stadium would devalue the church's property to such a degree that it would be unmarketable.

Early in the controversy, it was reported that the church would drop its opposition if the stadium was realigned so that it did not face the church. The city did alter the stadium's planned layout but denied it was in response to the church's demands. The controversy grew bitter as time passed, and the lawsuit threatened to block the stadium's construction. The mayor claimed that church officials were seeking to negotiate a deal with the city to close a street connecting the church and the park. He publicly referred to the church's leaders as "hypocrites" when they denied his claim.

Meanwhile, the Frederick Keys, renamed from the Hagerstown Suns, opened the 1989 baseball season in McCurdy Field with the governor, local officials, and Orioles representatives in attendance. The team was an immediate success with the fans.

The mayor and Terry Randall met in Annapolis in April, a few days before the lawsuit was to be heard in the courts, to appear before the state's Board of Public Works, which was scheduled to approve the second half of the state's funding. During lunch the mayor criticized the Keys owners for not taking a public stand supporting the city in the lawsuit. Randall was under the impression that although the team's owners were participating in the lawsuit, the city preferred them to keep a low public profile.

A few days later, the team owners held a press conference to explain that if the lawsuit blocked the construction of a new stadium, the team would be forced to relocate from Frederick because the agreement with the Carolina League guaranteed a new stadium would exist for the 1990 season. In fact, the agreement stipulated that for each year a new stadium was lacking, the team would be fined $50,000 by the Carolina League. This was money the owners were not willing to forfeit. Nor would the Orioles be content to have their players play in McCurdy Field for more than one year.

On May 8, 1989, the planning commission gave its final approval for the stadium. The mayor characterized the review process as "the most comprehensive consideration the planning commission has given any project in the 20 years I have been in public office" (Young, 1989). The chair of the commission disagreed.

In June 1989, the Frederick County Circuit Court ruled against the church. It found that the opponents failed to exhaust all administrative appeals before seeking judicial intervention, and it rejected the argument that deed restrictions prevented the stadium from being built at Loats Park. Site preparation began a few weeks after the court decision.

The Orioles remained detached from the stadium controversy and the lawsuit. The Orioles worked closely with the city and the team on the selection of an architect for the stadium and its design. Whereas a minor league team's owner may be satisfied with a new stadium if it contains amenities (such as concession stands and luxury boxes) that will help ensure profits, the major league officials have concerns about the playing field, its dimensions, and amenities that favor ballplayers (such as the clubhouse conditions).

The Lease, Stadium Construction, and Stadium Use

The Frederick Keys opened their 1990 season in Harry Grove Stadium, which still was not completely finished. Work on the stadium, mainly related to its skyboxes, progressed throughout the 1990 season, amidst cost overruns and further controversy.

City officials always made the point in their justifications for the stadium that it would be a community asset and would be used by city and county residents. The $3 million estimated cost for the stadium included money to improve the surrounding park and to provide parking lots that would be used not only by fans, but also by commuters during weekdays and by visitors to the park.

The lease that was negotiated was based on the Hagerstown Suns' lease. That lease called for an annual payment of $16,000 and $75 a game to cover the cost of the stadium lighting. Hagerstown's goal was to cover its stadium operating costs. Frederick, despite the higher costs of a new stadium, adopted the same terms in a lease that would extend to March 31, 1994.

The Frederick lease recognized potential conflicts in the use of McCurdy Field in 1989 and the likelihood of hosting regional and national amateur baseball tournaments during the length of the lease. The team agreed to give priority to the Babe Ruth League if any scheduling conflicts occurred over the use of McCurdy Field in 1989. It also agreed to give priority to a regional or national tournament in future years. The team was also prohibited from rescheduling postponed games on dates already reserved for youth league teams. The team was expected to play in Hagerstown (which it did on occasion in 1989) if any of these conflicts arose.

During the summer of 1989, it was discovered that original stadium cost estimates were approximately $1.5 million too low. Negotiations scaled back the stadium design to a projected cost of $3.2 million. The city agreed to supply the additional $200,000 if the team owners promised to try to raise that amount from the state. On the basis of a handshake, the owners promised if they could not raise the money from the state, they would reimburse the city.

Talks with the governor resulted in pressure to complete the stadium with most of its originally designed amenities, especially the skyboxes. The governor suggested that the state, the city, the county, and the team owners each contribute $300,000 to meet the costs of the original stadium design. The owners agreed. The Young administration is alleged to have agreed to a state loan of $300,000 to meet its obligation. The loan was to be repaid from the city's share of skybox revenues, which was to be negotiated with the team.

However, the newly elected Gordon was opposed to committing any additional city funds to the stadium, as were the county commissioners. This was made clear to team owners and the local legislative delegation in a meeting called to solve the financing problem. As a result, the team owners agreed to pay for the entire amount of cost overruns, estimated at the time to be $700,000 (but which actually approached $1 million), in exchange for a fifteen-year lease and the right to retain all skybox revenues. The team also agreed to pay the city additional rent of $200,000 over a fifteen-year period, at 8 percent interest, or $21,635 annually.

The stadium contains seventeen skyboxes, all but one of which were to be leased on the basis of a ten-year rental for $10,000 a year. (As of August 1990, thirteen of the skyboxes were leased for the 1991 season.) Randall claims it will take the owners fifteen years to recover the cost of their investment.

In August 1990, the city stopped construction on the skyboxes, with about 90 percent of the work completed. The team owners were refusing to reimburse the city $183,000 of an $858,000 construction bill for the skyboxes. They argued that government regulations required higher wages than they would have paid if the work had been contracted privately by the team. The city contended that if the team had contracted for the work, it could not have begun until after the work on the stadium structure was complete. This would have resulted delaying skybox construction for six to nine months. The team withheld its additional rent payment, and the city halted the construction work. The team eventually agreed to assume responsibility for all costs, except certain architectural fees, which amounted to approximately $60,000 as of January 1991.

Despite this controversy, the first three years of the Frederick Keys have been most successful for the Keys. Attendance in 1989 was 165,930, which was third highest (behind Durham and Prince William) in the Carolina League. In 1990, playing in their new stadium, the Keys attracted 277,348 fans, which was the second highest attendance (behind Durham) for all A-level leagues. The Keys, taking advantage of the proximity to Baltimore, played a few games in the Orioles' Memorial Stadium and were saluted before an Orioles game for finishing first in league competition. In addition, the Orioles moved their instructional league, composed of area college teams and Orioles minor leaguers, to Frederick for the 1990 season. In 1991, the Keys drew a record 318,354 fans, which was more than any other AA or A team's 1991 attendance.

The city, however, experienced a stadium operating deficit of $151,813 for 1990. Annual debt service on the variable-rate bond for the stadium was estimated by the mayor as more than $140,000. In addition, the city's financial commitment to the construction of the stadium had risen from the budgeted $1 million to nearly $2 million. A portion ($250,000) of this latter expense resulted from the planning commission's insistence that an overflow parking lot be paved. The new administration, therefore, had to "move around" capital budget funds (which totaled $15 million in fiscal year 1991), causing some planned projects to be delayed.

In 1991, the owners of the Keys, with the state's support, attempted to obtain an expansion AAA franchise, which they hoped to locate in Annapolis, the state's capital located approximately thirty miles south of Baltimore, or in the Washington, D.C., suburbs of Prince George's County. They were among five finalists for two teams, but they were not awarded a franchise.

NOTES

1. By 1990, the Office of Sports Promotion had a professional staff of two and a budget of approximately $650,000. The state suffered a severe and unexpected deficit during FY1991 and worse financial problems in FY1992. The Office of Sports Promotion's budget survived early cuts in the state's budget but was terminated in October 1991.

2. The Maryland State Games program was suspended in December

1990 amidst a scandal involving charges of nepotism and misappropriation of funds. The Maryland State Games were an annual event for Maryland's amateur athletes that were run by a nonprofit foundation, which was created in 1985. In 1987, the director of the foundation was appointed to a position within the Maryland Department of Health and Mental Hygiene to promote amateur athletic activities as a means of fighting alcohol and drug abuse. The foundation raised only $260,000 ($125,000 of which was in the form of a bank loan) of the total revenues of $891,000 between December 1988 and September 1990. More than $400,000 in federal alcohol- and drug-abuse prevention grants from the state's health department to the foundation were included in that total. Legislative auditors challenged $455,000 of its expenditures within that period. The function of promoting amateur athletics was reassigned to DEED in January 1991, and the games were held during the summer of 1991.

3. In 1987, local and state government officials, including the chair of the Advisory Commission on Sports and the Economy, made a presentation at the Carolina League's summer meeting. In September, Charles County commissioners signed an agreement with the owner of a team then located in Kinston, North Carolina, to complete a stadium by April. The county, which is located on the state's Eastern Shore, committed $1.5 million to build the stadium, and the state was expected to commit at least $2.5 million. A private developer donated fifty-two acres of land adjacent to a regional park for the stadium. The proposed relocation was approved by the league shortly thereafter. The team owner acquired a working agreement with the Cleveland Indians and began selling season tickets in Charles County for the next season. A November election brought into office new county commissioners. In December, an Army Corps of Engineers report halted stadium construction because of wetlands problems. This delay made it impossible to meet the April deadline. The new commissioners also discovered that the stadium would cost nearly a million dollars more than expected. As a result, the new commissioners voted to break the county's agreement, pay a $300,000 penalty to the team owner, and not build a stadium, rather than incur estimated annual deficits of $600,000 related to the stadium.

PART III

Franchise Relocation

The footloose nature of U.S. corporations receives much attention in the economic development literature. Corporations abandon communities where they have been located for many years, leaving those communities and their residents with a weakened economy and social structure and without any compensation or resources to assist recovery. This situation is often portrayed as a violation of a corporate moral obligation to the community and its residents. Some also believe that legal and financial obligations are broken when corporations relocate after accepting public subsidies (Bluestone and Harrison, 1980; White, 1988).

The public has come to perceive major league sports franchises as among the most footloose, primarily because of highly publicized threats by team owners to relocate their franchises and actual franchise relocations in various major league sports (Johnson, 1983). The media characterize team owners as greedy businessmen who are only concerned with maximizing their teams' profits and who have no loyalty to their host communities or fans. The media, however, simultaneously praise local officials for keeping or gaining a team and criticize them for providing the costly subsidies that accomplish the task of keeping or gaining a team.

Sullivan (1987) has recently called this stereotype into question in his study of the Brooklyn Dodgers' relocation to Los Angeles. Sullivan argues that the move was as much the result of political forces at play in both cities as it was Dodger owner Walter O'Malley's pursuit of profits. Indeed, Sullivan suggests that the move was actually a high risk venture that O'Malley undertook with inadequate analysis and preparation.

Henschen, Pelissero, and Sidlow (1989) have suggested that major league franchise relocations take place as a result of forces working to push and pull a franchise from its host community, which combine to overwhelm forces working against relocation. They identify the host community's land use and fiscal policies; sports team regulation; local institutional and political conflicts; and negative public opinion as factors that push a team away. The pull factors include another community's fiscal policies, land availability and economic development incentives; lack of sports team regulation; political support; favorable public opinion; and recruitment efforts.

Working against these factors are the host community's efforts to keep the team. These include new economic development incentives, changes in sports team regulations and fiscal policies, negotiations by supportive government officials, community support, and actions of various interest groups in the community.

This conceptualization of the dynamics of franchise relocation, as well as Sullivan's, emphasizes the political actions and public policies needed to persuade a team owner to remain in a community or to relocate to a new community. This implies that local governments are free to decide how best to negotiate with a team owner and that they do have latitude in such negotiations.

Part I concluded that even though franchise scarcity and instability coexisted in the minor leagues, the leverage that a minor league team owner has over local officials is not compelling (and is different than that of major league teams) because a minor league team is not economically significant and is geographically restricted to certain relocation sites. Also, local officials often cannot respond positively to a team owner's demands because of the limited resources available in smaller communities.

The cases presented in this section describe the events and negotiations that preceded the relocation of four minor league teams as well as those that forestalled the relocation of spring training and minor league operations of a major league team. They demonstrate the importance of stadiums in city-team negotiations, and they show how the business interests of team owners and the interests of local officials often conflict regarding the stadium issue.

The cases in this section provide radically different images of team owners. These images range from the stereotypical owner who is willing to leverage communities to maximize profits (e.g., George Steinbrenner and Joe Buzas) to those who see team ownership as the fulfillment of a dream but know little about marketing their product (e.g., Jordon Kobritz in Old Orchard Beach, Maine, and Dave Kramer in Fresno, California). The Birmingham and Charlotte cases present owners who, although they have very different personalities, are seen as the new breed of minor league team owner—someone who views minor league baseball as a business and develops business and marketing strategies that tie a team to its community and fans.

The team owner makes the decision to relocate a franchise. In some cases that decision will be made regardless of local development planning and the efforts of local officials to meet an owner's demands. Location decisions of owners tend to be business decisions that are designed to maximize their financial interests. For example, Joe Buzas, as owner of the Fresno Suns, chose not to remain in Fresno in the face of competition from the local university for fans and advertising dollars. Birmingham Barons owner Art Clarkson was determined to follow his market to the suburbs of Birmingham. Charlotte Knights owner George Shinn wanted a stadium that would be capable of hosting more than a minor league baseball team. To make his stadium plans work, Shinn had to avoid restrictions on the use of his stadium and needed more land than he could obtain in Charlotte.

In two of the cases, Charlotte and Birmingham, the teams remained within the metropolitan area, moving from the center city to a suburban community. In these two cases, the teams were owned by individuals who resided in the communities.

In two other cases, Fresno and Old Orchard Beach, teams relocated to distant communities. In both of these cases, local ownership was absent, and the sale of the team preceded the relocation. In the fifth case, the city of Fort Lauderdale, after arduous negotiations, continued to be the site for the New York Yankees' spring training and Florida State League team. George Steinbrenner, owner of the New York Yankees, however, appeared poised to relocate these operations to Tampa, where he has a residence and business interests.[1]

Team owners in each case, except for Old Orchard Beach, where a new facility was in place, made new facilities a condition for remaining in the community. Although local officials may try to keep stadium negotiations off their agenda, as Charlotte, Fresno, and Birmingham officials did in earlier years, they often are not able to control whether the stadium issue becomes a part of the public agenda or their own formal agenda. Events beyond the control of officials may occur unexpectedly. In Charlotte, for example, fire left the local team without a stadium, and in Fresno, a community college district found its stadium in such disrepair that it tore down the stands without consulting Fresno officials. Alternatively, a team owner may force the issue on local officials, as was the case in Birmingham and Fort Lauderdale.

The cases in this section suggest that minor league baseball is not so important that the decision to negotiate or to grant an owner's demands is a certainty (see also the Fort Wayne case). Each case questions the importance of minor league baseball to the local economy. In Birmingham, city council leaders suggested that developing a water theme park would be of greater economic significance than keeping the team. In Charlotte, the local chamber of commerce was not successful in raising funds from the local business community for a stadium. In Fresno, Old Orchard Beach, and Fort Lauderdale, city officials and business leaders disagreed among themselves about the importance of minor league baseball.

In each case, with the exception of Fort Lauderdale, there are accusations or evidence that local officials did not negotiate seriously with team owners. Local officials level the same charge against the team owners. The cases provide examples of the lack of communication (e.g., Fresno and Old Orchard Beach) and miscommunication (e.g., Charlotte and Birmingham) between team owners and local officials.

In each case, with the exception of Fort Lauderdale, local officials were willing to permit the team owner to go elsewhere rather than invest in a stadium or make more concessions. In the case of Fort Lauderdale, city officials were unwilling to lose spring training activities, which were the primary focus of negotiations rather than the minor league team.

The cases in this section find that none of the five communities possessed an explicit sports strategy, even though Birmingham and Charlotte invested heavily in professional sports and Fresno had a relationship with a state university's sports program. The Birmingham mayor's office appeared to have placed negotiations in a development context, and Fort Lauderdale officials were sensitive to the marketing potential of their relationship with the New York Yankees. The existence of plans, however, did not guarantee successful negotiation outcomes, as evidenced by the case of Birmingham.

The cases also call attention to intercity relations in a metropolitan region. Portland's ill will toward Old Orchard Beach for undermining its efforts to gain a team contributed to Old Orchard's failure to keep its team. Interviewees in Charlotte and Birmingham denied they had ill feelings toward their suburban neighbors for taking their teams. They insisted that the teams have not been lost but remain accessible to city residents. The fact is, however, both teams' attendance is now composed mainly of suburbanites rather than city residents, which is a change in their attendance patterns. The case of Fort Lauderdale illustrates intergovernmental cooperation to keep the Yankees' spring training.

In sum, the five cases in this section demonstrate the importance of the political environment within which stadium negotiations take place. Conditions in the host community, especially those affecting a team's financial position, often are the stimuli for relocation rather than the seduction attempts of another community or the motivations of team owners. Also, other issues on the local agenda and political actors other than the primary negotiators often influence the nature and outcome of negotiations.

The demands of minor league team owners do not necessarily receive priority treatment from local officials. Without an adequate playing facility, an owner has no choice except to demand a new stadium or to relocate. In other cases, minor league team owners attempt to leverage local officials for the maximum subsidies. In negotiations, it is important to create arrangements that satisfy the interests of the team owners without sacrificing the public interest. When this is not possible, local officials are ready to accept the relocation of a minor league team, as this section demonstrates.

NOTE

1. In August 1990, George Steinbrenner was barred by the Commissioner of Baseball from participating in organizational activities of the New York Yankees. Presumably, this would apply to decisions about the location of spring training and the Fort Lauderdale team, which the Yankees own.

Charlotte, North Carolina   5

Charlotte, North Carolina, which is located on the North and South Carolina border, is a part of the New South. Charlotte has a population of 395,934, making it the thirty-fifth largest city in the nation. It is the center of a metropolitan area of more than 1,112,000, which includes counties in South Carolina.

Charlotte aspires to be a regional center. It expends much effort pursuing national corporate headquarters and attempting to convince corporate executives to relocate to Charlotte. When Sears Roebuck and Company was considering relocating its headquarters from Chicago in 1988–89, Charlotte entered the competition and was among the final sites Sears considered.

The "Ch" factor has plagued Charlotte efforts to set itself apart as a leading city in the New South. Residents believe that people outside of the Carolinas confuse Charlotte with Charleston, West Virginia; Charleston, South Carolina; and Charlottesville, Virginia. They believe that the city's identity and location have been a mystery to most people.

City officials are convinced they have overcome the "Ch" factor since George Shinn brought professional basketball to the community. Shinn gained his wealth from ownership of a string of proprietary schools. In the early 1980s, he began to pursue ownership of professional sports franchises, which he wanted to bring to Charlotte.

At first, Shinn involved himself in the United States Football League, bringing two exhibition games to Charlotte. After that league folded, Shinn sought and won a National Basketball Association (NBA) expansion franchise. Shinn convinced NBA officials that the Charlotte *region* could support an NBA team, despite doubts among local officials and even within the Charlotte-Mecklenburg Chamber of Commerce.

Shinn's Charlotte Hornets began play in 1988 and sold every seat to every game they played in Charlotte in their first two seasons, setting NBA attendance records. According to interviewees, the Hornets' success has made residents more aware of living within a region rather than in isolated jurisdictions and has brought national attention to the city. The "Ch" factor is a problem of the past, they feel.

George Shinn, however, had sports goals other than ownership of an NBA franchise. In the summer of 1989, Shinn sought a National Football League (NFL) expansion franchise for Charlotte. He was in competition with Jerry Richardson, who is a former NFL player and owner of Hardee's, a fast-food chain. Richardson had plans to build his own stadium in Charlotte. Shinn also had purchased the Charlotte Knights, a minor league baseball team that plays in the AA Southern League, and relocated them across the state line in Fort Mill, South Carolina (see the case study of York County). This is an analysis of events leading to that relocation.

Negotiations with the Crockett Family

The Washington Senators/Minnesota Twins owned and operated a minor league team in Charlotte from 1941 to 1972. The team played in a ballpark built for the team by Senators owner Clark Griffith. At the end of the 1972 season, the Twins relocated the Charlotte team to Orlando, Florida. In 1975, James Crockett, Jr., a local businessman and promoter, bought the ballpark from the Twins for $87,500. Baseball returned to Charlotte in 1976, when Crockett and his family bought a AA-level Southern League team affiliated with the Baltimore Orioles.

A sister, Frances, was assigned to operate the team, newly named the Charlotte O's. The Crocketts were successful promoters of wrestling and other entertainment. Although Frances ran the team successfully for many years, several interviewees suggested that the baseball team was not a priority for the family.

The wooden stadium, renamed Crockett Park, was located in a neighborhood that increasingly complained about the games at the park. On March 16, 1985, Crockett Park burned to the ground. The land had become too valuable to continue to use it as a site for a baseball stadium. As an interim measure, however, a temporary stadium was built for the team at Crockett Park. The Baltimore Orioles gave the Crocketts two years to produce a new permanent stadium.

The Crocketts turned to the Charlotte-Mecklenburg Chamber of Commerce for advice about obtaining a new stadium. The Chamber of Commerce recently had hired Carroll Gray as executive director. Before coming to Charlotte, Gray had led a successful community effort to bring minor league baseball to Greenville, North Carolina. He was proud of that effort and believed he could lead a community drive to build a new stadium for the Charlotte O's.

The Chamber of Commerce therefore took the lead in attempting to site, finance, and construct a new minor league stadium. A former mayor was appointed chairperson of the effort. He approached the Charlotte city council with a proposal for financing a new stadium with revenue bonds to be paid off by the revenue from season tickets. The city council showed little interest in the project, partly because several council members felt animosity toward the former mayor and partly because the council was more concerned with the construction of a new $40 million coliseum. The coliseum was being built as part of an effort to regain the Atlantic Coast Conference's basketball tournament, which the city once hosted, and to secure the finals of the NCAA basketball tournament.

The Chamber of Commerce, rebuffed by the city council, launched its own fund drive. It set a goal of $4 million and promised that no public money would be used to construct the stadium. The fund drive was not as successful as hoped, however. After a city-owned site proved unsuitable for the stadium, a privately owned, nineteen-acre parcel adjacent to the new coliseum was identified as a desirable site. The city was asked to purchase the site for the stadium. The city council eventually agreed to take options on the land, but it placed a limit of $1 million on the purchase price. The options were scheduled to expire December 31, 1986.

Chamber of Commerce officials soon recognized they were not going to be able to build the stadium with private funds. They therefore sought the assistance of the county commissioners of Mecklenburg County. A proposal was put forth for the Chamber of Commerce to contribute $2.0 million and for the county to invest $2.7 million for a 5,000-seat stadium to be located on the site, which the city would purchase for $1.0 million. The city would operate the stadium through the Coliseum Authority.

The county traditionally left such projects to the city of Charlotte. County commissioners were divided over the proposal, but one commissioner in particular strongly supported the proposal "to save baseball for Charlotte." The commissioners decided to conduct the county's first "straw vote." A nonbinding referendum was scheduled for May 3, 1986, to decide a onetime tax of 1.7 cents per $100 assessed value to raise the $2.7 million.

Chamber of Commerce representatives led the campaign in support of the proposal. No organized opposition developed, although some officials spoke out against the proposal. Their principal argument was that because baseball was unlikely to leave Charlotte, there was not as much urgency to build a stadium as proponents were claiming. The issue passed by fewer than 500 votes, with less than 15 percent of the county's electorate voting. The results showed 17,825 in favor (50.6 percent) and 17,396 opposed. The commissioners hesitantly agreed to impose the tax to finance the stadium.

Negotiations between the Crocketts and the city continued through the end of 1986. The deadline for the city to exercise its option on the nineteen acres of land loomed over the negotiations. The city refused to exercise its options until a lease for the stadium had been signed by the Crocketts.

Interviewees, who participated in the negotiations for the city, questioned whether the Crocketts were serious about signing the lease. The Crocketts, however, pledged $450,000 to the Chamber of Commerce's fund drive and later pledged an additional $485,000. This was nearly half the total raised by the Chamber of Commerce, and it permitted the Chamber of Commerce to claim it had reached its goal.

The media reported that the city and the Crocketts were very close to signing a lease. The sticking point in December of 1986 was reportedly the Crocketts' demand that they keep all ticket and concession revenues from play-off games during the first four years of the proposed eight-year lease. The amount involved was estimated to be either $3,250 (by the Crocketts' attorney) or $10,000 (by the Coliseum Authority's attorney) per year. The city reportedly refused.

During this stage of the negotiations, Mayor Harvey Gantt described the negotiations as "one of the most complex $6 million projects we've ever done." He referred to three main difficulties: (1) the cost of the nineteen-acre parcel had increased from an initial estimate of $800,000 to $1.3 million by December 1986; (2) the Chamber of Commerce had not met its goal of $4 million to cover construction costs; and (3) the city staff had had to devote a great deal of time to the project, at an estimated cost of $134,000.

Gantt also noted that a large number of parties was involved in the negotiations. These included the city; the county; the Crockett family; representatives of the Charlotte Chamber of Commerce, who often acted as intermediaries between negotiators; landowners; the state government, which owned a farmers' market adjacent to the nineteen acres and was seeking its relocation; and the Coliseum Authority. The Coliseum Authority, which would operate the stadium, was negotiating with the Crocketts.

Finally, Gantt noted that the city council "never could control it [the stadium project] from Day One." The city manager echoed this sentiment when interviewed. He claimed that from the beginning the city was in a difficult situation—always reacting to someone else's proposals. The issue had become a part of the public agenda, fund raising was proceeding, a site had been identified, and fear of losing the team was being exploited. According to the city manager, the city council had no choice except to sort through the issues. Professional staff in the city manager's office had serious concerns about the project. By asking hard questions, however, the city manager's office appeared to be opposing baseball.

The principal concern revolved around the proposed stadium site's proximity to the new coliseum. City representatives were worried the Crocketts would sponsor nonbaseball events in the new stadium that would compete with coliseum activities. They were also mindful of the traffic and parking problems that would result when events were held on the same date. City officials also knew that the site's hilly terrain would necessitate careful engineering to house the stadium, and the cost implications of this had not yet been explored.

Even though no agreement was reached before the end of the year, the city took steps to purchase the nineteen acres. In August 1987, the parties were again close to reaching an agreement, but again negotiations fell apart. According to media reports, city officials demanded the Crocketts impose a surcharge of fifty cents per ticket to cover a projected $478,000 shortfall in the stadium budget. The Crocketts, concerned about their tax liability, refused. As an alternative, the Crocketts publicly offered to build the stadium with private funds if the city gave them the land. The city refused this offer as well and negotiations ended.

Two months later, in October, the Crocketts sold the team to George Shinn for slightly more than $1 million and withdrew their pledges to the Chamber of Commerce's fund drive. Shinn, who recently had won the NBA franchise and had negotiated a lease for the coliseum, believed he would be able to negotiate a stadium lease with the city. At the time, he was the local hero bringing major league sports to the community.

Negotiations with George Shinn

Shinn, in his earlier negotiations for the coliseum, had been forced to seek the intervention of city council members to finalize the deal. The council virtually "forced down the Coliseum Authority's throat" a lease that obligated Shinn to pay rent of $1 for each Hornets game, but it gave to the Coliseum Authority all parking and concession revenues. At the time it appeared that Shinn had cut a sweetheart deal for himself at the city's expense.[1] Coliseum Authority members resented the city council's intervention and the lease that was negotiated.

The negotiators for the city were not going to let the same thing happen with the minor league stadium lease. More important, Shinn did not want a stripped-down, $4 million stadium. He had visions of a modern stadium, capable of being expanded to host AAA baseball and eventually major league baseball. Such a stadium would cost more than $4 million and implied large crowds and nonbaseball events. A redesign of the stadium was paid for by the Chamber of Commerce from the funds it had raised.

The city negotiators, who were worried about the success of the coliseum, feared that Shinn, like the Crocketts, had plans to stage events in competition with the coliseum activities. They insisted on control over the scheduling of nonbaseball events, and they raised the concern about traffic and parking when both facilities were in use. According to city officials, failure to reach agreement on the control of nonbaseball events was the deal-breaker.

Shinn's attorney and chief negotiator, Spencer Stolpen, however, remembers the issues differently. He claims that Shinn conceded the Coliseum Authority's veto power over nonbaseball events. The deal-breaker, according to Stolpen, was disagreement over who would control the concessions. Shinn had continual conflicts with the Coliseum Authority over its ability to manage the concessions in the coliseum. Shinn wanted a professional concessionaire, not the Coliseum Authority, to manage concessions in the stadium.

A new city council showed little interest in the negotiations, when Shinn once again appealed for assistance. An election had replaced the mayor and several council members with fiscal conservatives. The stadium issue and minor league baseball were low priorities for the council members, who were pledged to improve roads and keep taxes low. Shinn was told to return to the bargaining table.

Instead, Shinn turned to the county commissioners for help and began to look for alternative sites. The county had raised the $2.7 million as a result of the onetime tax, although some argued that the money could only be spent on a stadium built on the nineteen-acre site adjacent to the coliseum. Shinn retained a real estate agent to evaluate potential sites in the county and elsewhere.

One thought was to identify a site that would be good for not only a minor league baseball stadium, but also an NFL stadium. Such a site would need to be easily accessible and would have to have at least a hundred acres. Shinn soon came to the conclusion that such a site in Mecklenburg County was too expensive.

The decision was therefore made to look beyond the county's borders. According to Stolpen, there were plenty of offers ("anyone with 100 acres and a field of dreams"), but no local government was willing to spend the $10–15 million to build the type of stadium that Shinn wanted.

Relocation

No further negotiations with Charlotte officials took place. In 1988, Shinn signed a development agreement for a stadium with York County, South Carolina, a Charlotte suburb. In 1989, the renamed Charlotte Knights, newly affiliated with the Chicago Cubs, played their first season in York County in a temporary facility, and in 1990, they moved to a permanent stadium there. The case study of York County provides additional details of the relocation and describes the nature of the agreement with York County.

Negotiations between the team owners and the city failed because both parties had side issues and agendas. City staff members struggled to control the stadium issue. They were primarily concerned about protecting the city's investment in the new coliseum. Shinn, looking beyond AA baseball, first thought of a stadium that could potentially accommodate major league baseball, professional football, and other forms of entertainment. Later, he viewed the project as a revenue-generating real estate deal. He was not interested in a stripped-down stadium.

NOTE

1. During the 1990 NBA season, Shinn demanded that the lease be renegotiated so that he share in the concession and parking revenues. He hinted he would relocate his team from the coliseum. This angered fans, who booed him at home games.

Birmingham, Alabama 6

The population of Birmingham, Alabama, like that of other core cities, has been declining steadily since the 1950s. Nearly 40,000 people left the city during the 1960s. Between 1970 and 1990, the city's population declined further, from 300,910 to 265,968. In 1990, it was the sixtieth largest city in the nation.

The Birmingham metropolitan area consists of five counties and encompasses 4,034 square miles. It has grown nearly 12.5 percent since 1970 and is projected to continue growing into the twenty-first century. The city is surrounded by more than thirty incorporated municipalities, nearly all of which have had positive population growth in recent years.

Birmingham experienced a dramatic change in its local economy in the 1980s. The city transformed itself from an industrial to a diversified economy. The modern Birmingham economy features biomedical research, medicine, and transportation. It no longer is characterized by the smoke stacks and pollution of the steel industry of the past decades.

The city's leaders, however, are concerned about the lingering image of Birmingham as a one-industry town. They tout the city's diversified economy and progressive race relations.[1] The city sees itself in competition with Atlanta, Georgia, as the regional center of the South.

In many ways the city's economic transformation parallels that of Pittsburgh, Pennsylvania. One difference between the two cities is that Birmingham does not have major league sports. It is not because Birmingham has not tried.

Birmingham and Sports in the 1980s

Alabama is football country. Legion Field in Birmingham has been the site of professional and major college football games, especially the annual Alabama University–Auburn University football game. As of 1989, however, that game would be played at Auburn every other year.

The Legion Field neighborhood, located on the east side of the city, frequently is criticized as being unsafe.

Birmingham's strongest sports desire is to obtain a professional football franchise. In the 1970s, the city played host to a franchise in the World Football League, and in the 1980s, it hosted a team in the United States Football League (USFL). Both leagues collapsed within a few years. The city made national news when it extended a loan to its USFL franchise to keep it in business.

Birmingham also attracted national attention in the mid-1980s with the announcement that it was entering the horse racing business. A major race track was planned for the east side of the city to attract racing fans throughout the region. Although the city never invested any money in the track itself, it did invest millions of dollars in public improvements, including the extension of infrastructure to the area of the track's location, with the hope that development would follow.

The initial effort to operate the track was a financial failure. At the time this research was being conducted, the track had reopened, and it appeared that it would be a viable operation. Development, however, was not occurring in the area of the race track as of the summer of 1989.

Birmingham, in the 1980s, participated in several highly visible and controversial ventures with sports entrepreneurs who promised major league status and national visibility. In the summer of 1989, interviewees were certain that the World League of American Football would locate a franchise in Birmingham, which it did. The World League of American Football is affiliated with the National Football League and began play with an international schedule in March 1991.

City officials gave professional baseball, despite its long history in the city, low priority throughout most of the 1980s. In fact, in 1986, the Birmingham city council indicated it would help finance a proposed water theme park rather than invest in a new stadium for the AA Southern League's Birmingham Barons. Although the water theme park deal fell through, interviewees asserted that the park would create a regional draw, which the Barons had not been able to do. City council members justified their decision at the time in terms of the proposed park's potential economic impact, compared with that of the Barons.

Baseball in Birmingham

Birmingham's professional baseball history dates back to 1885, when the Birmingham Coal Barons began play in the newly formed Southern Association. In 1910, the team's owner built Rickwood Field in the then-fashionable east side of the city. Babe Ruth, Dizzy Dean, Jimmy

Piersall, and Reggie Jackson are only a few of the stars who graced the field at Rickwood, which in the late 1980s was the nation's second oldest professional baseball stadium (Chicago's Comiskey Park, which was built earlier in 1910, was the oldest).

The city lost its minor league baseball team in 1975, when the franchise was relocated to Chattanooga, Tennessee. Five years later, an ownership group bought the Montgomery, Alabama, team and moved it to Birmingham. The team adopted the name of the Barons and settled in at Rickwood.

Rickwood's neighborhood was in a state of deterioration at the beginning of the 1980s. Like the Legion Field area, it was perceived as unsafe. Maintenance problems plagued the team throughout its stay at Rickwood, although the city and the team invested much money in stadium repairs and refurbishing. Plumbing problems and power outages during games, including the 1987 Southern League's all-star game, were common.

The team proved to be a success, however. Annual attendance exceeded 200,000 fans, and the team made a profit for its owners in the team's first three years in Birmingham. Parking was limited, though. Fans had to park in the neighborhood and walk the streets that many felt were dangerous. The team's general manager and principal owner, Art Clarkson, saw the stadium's condition and limited parking as the major barriers to the team's continued financial success. He claims the city became less responsive to his requests for repairs and stadium improvements and ignored his early suggestions that a new stadium be built.

In December 1985, Clarkson announced at a press conference that the team needed a new stadium. He issued a request for proposals from the city and surrounding communities. Only Birmingham and the suburb of Hoover pursued the matter seriously, although a number of inquiries were received.

The Birmingham mayor's office identified three potential stadium sites on the east side of the city by February 1986. The first proposed site was next to Legion Field. The proposal was to transform the Legion Field site into a sports complex. The city already was spending $2 million to renovate Legion Field and had plans to make significant street improvements in the area. The second site was Fair Park, which was the site of the Alabama State Fair. The city had made commitments to renovate the fairgrounds and invest in the rehabilitation of the surrounding neighborhood. A third site was identified near the new race track, but it was never formally presented to Clarkson. A downtown site was also considered briefly, but it was rejected by city officials. The city did not own enough land to house a stadium at either location. A downtown site would have been more expensive and would have taken more time to assemble than the city-owned sites at either Legion Field or the fairgrounds.

More important, from the perspective of those in the mayor's office working on the proposal, the Legion Field site and the fairgrounds site both fit into the city's ongoing redevelopment plans for the east side. Much of the corridor between Legion Field and the fairgrounds, which includes Rickwood Field, used to be an active entertainment corridor. Each of these sites contained its own history with which many residents still identified.

Clarkson, however, rejected outright the city's proposals. He had concluded that the team's market was moving south to the suburbs ("over the mountain"). As one interviewee stated, Clarkson was not in the redevelopment business. Clarkson publicly asserted that the city did not respond seriously to his request for proposals.

This claim caused ill will in the mayor's office, where the staff had spent considerable time putting together the two proposals and responding to Clarkson's demands. Clarkson's comments also added fuel to an already strained relationship between Clarkson and several city council members.

Five days after the mayor's office reported its proposals to the city council, the council voted five to two to permit the mayor's office "to finalize" a contract for $3 million to help build a water theme park. At the same council meeting, the president of the city council predicted that the council would kill the mayor's plans for a new minor league stadium. He asserted, "We're not going to break our necks to overly support the Barons," and he questioned whether the team's attendance justified a $5 million investment. He noted that "it would be in their [the Barons] best interest to relocate."

Clarkson and his consultants met with the representatives of the city sporadically after the exchange. The last meeting appears to have taken place in mid-1986. Clarkson, however, still maintains that the city did not respond seriously to his demands.

At least four suburban communities expressed interest in building a stadium for the Barons, but only Hoover persisted and demonstrated it was serious. Clarkson had hoped to leave Rickwood at the end of the 1986 season, but no agreement was reached with Hoover as 1986 came to a close. Clarkson had no choice except to remain another season in Rickwood.

In February 1987, the Hoover city council approved agreements to build a new stadium for the Barons on an undeveloped 1,300-acre site (see the case study of Hoover). In 1988, the Birmingham Barons played their first season in Hoover Metropolitan Stadium.

Conclusion

It is not clear when Clarkson decided to move from Birmingham. It is clear that the city attempted to link any new facility to redevelopment efforts, and Clarkson did not want any role in these efforts. Clarkson did not have any other attractive choices, beyond Hoover's efforts. He could have accepted one of the mayor's office's proposed sites, accepted a less expensive facility at a less desirable suburban site, relocated the team from the Birmingham area, or sold the team. Other Birmingham suburbs were not willing to expend the money necessary to build a stadium or did not possess suitable sites. Continued operation at Rickwood Field was not financially viable and was not in Clarkson's business interests. The strained relation between Clarkson and city council members made the swift implementation of any offer from the mayor's office uncertain, at best. An inadequate stadium, the conflict between public interest and a team owner's business interests, and strained political relations provided the preconditions for relocation in this case (see the case study of Hoover for subsequent events).

NOTE

1. The image of progressive race relations was damaged in the summer of 1990 by a controversy over the apparent discriminatory membership policies of Shoal Creek Country Club, which was the host of the 1990 Professional Golf Association (PGA) Championship. In fact, Shoal Creek is located in a suburb of Birmingham.

Fresno, California

The September 13, 1988, edition of the *Fresno Bee* carried a front-page story announcing the closing of Fresno's downtown department store. Gottschalks had been located in downtown Fresno for eighty-four years. Its departure from downtown intensified concerns about the future of downtown Fresno.

Buried in the sports section in the same edition of the *Fresno Bee,* an article reported that the Fresno Suns, an independent team in the A-level California League, were about to be sold and might be relocated from Fresno by the new owner. Fresno had hosted a California League team for more than forty years and, until 1987, had enjoyed a thirty-year relationship with the New York/San Francisco Giants.

The City of Fresno

Fresno is located in the San Joaquin Valley of central California. By automobile, it is three and a half hours to San Francisco, four hours to Los Angeles, three hours to the Pacific Ocean, and approximately two hours to three national parks, including Yosemite and Sequoia.

The city is part of Fresno County, which is 6,000 square miles in area and is known as the "agricultural capital of the world." Fresno County produces more crops with a greater economic value than any other county in the United States. The annual gross value of agricultural goods produced in Fresno County exceeds $2 billion. The county produces one-third of all grapes consumed in the United States.

The city's population has increased steadily since 1960 as a result of annexation and in-migration. The city annexed an annual average of 3.25 square miles between 1970 and 1988, increasing its total area from 41.80 square miles in 1970 to 99.16 square miles in 1988. Its population nearly doubled, from 165,655 to 308,700, during that same time period, and by 1990 it had reached 354,202. The city is the eighth largest city in

California and the forty-seventh largest city in the nation. State and city population projections estimate that the metropolitan area will continue to grow at an annual rate of 1.4 percent to 1.9 percent well into the twenty-first century.

The city's population base has moved steadily northward and eastward from downtown. More recently, some growth has begun on the city's western fringe, across Freeway 99, which serves as the city's western border.

The city's downtown area is relatively quiet during the workday. Government offices and other public buildings, such as the public library, appear to be the main attraction for those who are downtown during the day. The downtown is virtually empty on weekends and at night.

Those interviewed described Fresno as a growing community, wealthy but with economic problems. California's Proposition 13 has restricted the city's ability to pay for the costs that growth entails. The city's annexation policies have caused bitter conflicts with county officials over tax revenues. The city raised its hotel and motel tax from 9 percent to 12 percent in the late 1980s to balance its budget.

Such a tax is lucrative in Fresno because of the large number of motels lining Freeway 99 within the city's borders and because of the convention trade the city attracts. The city ranks among the top three convention cities in California, due primarily to its central location in the state.

Fresno was one of the first California cities to build a convention center (in 1966). Fresno's convention center is part of a downtown complex that includes a conference center, an exhibit hall, a 2,300-seat theater, and an 11,000-seat arena originally built for the basketball team of California State University–Fresno (otherwise known as Fresno State University).

Fresno hosts several state conventions that are larger than many of the national meetings that other cities attract. For example, meetings of California organizations in Fresno have drawn 6,000–7,000 attendees. In the summer of 1989, the city was in danger of losing its larger conventions because of insufficient exhibit hall space, which ranked ninth in the state. The Visitors and Convention Bureau, which oversees the convention center complex, was pressing local officials for a new $15 million addition to the exhibit hall and a downtown hotel.

Although the low-priced freeway motels contribute to the city's revenues, interviewees noted that they also contribute to the city's image problem. They described Fresno as having no image beyond the state's borders and a negative image within the state. Its image within the state tends to be that of a small farm community, with nothing to offer visitors or businesses. One interviewee described Fresno as a one-hour town—a place to get gas and a quick bite to eat before continuing on to your destination.

Local leaders, however, believe the city is maturing and is becoming a regional center for central California. They are proud of the cultural amenities the city possesses and, in the summer of 1989, were seeking ways to add to those amenities. One of the amenities Fresno residents had enjoyed for more than forty years was professional baseball. In 1989, that no longer was the case.

Professional Baseball in Fresno: Franchise Sales and Relocation

Fresno was a charter member of the California League when it organized in 1941. The Greater Fresno Youth Foundation owned the franchise until the early 1980s. The foundation, a nonprofit organization, used surplus revenues to help support amateur baseball in the Fresno area.

The Fresno franchise enjoyed the longest (a thirty-year) affiliation with a major league club (the New York/San Francisco Giants). In 1987, however, the Giants terminated its Player Development Contract (PDC) with the Fresno franchise. Throughout its history, the team played at John Euless Ball Park, which was owned and maintained by the State Center Community College District.

Euless Park was constructed in the early 1940s. The first renovations of Euless Park's wooden grandstands were made in 1967. New construction was placed directly on top of the original construction. It was obvious by the early 1980s that significant stadium improvements were needed.

City officials and community college district officials failed to respond to requests from the foundation, however. The foundation, realizing that it could not afford to finance the necessary repairs itself, sold the franchise to Robert Piccinini for $40,000 at the end of the 1982 season. Piccinini owned a string of grocery stores.

The new owner invested approximately $150,000 in stadium renovations in 1983, but the repairs were mainly cosmetic. They included more lighting, additional outfield fencing, improved concession areas, repainting, repairs to the walk deck and its surface, new carpeting, and repairs to the structure below the grandstand. No other significant renovation efforts or repairs were made after 1983.

According to interviewees, the facility was not in good condition and was in a neighborhood that was difficult to navigate. Interviewees asserted that the stadium's condition made attending games less attractive. One individual said it was an embarrassment to bring visitors from out of town to the stadium to show them Fresno's minor league team. Another interviewee related that a photographer from city hall assigned to take a picture at the ball park was unable to find it.

According to the former general manager of the Fresno Giants, Bill Thompson, Piccinini was able to increase annual profits from the $20,000–30,000 level that the foundation earned to $75,000–130,000. The increased revenues were related to more signs on the outfield fences and a larger number of promotions marketed through the owner's grocery store chain. Nevertheless, according to Thompson and others, the Giants were never the "game in town."

The game in town, especially in the late 1980s, was Fresno State University. The university's football and basketball teams enjoyed success on and off the field in the 1980s. The community supported these teams not only by attending their games but also by financing the construction of the school's football stadium and an addition to the city's indoor arena, where the basketball team plays. Attendance at Fresno State football games is part of Fresno residents' fall social calendar.

The university's baseball team has become one of the nation's most successful college teams. Its stadium, also built with community contributions, is one of the best college stadiums in the nation and is superior to many AAA facilities. It is a 3,500-seat stadium, but with bleachers it can accommodate another 3,000 fans.

The university sells 3,000 season tickets for its forty to forty-four home baseball games. The team's thousand-member booster program is the nation's largest for college baseball. Annual attendance ranges from 170,000 to 180,000, which led the nation's colleges in 1988, 1989, and 1990. The Fresno State baseball team was ranked among the top twenty college teams in the nation in the late 1980s. It won its conference in 1988 and 1989, and it played in the College World Series in 1988. Major league clubs drafted ninety-four Fresno State baseball players between 1965 and 1989, placing the school ninth in the nation for the number of players drafted ("Colleges, Most Players Drafted," 1990: 35).

According to Thompson, Piccinini expressed his intention to sell the franchise at the beginning of the 1987 season. Near the end of that season, in which the team won the league championship and attracted nearly 108,000 fans, officials of the San Francisco Giants severely criticized the condition of the facilities at Euless Park. On September 15, 1987, Piccinini sold the franchise to Bill Yuill for a reported $560,000.

Yuill was described by newspaper accounts as a Canadian media mogul and owner of several other minor league teams.

At about the same time, the Community College District commissioned a survey of the structure supporting Euless Park's wooden grandstand. The engineering report, which was completed in October, concluded that "the grandstand structure is unsafe in its present condition" and that "the cost to rehabilitate the structure to current code standards would exceed the cost to demolish and replace it . . . " (William M. Brooks, Inc., 1987: 3). The report recommended the demolition of the grandstand.

The San Francisco Giants soon announced they were assigning their PDC to San Jose, which had operated as an independent club in 1987. Demolition of the wooden grandstand began in January 1988. This left the Fresno club with neither a PDC nor a stadium.

Yuill sold the franchise for a reported sale price of $615,000 within four months of his purchase of the franchise. Dave Kramer, a southern California businessman, was the buyer. Interviewees described Kramer as a baseball fan pursuing his dream of owning a professional team. They agreed that he knew little about operating a minor league team.

The franchise was renamed the Fresno Suns. The team played the 1988 season as an independent club, using players from the San Francisco Giants, the Baltimore Orioles, and a Japanese team, the Hanshin Tigers. It played at Euless Park and fans sat on portable bleachers that the team rented. Trailers served as dressing rooms, concession stands, and team offices.

The team set a California League record in 1988 by losing twenty straight games and finished the season with the second worse record in the league. Attendance fell to 35,000.

Kramer lost a great deal of money operating the team and sold it at the end of the 1988 season to Joe Buzas, a minor league baseball entrepreneur. Buzas has owned and operated twelve minor league teams in seventeen cities since 1956. He reportedly has been active longer than any other owner in the minor leagues (Steinbreder, 1990: 65). He boasts of purchasing the Reading, Pennsylvania, franchise for $1 in 1976 and selling it for $1 million in 1986. In 1988, Joe Buzas owned the AAA-level Portland Beavers of the Pacific Coast League and served as chairman of that league's expansion committee.

In late October, shortly after his purchase of the Fresno franchise, Buzas announced at a news conference held at Fresno's Chamber of Commerce that Fresno was the "number one candidate" for a team if the Pacific Coast League expanded, which it was expected to do for the 1991 season. He assured the community that as owner of the Fresno territorial rights he would not block a AAA team from coming to Fresno and that until a AAA team came to Fresno he would operate the Suns in the city, if improvements were made to Euless Park. He gave the city until December 15 to work out a solution to the stadium problem.

Buzas had fueled discussion of bringing a AAA club to Fresno a year earlier by telling a *Fresno Bee* reporter that Fresno could support AAA baseball. At the time, he was negotiating his Portland lease, and speculation developed that he would relocate the Portland team to Fresno (see also the Colorado Springs case study). That speculation continued in 1988, although Buzas refused to comment on the possibility of relocating the Beavers. He did announce that he was interested in owning a second Pacific Coast League team and locating it in Fresno. It is contrary to Pacific Coast League rules for one owner to own two franchises in the league, but Buzas said he could circumvent the restriction (McEwen, 1988).

Officials from the city and the State Center Community College District worked on a plan to make Euless Park a satisfactory facility for Buzas. The cost was estimated to be $100,000, in addition to donated labor. Buzas did not intend to invest his money in Euless Park or in a new stadium. According to Buzas, "If a city wants me, then it must do something for me. It's important that a city does a lot for you."

Buzas also explored using the stadium at Fresno State University. According to Buzas, the university asked for half of the ticket revenues and all of the concession revenues. No advertising on the outfield fences would be permitted. These terms were unacceptable to Buzas, as they would have been to almost any owner.

According to Fresno State University's athletic director, Gary Cunningham, the Suns' use of the stadium would have caused too many conflicts. The university could not permit advertising on the outfield fence because of existing contractual commitments. It also had contractual commitments to its concessionaire. Even though there would have been little overlap with the university baseball team's schedule, there would have been conflicts with summer activities at the university, especially with football practice, which is held next to the baseball stadium. Cunningham also noted that maintenance work on the field and in the stadium was done during the summer.

On November 19, Buzas formally requested permission from the California League to relocate the Fresno franchise to one of three cities. This was nearly a month before the deadline Buzas gave to the city. Two days later, he announced publicly that he would move the team from Fresno to Salinas, California. He justified the decision by citing the lack of an adequate stadium and the competition from Fresno State University.

City and community college district officials said they were surprised at the announcement. The chancellor of the community college district, however, stated that the district "was not in the baseball business. We are in the education business."

In 1989 and 1990, Buzas operated the Salinas franchise as an independent club, using players from the Giants and Japan. In 1990, he operated under an agreement with the Fukuoka Daiei Hawks that was reported to be as generous as a traditional PDC. The agreement included the provision of a Japanese manager for the team, which was a first for professional baseball in America. The eight Japanese players assigned to the team reportedly earned an average annual salary of $50,000, compared with the American players' compensation of an average $500 a month for the playing season. The Salinas team attracted the fewest fans in the California League in 1989 (47,609) and 1990 (33,465). By the beginning of the 1991 season, Joe Buzas had sold the team.

Fresno Stadium Politics, 1988–89

Efforts to gain support for a new, publicly owned stadium began in 1987, after the Euless Park engineering report was made public. As of the summer of 1989, discussion of a new stadium was marked by a consensus among city officials that Fresno wanted a AAA franchise to play in a multipurpose stadium located downtown, near the convention center complex. Such a stadium was viewed as complementary to the convention center complex, an important asset to downtown revitalization plans, and a means by which each of three local high schools could play all of its football games on Friday nights, which was not then possible. There was no consensus, however, on what priority should be given a stadium relative to other needs of the city.

Several different groups were active in advocating or studying the stadium issue, which gave the appearance of a fragmented movement with no effective leadership. The most visible and vocal champions of a new stadium were Rod Anaforian, a member of the city council, and Robert Coleman, president of the Fresno Baseball Boosters, formerly known as the Giants Boosters. In January 1988, Anaforian sought city council approval of a resolution to direct city staff to study the feasibility of building a multipurpose stadium. Prior to the January city council meeting, several newspaper articles had discussed the need for a new stadium to attract a AAA baseball team and the support for such a project.

Coleman had launched a letter-writing campaign directed at city council members, claimed to have 10,000 signatures on a petition advocating the project, and predicted a turnout at the council meeting of 450–500 supporters. One council member described the meeting as the most publicized meeting the city council ever had. The meeting was held in Memorial Auditorium in anticipation of a large audience.

A week before the meeting, Yuill sold the club to Kramer, and demolition work started at Euless Park. The *Fresno Bee* noted reports were circulating that Kramer would move the team to Southern California, thereby "opening the way for triple-A baseball in Fresno for 1989." It was hoped Buzas would relocate his Portland club to Fresno if a stadium was built. In response to such rumors, the California League President met with Kramer, Anaforian, and the city manager that same week to clarify franchise and territorial rights and the rules of minor league baseball.

The January city council meeting was attended by seventy-five people. The city council rejected Anaforian's proposal by a vote of four to three. Karen Humphrey, who was a council member at the time and later became mayor, stated in a summer 1989 interview that the motion failed because there was concern about making a commitment to a project whose importance had not been fully demonstrated. Private sector interest was not apparent, and there was no larger context within which to place the project. Council members at the meeting called for a commitment from a AAA team and from private enterprise before the city made a commitment to move forward.

When it approved the 1989 budget several months later, however, the council did authorize staff to study the feasibility of a stadium. Anaforian alleged the January defeat was pure politics directed at him. Interviewees described Anaforian as a minority of one on the council, who had burned too many bridges. They did not think he was capable of leading a successful campaign for a major project.

According to Mayor Humphrey, the change in the council's position resulted from the development of a central area plan that included a downtown stadium and an expanded exhibit hall, increased community interest in the stadium proposal, and increased interest in private funding. Anaforian countered that nothing had changed from one vote to the other.

Another source of support for the stadium project came from the Fresno Chamber of Commerce, which created a task force to support a downtown multipurpose stadium. The task force was in contact with the Pacific Coast League, the California League, and Joe Buzas. It had tried to raise private money to upgrade Euless Park before Buzas left but could not meet Buzas's timetable. The task force was maintaining its contacts with Buzas in 1989.

Still another group that became involved with the stadium issue was the Ad Hoc Committee for Community Enrichment-Fresno County. This group was formed to develop a means to raise money for several large capital projects necessary for establishing a community's cultural identity. The committee included several individuals who had contributed to various projects in the past, including Dennis Whitehurst, who served as mayor of Fresno from 1977 to 1985.

According to Whitehurst, Proposition 13 has prevented the city from raising the revenues needed to initiate several projects. In the absence of large corporate sponsors, the same individuals were being solicited time after time to support a variety of community projects. These residents felt they were nearing their giving limits and could not possibly support all the worthwhile projects being proposed.

As of the summer of 1989, this group was still trying to plot its strategy. It had sponsored a seminar, attended by two hundred people, that reviewed the experiences of Denver and Indianapolis. The committee had identified a "wish list" of projects to be supported. This list was heavily weighted toward cultural arts projects, which reflected the membership's interests. The list also included an on-campus basketball arena for Fresno State and a new stadium to house minor league baseball. The stadium was included with the approval of city officials.

The committee's leaders were leaning toward seeking a half-cent increase in the sales tax to serve as the funding mechanism for the projects. They believed they were capable of using the wish list to forge a coalition powerful enough to pass such a tax. They were certain that local officials would not be able to lead such an effort. However, they still had not developed a means for carrying out their plans if such a tax increase was approved by the county's voters. Proposition 13 prohibits earmarking funds.

Finally, city staff had been working quietly on a stadium study. An assistant city manager was assigned to the project and had spent much time gathering data and visiting stadium sites across the nation. He saw the stadium project as one of several high-priority issues for the city council, but he did not believe it was at the top of the city council's list. Indeed, interviewees thought an exhibit hall expansion was more important than a stadium, especially in terms of economic impact. The assistant city manager also suggested, and others confirmed, that from a strictly recreational perspective, green areas, neighborhood parks, and regional parks had higher priority than a stadium.

Several of the interviewees noted that the stadium was an important issue for only a small number of residents—the hard core baseball fans. The former mayor noted that those who could bring people together in support of a community project had not made the stadium a priority. He believed it was a nonissue for most citizens because the Suns were not popular.

Of those interviewed, only Anaforian, Coleman, and Chamber of Commerce representatives claimed that the loss of the team hurt the city economically. Those involved with economic development activities and with visitors and convention activities saw it as a minor loss, if any. They noted that neither the Giants nor the Suns was important to their activities. For baseball fans baseball is still available at Fresno State in the spring and a few hours away in San Francisco and Los Angeles during the summer.

Conclusion

In the summer of 1989, Fresno appeared to be on a slow but steady path toward building a downtown, multipurpose stadium. However, all city officials and Chamber of Commerce representatives who were interviewed strongly stated that they would consider no location for a stadium other than downtown. The stadium must serve the purpose of downtown revitalization. Others, including Joe Buzas, questioned the wisdom of a downtown location. They believed it would have a higher probability of success north of downtown, where residential development was occurring.

The number of groups and interests active in stadium advocacy promised to be a hindrance to eventual success. Potential for conflict was high. For example, several interviewees questioned the influence and ability of the leadership of the Chamber of Commerce as well as that of the city government.

Coleman's group appeared to be a front for Joe Buzas. Coleman was identified as the vice president for the Salinas club and was expected to lead any effort to sell seat options in the new stadium, which proved to be a successful financing tool for the university's football stadium. The Ad Hoc Committee was far from implementing its strategy and would need voter support for an increased tax. Many believed that the group's constituents would not rank a stadium very high on its list of priorities.

Finally, Fresno State University's role would be pivotal. Although an A team does not represent much competition for the university's team, a AAA club would compete for advertising revenue and fans' dollars, as well as for media exposure. No interviewee, however, believed the university would attempt to prevent a AAA team from locating in Fresno. Even the university's athletic director admitted that such behavior would result in unacceptable political costs.

The university might be persuaded to permit a AAA club to use its stadium on a temporary basis in exchange for permission from the city to escape from its commitment to play basketball in the city's arena through 1995. Without some contingency arrangement to use the stadium, the effort to attract a AAA team to Fresno would be most difficult. In fact, Fresno dropped out of contention for a AAA expansion franchise in late 1990.

Old Orchard Beach, Maine   8

Harry Wessel

Sports Illustrated called Old Orchard Beach "the best little AAA park in the game" in the summer of 1984 (Wolf, 1984: 42). In the summer of 1989, Joe Burris of the *Boston Globe,* in reference to the park's new function as a concert arena, called it a "field of screams" (Burris, 1989: 47). This is the unusual case of Old Orchard Beach, Maine, and professional baseball.

Old Orchard Beach is transformed into a vacation resort dominated by French Canadians during the summer, when its population swells from 6,400 residents to nearly 100,000. The beach, which is cleaned daily, is one of the most attractive on the East Coast.

Yet there is much about Old Orchard that is not very appealing. Most day tourists see Old Orchard as a classic honky-tonk beach town, with a tacky amusement park, greasy spoon fast-food restaurants, and stores peddling "tee shirts, tatoos, and vibrators."[1] Throughout the 1980s, the town sought to change its image as a summer resort area that only catered to the prurient interests of working-class Mainers and French Canadians. In 1983, the town embarked on a project that officials thought would put Old Orchard Beach "on the map."

Baseball Comes to Old Orchard Beach

In the summer of 1982, Jordon Kobritz purchased the Charleston Charlies, a Triple A affiliate of the Cleveland Indians located in West Virginia. Kobritz planned to bring his team to Portland, Maine, a city of 65,000 just twelve miles north of Old Orchard Beach. Maine, Kobritz's home state, has had a minimal and dubious baseball history. The only baseball team ever to play in Maine was the Portland Pilots, a Class B New England League team that folded in the 1950s.

Kobritz approached the mayor of Portland with the idea of relocating his team to Portland at about the same time that a Portland city councilor had worked out a plan to move the Double A Bristol, Connecticut, franchise of the Red Sox to Portland. The passage of a city referendum authorizing the upgrading of a field located behind the Exposition Building in Portland was all that remained to finalize the Bristol franchise relocation near the end of 1983.

Kobritz blames Councilor Traub, the principal proponent of the Bristol deal, for committing to the Bristol franchise relocation without seriously considering his offer to bring a Triple A franchise to Portland. Nevertheless, Kobritz's offer apparently influenced the Portland city council. After Kobritz's eleventh-hour offer and the ensuing city council debate over the advisability of bringing any professional team to Portland, the city council rejected placing the issue before the citizens of Portland in the form of a referendum.

In January 1984, Jerome Plante, town manager of Old Orchard Beach since 1977, convinced the Old Orchard Beach City Council to grant Kobritz an option to purchase nearly fifty acres of town-owned land for $50,000, after it became clear that Portland was not interested in hosting Kobritz's baseball team. Plante explained how Old Orchard came into the picture:

> When I read about [Portland City Council's vote to reject a referendum] in the paper, Kobritz had no idea about coming to Old Orchard Beach. I called him and said, "How about taking a look at us?" He came down on a Sunday. We showed him the facilities that we had. He had certain criteria. One, it had to be accessible. Coincidentally, the state had exit 5 [off Interstate 95] under construction at the time. Two, there had to be community support. [Community support] was there to such an extent that we worked out a unique agreement, a secondary obligation of sorts. We said to the Finance Authority of Maine [FAM, formerly the Maine Finance Authority], "We will assume a contingent liability if there is a foreclosure, and a subsequent default. The town would be responsible for the outstanding bonds."[2]

Kobritz approached FAM for a $2.2 million private loan to build a stadium in Old Orchard. Kobritz would be sole owner of the stadium. According to Timothy Agnew, director of FAM, Kobritz's loan was rejected by the guarantee board because his credit history was not strong enough and his collateral was too weak. When the agency balked at the request, the Old Orchard City Council, primarily at the behest of Plante, agreed to purchase the park in the event of a default (Burris, 1989; and interviews with Plante and Kobritz).

The agreement between Kobritz, FAM, and Old Orchard provided

Kobritz with $2.2 million to purchase 48.8 acres of town-owned land and build and operate a stadium. After five years, when the loan was due to be repaid, Kobritz would acquire sole title to the facility. In the event of default, Old Orchard would buy the bond from FAM and assume ownership of the stadium; Kobritz's personal assets were protected. The no-recourse loan agreement was included at the request of Plante.

If the city had financed the stadium, it would have secured a lower interest rate than Kobritz obtained. Kobritz complains that if Old Orchard had purchased the bond outright, the town would have been charged a 6 percent interest rate, which was considerably below the 10 percent rate FAM charged Kobritz. A city bond arrangement, however, would have required town approval in the form of a referendum vote.

According to Plante, it was unlikely that the town would have provided any additional financial assistance beyond the bond guarantee: "I don't think that politically [Old Orchard Beach purchasing the bond and refinancing to Kobritz] would have been feasible. The contingent liability was all that we could do. This is a town with a lot of small entrepreneurs. We issue more licenses than any city in Maine, with the exception of Portland. So we have a climate that is so used to free enterprise in the pure sense, it's pretty hard to say that because this guy owns a ball team we ought to give him a helping hand beyond what we did." This is a moot point because, as Agnew noted, the Finance Authority of Maine was not empowered to provide loans directly to municipalities.

It appears, however, that Kobritz never requested additional financial assistance beyond the contingent liability assumed by Old Orchard. When asked if he had ever requested assistance from the town, Kobritz declined comment (Burris, 1989: 47).

The town council of Old Orchard Beach unanimously approved the loan guarantee for Kobritz in early 1984. Plante cited the unanimous vote as proof of the broad community support for the project: "This town is very, very lively politically. A tough town to function as far as politicians are concerned. So the vote clearly signified the tremendous community support."

Other community leaders gave a very different interpretation. They said the agreement was approved because of Plante's considerable political influence in the community. Plante had lived in Old Orchard Beach since he was a small boy and was on a first-name basis with almost the entire business community. Not only had Plante been town manager of Old Orchard Beach since 1977, but, in 1984, he also served as the town's tax collector, welfare commissioner, road commissioner, and chair of the school building fund.

Plante sold the plan to the town as a no-lose proposition. No public monies or community assets would be involved in the deal. The idea of default apparently seemed remote to the town leaders.

Agnew acknowledged that while the Kobritz loan was viewed as too risky without the contingent liability assumed by Old Orchard, FAM did evaluate the venture positively. Agnew stated that the guarantee board concluded the potential public benefit of a baseball team in Old Orchard justified the issuance of the bond. Agnew also said that FAM decided the overall positive effect on the quality of life in Old Orchard justified issuing the contingent loan. This conclusion was based on performance projections that included such intangibles as spillover benefits to the related businesses in the area, citing the ever-elusive multiplier effect, as well as the more tangible creation of jobs.

Agnew noted that the arrangement between FAM, Old Orchard, and Kobritz was unique for the state of Maine at that time. It was his understanding that sport development is usually financed through public underwriting of private commercial bank loans.

Old Orchard Beach acquired a Triple A team because of the entrepreneurship of Jerome Plante. Town officials, community leaders, and the citizens of Old Orchard were not involved in the decision to begin the process of bringing Kobritz's franchise to Old Orchard. Plante simply seized the opportunity when it presented itself.

Baseball in Old Orchard Beach

The site that was later to become the "best little ballpark" was a mosquito-infested forest. It was perhaps an omen that a worker died when a tree fell on him during the construction of the park (Wolf, 1984: 54). But there was little thought of fate when Kobritz's wife threw out the first ball for the newly renamed Maine Guides on opening day in 1984. The Ballpark, as it was called, was filled to its capacity of 6,104 that day. George Ouellette, executive director of the Old Orchard Beach Chamber of Commerce, and for the first two years the public address announcer, sang the national anthem.

One need not have been a psychic to predict that Old Orchard Beach baseball would likely fail. Maine's climate is hardly conducive to baseball. Spring in Old Orchard often means snow, extreme cold, mosquitoes, and fog. As Jeff Barkley, a Maine Guides pitcher in 1984, put it, "The coldest winter I ever spent was a summer in Old Orchard Beach" (Wolf, 1984: 56).

There were also signs of trouble ahead. The Maine Guides were a Cleveland Indians franchise in Boston Red Sox territory. The Guides became "visitors" in their own park when the Red Sox franchise played in Old Orchard Beach. Although they seemed grateful to have a professional baseball team, local residents made it abundantly clear they would have preferred a Boston affiliate.

Nevertheless, it initially appeared the venture would succeed. Kobritz built the stadium in six months. During the team's first year, the Guides averaged 3,000 fans per game. Games were broadcast on a statewide, ten-station radio network, and approximately ten games were telecast on the local CBS and NBC affiliates. The following year, the stations bid for exclusive rights, and the NBC affiliate won. It telecast games for three years (Burris, 1989: 47). More than 1,000 season tickets were sold for the first two seasons.

The Guides' novelty soon wore off, even though they were competitive during their second season. The weather, which had been unseasonably warm in 1984, reverted to its usual chill. By 1986, attendance had fallen off tremendously. Annual attendance during the 1986 and 1987 seasons totaled 105,578 and 104,219, respectively, which was much less than the 200,000 Kobritz had estimated was necessary to make a profit.

The question of why the team did not sustain the level of fan support it needed is hotly disputed. Plante contends, and other residents agree, that the town initially supported the franchise. Once the team was committed to Old Orchard, Plante said, "We assisted him [Kobritz] in selling season tickets. During the first year they drew 800–900 season tickets. If they could have maintained that, and drew upon that, there is no doubt that Triple A baseball would have survived here and been successful." On this point Kobritz agreed: "Everything is based on attendance. During the first year the team was successful beyond a doubt. Attendance began to drop the second year, and by the third and fourth year had bottomed out."

Who, then, was to blame for the drop-off in attendance? Members of the community were in nearly universal agreement. "The combination of Kobritz's managerial skill, and his personality, which left much to be desired, was the problem. He was very talented in acquiring the franchise and building the stadium, but he couldn't sell himself," stated Plante. Plante compared Kobritz's performance with that of the Red Sox AAA team in Pawtucket: "They started with low attendance and a dilapidated stadium, they built it up slowly and on the basis of their personnel. They sold themselves first before they tried to sell tickets and that Jordon couldn't do."

Others agreed. Town officials clearly thought Kobritz's personality was the problem. Paul Ladakakos, chairman of the Old Orchard Beach town council, said that Kobritz alienated himself from the townspeople and didn't ask for help when he needed it. On the team's failure,

Ladakakos said, "My feeling was that it was [Kobritz's] personality toward the people, toward the town itself" (Burris, 1989: 47).

Ouellette concurred with Plante's characterization. Ouellette believed that the financial success of baseball in Old Orchard was contingent on effective public relations. "Jordon didn't promote as he should have. He treated [baseball] as something that promotes itself. Kobritz needed to be hokey," stated Ouellette. "Apparently, Kobritz believed that the 'grand old game' would carry itself. Baseball isn't what brings people to Old Orchard, it's the beach."

Ouellette also criticized Kobritz's managerial style. He noted that Kobritz irritated season ticket holders by raising parking prices and not giving them additional parking, a perquisite that often comes with the price of a season ticket at other minor league ballparks. "He was stand-offish, he wasn't a warm person."

He also agreed with Plante on the town's welcome to the team. "The town couldn't have gotten more involved," stated Ouellette. Ouellette did acknowledge that the town had reservations, however: "Citizens weren't prepared to gamble [financially] on his dream."

Kobritz, not surprisingly, had a different interpretation of events. Kobritz refused to assume any of the responsibility for the team's demise. In fact, he took issue with the statement that the franchise failed. Kobritz said that the team was very successful financially during the first two years. He was able to pay the mortgage and averaged an annual profit of $600,000. Kobritz claims that the profit, however, was reinvested in the operation of the stadium. "The team didn't fail," Kobritz said. "The conditions were such that it became impossible to manage a successful professional baseball franchise in Old Orchard Beach."

Kobritz's greatest frustration seemed to be the inability of Old Orchard's government and business community, not to mention local residents, to understand his working relationship with the major league organization. For example, Kobritz pointed out that most people assumed that the team is actually owned by the major league affiliate and that the franchise owner receives compensation for the operation of the franchise, which is not accurate.

Kobritz noted that the town provided no assistance in covering the expenses incurred in the operation and maintenance of the stadium. He said the Pawtucket Red Sox had a far more advantageous arrangement with their host city than the Maine Guides had with Old Orchard Beach. "The Paw Sox agreement requires that the owner pay $25,000 rent, while the city takes care of everything else." Did Kobritz ask for help? As in the earlier *Boston Globe* interview, he declined to answer that question.

Ladakakos said Kobritz did not ask for help. Plante also mentioned

Kobritz never proposed that the town assist in managing and operating the stadium. Kobritz wanted sole ownership of the stadium. Plante reiterated that the town probably would not have approved the bond guarantee if the contract had required the town to make an up-front financial commitment to the stadium deal.

Kobritz also disputed the claim that he did not promote the team: "I advertised, we took out forty-two highway billboards promoting the team in Saco, Biddeford, and Portland, with only two to five in the Old Orchard Beach area. Of the 1,200 season tickets that were sold during the first two years only 100 were from the Old Orchard area." The claim about advertising the team was confirmed by residents.

Lack of support from city officials in Portland was another factor that contributed to the demise of the Maine Guides. Portland and Old Orchard Beach are only twelve miles apart, and their relationship has been characterized by competition and conflict over efforts to attract new businesses. Although the Guides resided in Old Orchard, Portland benefited from having the team nearby.

Kobritz noted that most suppliers to the Ballpark were based in the Portland area and that there were obvious benefits in exposure and publicity in having a baseball team just twelve miles away. Nevertheless, Portland officials, having failed to acquire a professional baseball team of their own, demonstrated little interest in promoting the Old Orchard franchise. It was unlikely that the Guides could maintain the financial success of the first year without the Portland community's active support.[3]

Finally, Old Orchard Beach officials refused to allow Kobritz to schedule certain rock concerts that he believed would bring in necessary additional revenues. Town officials resisted Kobritz's booking certain heavy metal bands, such as Def Leppard, because of the noise, traffic congestion, and "undesirable" fans that these concerts attracted.

Ouellette disagreed that concerts, of any type, would have offset Kobritz's financial losses in Old Orchard. "SeaPAC [see below] isn't having, I think, a good year. The noise is a problem and the country western bookings have been a flop," he said. As executive director of the Chamber of Commerce, Ouellette was understandably biased: "Local business doesn't benefit particularly [from concerts]. When Old Orchard Beach is full, it is full. Concerts have little positive financial impact on the town. Young people have little money, and they don't spend that money in the town."[4]

The prevailing view among community leaders was that when attendance was good at a baseball game, the spillover effect on the town's economy was substantial. Some merchants disputed this, however, claiming that baseball had little or no positive effect on business. Those who said the team helped the town economically were almost always baseball fans.

Regardless of this point, if the town had let Kobritz book financially profitable performers he might well have been able to use the profits to subsidize the costs of operating the Ballpark. Clearly, however, a rift had developed between the team owner and local officials.

Old Orchard Beach Says Good-bye to Baseball

At the end of the 1986 season, Kobritz sold his franchise to a group in Scranton, Pennsylvania, for $1.2 million and the option to buy the AA-level Eastern League's Waterbury, Connecticut, franchise. If the sale of the Waterbury franchise to Kobritz was not approved, Kobritz was to receive an additional $400,000 in cash and $10,000 a year for ten years. The Eastern League failed to approve the sale of the franchise to Kobritz, and the Scranton group eventually relocated the Waterbury team to Williamsport, Pennsylvania (see the Frederick case study).

Kobritz immediately sued to void the deal and won, allowing him to operate the team for the 1987 season. During the fall of 1987, the Scranton group appealed the lower court's decision to the New England Court of Appeals in Boston and won. The high court ruled that it was a straight sale and that Kobritz was not entitled to the AA team. The newly named Maine Phillies played out the 1988 season in Old Orchard Beach under ownership of the Scranton group and then relocated to Scranton for the 1989 season.

In 1987, the town assumed the liability on the notes for the stadium and paid $50,000 in taxes to the state of Maine for the year. The city council considered leasing the Ballpark for $1 a year while a group of local townspeople attempted to purchase a Double A team, but the council rejected this proposal by a vote of three to two, after a half-hearted attempt by Kobritz and a group of townspeople to convince the town council to intervene (Burris, 1989: 47).

The more immediate and feasible alternative was to utilize the Ballpark for concerts. The problem was that the Advisory Committee to the Old Orchard Beach City Council in charge of decisions affecting municipal entertainment was opposed to concerts at the Ballpark. The reason was simple. Concerts would not benefit the town directly and would attract "undesirables."[5] This policy was abandoned when Dale Blow and associates assumed responsibility for the stadium and the outstanding bond.

The Ballpark was sold to Dale Blow, a local businessman, and Frank Russo, a Rhode Island concert promoter, who agreed to assume the responsibility for the outstanding bond and pay over three years the back taxes that Kobritz had accumulated. The stadium was renamed Seashore Performing Arts Center (SeaPAC) and has been used to host concerts by Bon Jovi, Bob Dylan, the Beach Boys, and Chicago, among others. No alcoholic beverages could be sold at events attended primarily by adolescents, and no heavy metal or rap groups were permitted during the first year of operation.

The new owners made minor renovations at the park. They took out the dugouts and removed the fences and the backstop, but they left the posts so it would take only a few days to convert back to a regulation playing field. Many of the residents of Old Orchard Beach argue that with a seating capacity of 15,000 and a summer schedule that is more realistic given the climate, SeaPAC is a much better business venture for the town than the Ballpark was.

Conclusion

Once the opportunity to acquire a professional baseball franchise presents itself to a community, there is a very strong argument to include as many community leaders, private and public, in the decision-making process as is practical. The failure to include the town council in a protracted discussion of alternative financial arrangements in attracting the Kobritz franchise to Old Orchard deprived the decision makers of the opportunity to examine the potential costs and benefits involved in underwriting the Kobritz loan.

In fairness to Plante, the town council anticipated the business community's reluctance to commit any immediate financial support to the project and was predisposed to accept Plante's assurances that Kobritz could make the franchise financially successful. The worst case scenario, which in fact occurred, was that the town would have to assume responsibility for the outstanding loan but would inherit a first-class sports (entertainment) facility.

While the lack of planning on the part of the officials of Old Orchard Beach should not be downplayed, the loss of the Guides was probably decided by events beyond the control of all the participants. The novelty of the team wore off, the weather failed to cooperate after the first year, the franchise was not a Red Sox affiliate, and the team played worse than it had during the first two years. These factors and others contributed to the franchise's financial demise, but these explanations are rarely mentioned by the participants in the experience. The blame is rarely placed on anything so uncontrollable as the weather. In the eyes of many of the participants in Old Orchard

Beach's baseball experiment, the blame clearly rests with the owner, Kobritz.

Will baseball return to Old Orchard Beach? It is unlikely. During 1988, Blow approached two teams that flatly refused to consider Old Orchard Beach. The teams felt that the weather was not suitable for baseball. In addition, Blow said that both teams essentially wanted the town leaders to underwrite the franchise in the event that it again failed financially. Although it was never said outright, Blow was certain that Old Orchard Beach's "reputation" after the Kobritz fiasco negates any possibility of relocating a team to Old Orchard Beach.

NOTES

1. This is a common characterization of Old Orchard often made by the town residents. The origin of the phrase is unknown.

2. All quotations in this case, unless otherwise noted, are taken from interviews with the principals conducted during the summer of 1989.

3. According to Plante and Kobritz, the mayor of Portland, after hearing that Kobritz would locate his franchise in Old Orchard, wished the town and Kobritz good luck but indicated that Portland had no interest in promoting the venture.

4. Ouellette interview. The prevailing view among town leaders, supported by a market study of Old Orchard Beach commissioned in 1987, is that concerts have little to no positive impact on the local economy (Market Decisions, 1987: 79).

5. SeaPAC was under attack in 1989 because of the noise generated by rock concerts. As one local official described the problem in an interview, "The town never realized the difference in sound levels generated by screaming adolescents compared to the sound a home run produces" (Cohen, 1989: 21).

Fort Lauderdale, Florida   9

Robyne Turner

Florida cities that host spring training and minor league seasons vary from the burgeoning, yet isolated, retirement center of Port Charlotte, with a population of about 30,000, to Fort Lauderdale, which has a relatively stable population of 150,000 and is the central city of a metropolitan area of 1 million people. Fort Lauderdale and Broward County, the county in which it is located, are working to diversify their economies from primarily a tourist base to one of offices, retail activities, and high-technology enterprises. Yet the continued reliance on tourism keeps local government committed to professional baseball in the form of the New York Yankees' spring training and minor league baseball seasons.

This commitment is made in an environment where competition between cities to host a team is fierce. For example, in the spring of 1990, eighteen major league teams trained in sixteen Florida locations, and fourteen minor league teams were hosted by most of those same cities. Three Florida cities were also among six finalists in contention for two major league expansion franchises. St. Petersburg had a domed stadium built, and Orlando had the revenue sources committed for a franchise. The availability of Joe Robbie Stadium, home to the Miami Dolphins football team, made Miami a third (and ultimately successful) contender for an expansion franchise.

Spring training is a highly competitive tourist attraction in the state of Florida. Florida cities have been hosting major league spring training camps for over forty years. The major league players are familiar names that draw tourists and fans from all parts of the nation for six weeks in February and March of each year.

The results of a 1987 survey estimated fan attendance for the exhibition season in Florida to be 150,000 persons, an estimated 100,000 of whom are out of state tourists (Florida Department of Commerce,

1987). A majority of these tourists claimed that spring training was a major reason for their trip to Florida. Baseball's popularity is expected to translate into regular tourist visitors and tourist dollars for the cities that host spring training. Spring training activities and the fans attending exhibition games generate an estimated $330 million for the state's economy.

Spring training's contribution to total state tourism is small, however, when compared with the estimated $30 billion that the 37 million tourists visiting the state annually pump into the state's economy ("Statistical Overview of the State," 1989). Many winter tourists who come to Florida for baseball have a secondary residence in Florida. Estimates are that only 7 to 17 percent of lodging revenues in spring training cities come from baseball fans during the season.

A survey of local tourists conducted by the Broward County Convention and Visitors Bureau (CVB) showed that sports in the urban area had low visibility and low priority among tourists (Broward County Convention and Visitor Bureau, 1988). The CVB estimates gross tourist revenues for all tourist activities in Broward County to be about $7 million annually (Broward County Convention and Visitor Bureau, 1988). The focus of tourism, however, is the beach and other water-related activities, which are year-round activities that generate approximately 3.4 million tourists annually (Broward County Convention and Visitor Bureau, 1988). There are no plans by the city or the CVB to emphasize baseball (either spring training or the minor league season) as part of the county's tourist strategy.

Leaders in Fort Lauderdale, however, continue to think the Yankees attract New York residents, who will spend their winter vacation wherever the team plays. It is estimated that as many as 5,000 New York residents who vacation or own property in the county have a commitment to follow the team to spring training. The Yankees are the second most followed spring training team in the state (Florida Department of Commerce, 1987). This specialized market of potential tourists keeps the city committed to supporting the Yankees.

Benefits of Minor League Baseball Vary

Most cities that host a spring training team also host a minor league team. This gives Florida cities two teams and two seasons. The Florida minor league teams compete primarily in the A-level Florida State League, a complex-based Rookie league, in instructional leagues, and in spring training with their major league affiliates. Jacksonville is the only Florida city with a minor league team higher than A level.

Minor league teams are often a part of the agreement to host their major league teams' spring training. For example, Fort Lauderdale must agree to host the Yankees' minor league club as a condition of keeping the valuable spring training operation. Larger cities, such as Fort Lauderdale, consider this arrangement a tourism marketing "loss leader."

Larger cities have many recreational and entertainment outlets. The minor league baseball games must compete in a crowded arena for a population with varied interests. The city cannot promote this attraction to the exclusion of others, unless minor league baseball can present itself as a major economic development force or a major generator of tourism. Minor league baseball may therefore languish in big cities, hostage to the focus on spring training.

Smaller cities, however, find that the additional minor league season is a welcome recreational and entertainment amenity. For example, the Vero Beach Dodgers, who play in Vero Beach (population 18,000), are the focus of the city's summer population. The team is a major activity for the small town and is genuinely supported by the public, business, and government.

Another consideration is the degree of effort made by the minor league team to make its presence known in the community. In Fort Lauderdale, the minor league team is owned and operated by the parent club. Neither game attendance nor concession revenues is the top priority because the team is fully subsidized by the major league club. A minor league team owned by its major league affiliate may not be as motivated to turn a profit as would be a club that is a business venture for the owner. Since the Fort Lauderdale minor league club is not run as a self-sustaining business, it does not have to be too concerned about its presence in or contribution to the host community.

City support and any other benefits the minor league team receives, such as stadium improvements, are a result of the coattails of the spring training season. Since the city subsidizes spring training through improved facilities and contract revenues, the minor league team benefits and does not have to improve its presence in the community. It acts as a free rider.

Fort Lauderdale's minor league team uses the same stadium and facilities as the Yankees do for spring training. Although the minor league team pays the city for the use of the stadium, the fee does not cover the cost of stadium operations. Much of the actual cost of supporting the minor league team is written off by Fort Lauderdale as the cost of keeping the spring training team. The city loses money on the minor league season but justifies it with the assumption that a net gain is made by hosting the Yankees' spring training. The city, however, does not calculate figures to document this assumption.

Changes in the Rules of Intercity Competition

In the 1980s, the relationship between the major league teams and their host cities turned into a competitive business arrangement. Florida communities committed to an all-out financial war over baseball as a means to promote growth and tourism, with spring training teams as the focus of the rivalry. Cities spend millions of dollars, mainly through tourist-tax revenues, to keep teams satisfied and to coax teams to relocate. The competition for teams to relocate has produced a bidding war, footed by public and corporate financing. According to the Florida Division of Tourism, the free-wheeling relocation of teams is "a buyers' market. It's free enterprise" (Altaner, 1988).

In addition, private developers have become partners with cities and counties to finance amenities necessary to attract teams. Teams now expect to be treated to new and refurbished stadiums, training facilities, offices, living accommodations, hotels, and housing developments. These are the new standard terms in their negotiations with host communities. This is a major change from the small stadiums that such cities as Fort Lauderdale have maintained.

Undeveloped areas are the most successful new entries in this competition. These communities are aggressively pursuing spring training teams by offering new, state-of-the-art facilities. They can make such offers because they have abundant vacant land available to build the new facilities. The teams that relocate have better training facilities, which they feel provides them with a competitive edge over rival teams. The strategy adopted by these cities is to lure baseball teams and use their presence to promote growth and development for the area, instead of relying on the tourist aspect of baseball.

For example, Port Charlotte is a small town on the southwest coast that has been created by developers as a residential retirement location. In 1987, the city provided a real estate deal to the Texas Rangers to lure their spring training operation from Pompano Beach (adjacent to Fort Lauderdale on the north) and to attract the Rangers' minor league team located at Plant City (near Tampa on the west coast). This deal included not only a new stadium and premier team facilities, but also a hotel to house the players, visitors, and tourists. The team manages the hotel and receives the profits from its operation. The city has the team and hotel to use as a development incentive and expects to triple its population by the mid-1990s (Justice, 1989).

Charlotte County, like many other counties, has pledged all revenues from its 2 percent tourist-tax to finance the stadium costs. Florida counties are allowed to levy a 2 percent or 3 percent tax on the room rate of all hotels and motels in the county. These tax revenues must be spent on tourist-related activities. In 1985, the state approved baseball as an eligible tourist-related activity, thus providing local governments with a revenue source to finance new stadiums. This has worked well in counties where tourism and baseball are new. However, in established areas, such as Fort Lauderdale/Broward County, tourist-tax revenues must be reallocated for any new baseball financing. This requires a political choice among competing tourist expenditures.

Port St. Lucie, located north of Fort Lauderdale on Florida's southeast coast, is another example of successful development facilitated by baseball. In 1988, the New York Mets' spring training activities and minor league team were lured from St. Petersburg by a new, $10 million state-of-the-art stadium and training facility. The land for the stadium was provided by the city and funded through the county's tourist-tax revenues. The stadium developer, Thomas J. White Development Company of St. Louis, also is building a $2 billion residential and commercial project adjacent to the stadium. Mets team members are involved in the project's marketing strategy.

Port St. Lucie views this as a winning policy. The city nearly quadrupled its population, from 14,000 in 1980 to 55,866 by 1990. It has expanded its tax base, and baseball provides an amenity package to attract residents. The developer has a stadium located next to his development, which draws prospective buyers. The team uses a new premiere facility, subsidized by local government for spring training and its minor league team.

This new competitive strategy of growth through baseball is a major threat to established host cities, such as Fort Lauderdale, which are not growing and do not have vast land resources on which to build new facilities. Oftentimes these cities already have committed their future tax revenues to other tourist ventures that likely will generate more visitors than baseball will. Yet to keep their baseball teams, they are forced to up the ante with public dollars to fund expanded fields and modernize their stadiums and training facilities. This is a difficult task, considering the scope of the public-private development ventures used by other cities. Fort Lauderdale's budget has been hit especially hard by the rising stakes in baseball competition.

The Yankees, as well as other teams, determine their location based on the best deal they can assemble. Team emphasis on spring training is just that—training. While fan support is a morale booster and generates gate receipts, the quality of the facility is what makes the deal work. A spokesman for the White Sox stated that "if you have a fantastic deal, you could break even, but that's not the point, . . . first class facilities is the objective" (Altaner, 1988).

Whatever hardship the city might face concerning subsidies for the team is not a factor to the team making location decisions. The team considers its contract with the city to be a business arrangement, which requires that the team conduct its negotiations as a business organization first and as a "home team" second.

City governments perceive spring training as a local money multiplier that justifies the intense bidding for teams. Baseball is expected to stimulate growth, be an economic force, and generate tourists. Local voters are willing to gamble that potential tourists will foot the bills for team demands when they pass a tourist-tax referendum (as they did in the city of Sarasota in 1988) as a means to pay for new or upgraded facilities.

Business Support for Baseball in Fort Lauderdale

Fort Lauderdale and Broward County could justify their contract concessions to keep the Yankees if there were evidence of community and business support for baseball. City officials traditionally rely on business support to justify economic development activity by local government. The business community should therefore be expected to support spring training and minor league baseball. There is no organized business support for a baseball presence in Fort Lauderdale, however.

Other cities do receive that support and use it to justify and supplement baseball expenditures. For example, when the Red Sox considered leaving Winter Haven in 1989, a group of fifty business and community groups quickly organized a strategy to keep the team in town. Conversely, Fort Lauderdale's corporate and business support was limited to well wishes during the 1989 negotiations with the Yankees (described below).

The business community in Fort Lauderdale does not see baseball as having a significant impact on its businesses. Other sports are on the local business agenda. The Broward County CVB has been active in organizing sailing, boat racing, and fishing events to attract national attention and tourists. In addition, the Broward County Economic Development Board has organized a sports committee to act as a clearinghouse for information on facilities and support services for any sporting event. The staff of the Economic Development Board consider the Yankees important, but the board's private sector business members have not elevated the Yankees to the board's agenda.

The Yankees do not have a financial stake in the city, and the team owner does not have any economic grounding in the area. More important, since the business community does not perceive the Yankees to be a major financial contributor to the local economy, it does not pay much attention to the Yankees and baseball. According to the Chamber of Commerce, there was little concern in the business sector over the possibility of losing the 1990 spring season (Pitt, 1990).

Fort Lauderdale and the Yankees: A Negotiated Relationship

The New York Yankees, which have been training in Fort Lauderdale since 1959, renegotiated the terms of their agreement with the city of Fort Lauderdale in 1988–89. (See the chronology of events in Table 9.1). At the same time, the team's owner, George Steinbrenner, was negotiating with the city of Tampa for training facilities and a stadium. The city of Fort Lauderdale was forced to rely on the intergovernmental cooperation of the county and other neighboring cities for land and revenues to meet the Yankees' demands and to counter the incentives Tampa offered the Yankees. The remainder of this case study is devoted to the 1988–89 negotiations between Fort Lauderdale and the Yankees.

During 1988, the Yankees opened negotiations with the city of Fort Lauderdale by asking for improvements to the city-owned stadium, offices, and practice fields and for new facilities to accommodate minor league spring training. Steinbrenner reminded Fort Lauderdale and Broward County officials that other teams in Florida had better facilities and cited the improvements Sarasota made for the White Sox.

The contract negotiations hinged on meeting the Yankees' request for facility improvements as well as an important new demand—making additional spring training facilities available for the minor league players. The Yankees wanted new minor league fields and training facilities so their minor league teams could all train at a site near the major league team.

It is desirable for minor leaguers to train near the main spring training site so they can easily be called up to participate in an exhibition practice or game. Prior to 1988, the Yankees' minor league teams held spring training in Hollywood (just south of Fort Lauderdale). Steinbrenner moved those activities to Tampa, where better facilities were offered. Providing spring training accommodations for minor league players, and thereby hosting major and minor league spring training as well as the minor league playing season, would be an additional activity undertaken by Fort Lauderdale.

Table 9.1: Chronology of Events

Date	Action
March 1988:	City approves $275,000 for one-time stadium improvements to be balanced by advertising in Yankees media outlets and a two-year contract extension. County's Tourist Development Council (TDC) agrees to extend the availability of $425,000 of tourist-tax revenues to Fort Lauderdale for stadium improvements through April 1989.
June 1988:	TDC agrees to an additional payment of $680,000 from reserves to help finance a park in Coral Springs to be used by the Yankees' minor league players during spring training season.
July 1988:	Yankees make Fort Lauderdale contract contingent on the availability of a separate training facility for minor league teams and refuse to sign until Coral Springs contract is signed. Yankees enter into formal negotiations with Coral Springs to use a proposed county park for minor league training during the regular spring training season.
September 1988:	Yankees make new demands of $550,000 for stadium improvements in lieu of a $1 million new clubhouse (saving the city $500,000). City agrees to take $300,000 from Parks and Recreation capital improvements fund and $200,000 from school board payment for use of Lockhart Stadium (football field adjoining Yankee Stadium).
October 1988:	City agrees to use $425,000 from Broward County TDC for additional $550,000 of stadium improvements and to pay $75,000 in 1990 for team housing subsidy during spring training.
November 1988:	Yankees sign a two-year extension with Fort Lauderdale to go through the 1990 season. Will sign for another three years if Coral Springs deal is made.
December 1988:	Yankees make contract with Coral Springs contingent on the team's use of the park for ten months a year instead of four.
April 1989:	Tampa Sports Authority agrees to build an $8 million spring training/minor league baseball complex; talks begin with Yankees.

Table 9.1 (Continued)

Date	Action
May 1989:	Yankees and Coral Springs cannot come to agreement over the time period the team can use the county park/training fields. Yankees ask Tampa to extend their two-year minor league training contract for another fifteen years.
June 1989:	Broward County sets a deadline of June 9 for Yankees to sign a contract with Fort Lauderdale. On June 20, Fort Lauderdale agrees to additional stadium improvements and travel/lodging subsidies over the next four years to get an additional two-year extension of the contract. Yankees sign additional two-year extension through 1993 season, in return for $1.6 million in stadium improvements, including locker room, press box, new fields, improved seating, concession stands, 1,000 new bleacher seats, batting and pitching cages, and new offices, and $475,000 in lodging and travel subsidies.

FORT LAUDERDALE MAKES AN OFFER

The city of Fort Lauderdale owns Yankee Stadium, where the team's spring training is conducted and minor league games are played. The Parks and Recreation Department has responsibility for stadium operations and maintenance. The stadium seated 7,500 people for spring training before improvements in 1989 increased stadium capacity to 8,500. Prior to 1989, approximately 91,000 fans annually attended games and practice sessions during spring season (City Fort Lauderdale, 1986). Estimates of fans per season after the 1989 stadium expansion are closer to 100,000. Annual attendance for the Yankees' minor league team has fluctuated from more than 50,000 (in 1987 and 1991) to less than 35,000 (in 1990) in recent years. Most fans are permanent residents of the area.

The city's contract with the Yankees covers the standard terms, such as gate receipts, lease payments, concession revenues, stadium maintenance, parking, and security (see Table 9.2). The city receives 15 percent of the gross gate receipts for spring training; a flat fee of $14,000, plus a percentage of gate receipts in excess of $140,000, for the minor league season; and a percentage of the concession and parking revenues. The team pays for internal operations, such as ticket takers and stadium security. The city pays for the rest of the maintenance and operational costs during both seasons, all of which totals approximately $725,000 per year. The city annually subsidizes the baseball seasons. Accurate figures for net costs or revenues are not readily available, however, because of combined record keeping with other city facilities.

It has been customary for the city to maintain a reserve account ($50,000 in 1989) for annual improvements to the stadium. The budget describes the fund as an "account established for the purpose of making annual improvements in preparation for the New York Yankees spring training season." No mention is made of the minor league team's use of, or benefit from, the stadium (City Fort Lauderdale, 1988a). In 1989, however, the Yankees' demands for stadium improvements required guarantees of much larger expenditures (see Table 9.3).

At the opening of negotiations in early 1988, the city of Fort Lauderdale agreed to provide an additional $275,000 of improvements if the Yankees would extend the current contract for two years. Seating improvements, field upgrades, and clubhouse amenities would be provided for the team. In return, the Yankees agreed to provide the city with advertising in the Yankees media outlets, such as the team magazine and game programs, diamond-vision advertisements at Yankee Stadium in New York, and mentions during Yankees broadcasts. The print ads have a market value of about $4,500. The exposure value of the advertising and diamond-vision marquee announcements are worth much more. The city valued this advertising package at $275,000. Nonetheless, when a city commissioner asked if the city would make money from its deal with the Yankees, the city manager replied that "she could not state that the city did; however, she was certain the economy of the county overall was improved by their presence" (City Fort Lauderdale, 1988b).

As quickly as the initial demands were made and met, new requests were added before Steinbrenner would sign a contract extension. By the end of March 1988, the city requested an extension of a $425,000 grant from the county's Tourist Development Council (TDC) through April 1989. This grant would help pay for the original demands and the additional demands.

Revenues from the county tourist-tax are administered through the quasi-governmental TDC. This body is made up of elected officials from the county, Fort Lauderdale, and one other city as well as private sector representatives from the tourist and hotel industries. Total 1989 TDC tourist-tax revenues were expected to be close to $10 million. Fort Lauderdale asked the TDC for the funds on the basis that the Yankees generate tourism benefits for the entire county, not just Fort Lauderdale. The TDC agreed with this argument.

Table 9.2: Contract Terms between
Fort Lauderdale and New York Yankees, 1988–93

	Ft. Lauderdale	Yankees
Revenues		
Spring Training:		
	15 percent of gross admission	advertising parking souvenir concession
	in-kind publicity through Yankee media outlets	broadcasting
		15 percent of concession (1988–91)
	15 percent of concession (1991–93)	
Minor League:[a]		
	10 percent of gross admission over $140,000	
	$14,000 lease rent (less security personnel)	
Expenditures		
Spring Training:		
	stadium maintenance operation personnel	parking personnel
	security personnel	
	net utilities	field light utility cost
	travel and lodging $94,000 (1990) travel and lodging $95,000 (1991)	
Minor League:		
	stadium maintenance and operation	security personnel

[a]Minor league contract terms reflect deviations from Spring Training contract terms.
Otherwise all terms are the same for both Spring Training and Minor League seasons.

Table 9.3: Yankees Facility Improvements

Revenue Sources	Actual Expenditures, Yankee Stadium at Fort Lauderdale	Proposed Expenditures, Minor League Training Park at Coral Springs
Fort Lauderdale		
Original locker room	$ 538,000 (1988)	
Field improvements, additional press box	515,000 (1989)	
Office, fields, 1,000 new seats, refurbished bleachers, etc.	350,000 (1989)	
Lodging, travel	470,000 (1990–93)	
Architectural fees	37,500 (1988)	
Broward County Tourist Development Council	425,000 (1990–93)	$ 680,000
Broward County		
Park		850,000
Roads		2,500,000
Coral Springs		
Annual operations		300,000
Total	$2,335,500 (1988–93)	$4,330,000 (proposed)

THE YANKEES RESPOND

The city was prepared for costly demands from the team. The city was not, however, prepared to meet the new request from the Yankees: additional practice fields and facilities to accommodate minor league players during the spring training season. Fort Lauderdale's stadium has no adjacent land on which to expand. Other cities in the county were therefore sought as partners in this deal to provide land for a new site to accommodate the Yankees. The cost of providing these additional minor league facilities was estimated to be $2.2 million. The team insisted that its contract with Fort Lauderdale was contingent on the additional site. Fort Lauderdale was consequently forced to negotiate a complicated intergovernmental deal to keep the Yankees in town.

In July 1988, the intergovernmental aspects of the contract negotiations began to take shape. The Yankees began formal negotiations with the city of Coral Springs in western Broward County. The county already had plans to locate a major regional park there, and Coral Springs was willing to work with the team regarding use of the park during spring training season. In addition, the TDC agreed to contribute to the effort.

Coral Springs agreed to let the Yankees use the park for four to six weeks in the spring free of charge. The city would pay $300,000 per year for park maintenance. A major developer in Coral Springs, Coral Ridge Properties, also agreed to contribute to the project.

By the fall of 1988, a contract extension between the Yankees and Fort Lauderdale remained unsigned. The Yankees made new demands. In light of the quality of facilities provided for other teams around the state, Steinbrenner requested another $550,000 in improvements be made to the Fort Lauderdale stadium and facilities. New fields, a better press box, and a thousand additional bleacher seats became necessary to make a deal.

In the interim, the cost of the original improvements had increased. Fort Lauderdale had a portion of the TDC grant of $425,000 remaining, which could help fund these additional improvements. The city also expected to use $300,000 from the lease of another recreational facility, as well as $200,000 in capital expenditure funds available in the city's Parks and Recreation capital plan budget.

The city agreed to make these improvements only if the Coral Springs deal for minor league facilities was negotiated separately. In addition, the city agreed to provide $75,000 for lodging expenses for the team, in Fort Lauderdale, during the 1990 spring training season. This was a unique arrangement in spring training contracts.

Other aspects of the city's final negotiations centered on the terms of the contract's annual revenues and expenditures. The contract negotiated by the city with the team covers both the spring training and minor league seasons. The terms of the new contract were changed in several respects to sweeten the deal for the Yankees. Among the changes was a transfer of the concession and parking revenues from the city to the Yankees, valued at about $10,000 in 1988.

Steinbrenner agreed to the terms. He won new improvements and a very attractive travel subsidy. He could also continue to pursue the minor league facilities.

City officials decided they were over a barrel and, therefore, agreed to the team's demands in order to get a contract signed. A two-year extension (1989 through 1991) to the contract was signed in October 1988. An addendum was included specifying that if an agreement was reached with Coral Springs, the contract with Fort Lauderdale would be extended automatically for an additional three years. According to the city's Parks and Recreation director, Tom Tapp, "It is not a typical lease in which the city's interests are carefully protected, because we have not been negotiating from a position of strength. . . . We want to keep the Yankees, they know that, and they have other options" (Vlahou, 1988).

INTERGOVERNMENTAL PARTNERS EXTEND THE NEGOTIATIONS

Coral Springs continued negotiations with the Yankees and agreed in late 1988 that the team would use the facility during four months (extended from four to six weeks) in the spring. As negotiations seemed to near closure, the Yankees again made additional demands. Steinbrenner proposed that the Coral Springs park be available to the team for ten months out of the year instead of four. The team wanted its entire year-round minor league operation to be housed at one site (it operated the A-league team during the spring and summer in Fort Lauderdale, the spring training and year-round players' rehabilitation in Tampa, and an instructional league team in Sarasota).

Coral Springs vehemently opposed this request. The mayor stated that the demands were "absolutely, positively, utterly impossible," and a commissioner stated that "anything that's a change in the original deal stinks and should not be accepted" (Doto, 1988).

This strong negative reaction can be attributed to several factors. One is that Coral Springs felt it already was compromising its park by giving up public use for four months. Coral Springs is an upper-middle-class, amenity-conscious community. The deal was seen as a major sacrifice, but somewhat balanced by the opportunity for residents to watch professional, if only minor league, baseball players practice. The additional demand to give up the park for ten months would mean that city-sponsored youth league activities would be sacrificed. That is politically unacceptable in Coral Springs.

Second, the negotiation had been a protracted affair. Broward County did a great deal of arm twisting with the Yankees, and Fort Lauderdale put pressure on Coral Springs to finalize the park agreement. Coral Springs did not appreciate being put in the middle. The city saw its position go from originally having a county-funded year-round park for its residents, to sharing it with the Yankees, to having minimal use of the park and footing the bill for the Yankees' benefit.

Finally, Coral Springs had no incentive to stick with the negotiating process at this point. Coral Springs did not have the loyalty or economic ties to the Yankees that Fort Lauderdale did, so its support was tentative throughout.

Fort Lauderdale was not in a position to demand anything from Coral

Springs and could only approach the process as one of intergovernmental cooperation. Broward County has twenty-six municipalities. Intergovernmental cooperation is difficult at best, and in this case it carried no advantage for Coral Springs. Fort Lauderdale had very little leverage to make the second extension of the contract a reality.

The county entered the negotiations as another intergovernmental party to the minor league facilities contract. Broward County was willing to use $850,000 of its Park Department funds for the project. The county also pledged $2.5 million in future road improvements to the area to facilitate the year-round use of the park (some of which was an increase over the cost that would be necessary even if the Yankees did not use the park). The county's Tourist Development Council was another intergovernmental party to the new minor league park. It agreed to contribute $680,000 of county tourist-tax revenues to the cost of the Coral Springs facility to build practice facilities and a clubhouse for the Yankees to use at the park.

When Steinbrenner pressed for more concessions in spring 1989 and the deal for the minor league park at Coral Springs faltered, the city of Tampa made overtures to the Yankees by proposing a new stadium. Steinbrenner asked Tampa for a fifteen-year extension of his current minor league contract, thus hoping to squeeze the Fort Lauderdale negotiations to a quick settlement.

At this juncture Broward County, through the county chairperson, stepped in as the negotiator for Fort Lauderdale. She gave the Yankees a deadline of June 9, 1989, to sign an agreement with Fort Lauderdale. The county and the TDC would release their funds earmarked for the baseball facilities if an agreement was not reached. The chairperson of the county commission, who also was the chair of the TDC, felt that the offer was too good for the team to refuse and stated that "he [Steinbrenner] cannot possibly demand anything more than what we're offering him" (Vlahou, 1989).

The local newspaper, the *Ft. Lauderdale News and Sun Sentinel,* echoed those sentiments by issuing an editorial that criticized Steinbrenner's demands. It admonished that "after so many people have worked for so long trying to find ways to finance Steinbrenner's many requests for improvements to his training facilities, that [his additional demands] is a highly unprofessional reason to again drag his feet" ("Steinbrenner Demands Off Base," 1989).

The negotiations with Coral Springs finally ended because no satisfactory agreement could be reached. The Yankees did agree to an additional two-year extension of the contract with Fort Lauderdale (taking the contract through 1993). Once again, the city agreed to make additional stadium improvements, which included seat and field improvements and new restrooms, concession areas, and sound system. All stadium improvements would cost a total of $1.6 million over the four-year contract. In addition, the city agreed to subsidize travel and lodging over four years (instead of one) at a cost of $475,000.

INTERGOVERNMENTAL COMPETITION IS THE YANKEES' LEVERAGE

Tampa has been part of a round-robin of baseball relocations and attempts to establish a professional baseball presence in the Bay area. Several years ago, the state authorized the creation of the Tampa Sports Authority (TSA). One of its goals is to acquire a major league baseball franchise. Across Tampa Bay, St. Petersburg has the same goal. It built a publicly funded, domed stadium to prove its seriousness. At that point, Tampa fell behind in the race to impress the major league team owners.

Instead of acquiring a major league franchise, Tampa decided to construct a premier minor league and spring training facility, funded through tourist-tax revenues. Until 1988, Tampa hosted the Cincinnati Reds' spring training operations at the city's Redsland facility (now called the Yankees Complex). When the Reds relocated their spring training operations from Tampa to neighboring Plant City, the TSA decided to construct by 1992 a baseball complex that would include an 8,000-seat stadium costing $5–8 million. Tampa had to gamble that it could build new facilities to lure another team. The Yankees are that team.

The Tampa Sports Authority lured the Yankees' minor league training from Hollywood, Florida, in 1988. During the 1988–89 negotiations with Fort Lauderdale, Steinbrenner signed a five-year agreement with Tampa that will end in 1994, a year after the Fort Lauderdale agreement ends. He agreed to extend the contract for minor league spring training and to locate in Tampa all the Yankees' Florida minor league activities except for the Florida State League team, which would remain in Fort Lauderdale.

The TSA expected to lose $540,000 over the five years, but it justified the contract terms as a "calculated gamble" to get the Yankees to move from Fort Lauderdale (Selman, 1989). In return, Steinbrenner committed $1 million to facility improvements in Tampa, which he felt would "show commitment on our part to the community" (Henderson, 1989). A comparable offer was not made to Fort Lauderdale, and there is no recent evidence of good-faith investment by the Yankees in Fort Lauderdale.

The Yankees threatened to relocate if Fort Lauderdale did not provide expanded spring training facilities that could accommodate their minor league players. This threat was made just as Tampa made its offer to build its minor league center. Tampa was unable to make the facilities available for the 1989–90 seasons, and the Yankees elected to drop the demand that Fort Lauderdale provide the minor league facilities.

At this point the negotiations between the Yankees and Fort Lauderdale were back to square one: negotiating for spring training and the minor league season. Fort Lauderdale, however, did not seize the advantage of this change in conditions at the bargaining table. The Yankees could not move their spring operations to Tampa in 1989 or the next year, but they made extensive new demands in lieu of the minor league training facility. It is questionable whether Fort Lauderdale needed to agree to extensive short-term demands, because the Yankees had few if any sites available.

Fort Lauderdale is well aware of Tampa's competitive position and realizes that the Yankees may relocate. Steinbrenner has a residence in Tampa and owns several lucrative business ventures there. This fact adds to the speculation that the Yankees will move their entire Florida operation to Tampa as soon as possible. The Tampa stadium, however, will not be completed until 1994, at the earliest. Fort Lauderdale could attempt to attract a new team, but Fort Lauderdale and Broward County officials are dedicated to the Yankees, not just baseball, partly because of the large number of immigrants from the state of New York who live in Florida, especially in south Florida. Of all the states, New York supplies the most new immigrants (42,076 persons statewide in 1988) ("Statistical Overview of the State," 1989).

Fort Lauderdale expects its current investment in its stadium to pay off, even if the Yankees do leave. A new team would be sought to fill the stadium and facilities.

Conclusion

Fort Lauderdale supports baseball because it supposedly attracts tourists, produces such intangible benefits as civic pride and identification, and provides another amenity for winter visitors and full-time residents. However, the traditional indicators of a policy's viability, such as political support, demand articulation, and revenue contribution, are not evident in Fort Lauderdale. The decision to support the Yankees is motivated mainly by tradition and civic pride. Although these are noble factors, one must question whether spring training and minor league baseball in Fort Lauderdale are worth the escalating price.

There is no doubt that hosting a team can be a valuable endeavor, especially in smaller, growth-oriented communities. Smaller communities that are attractive development areas have been able to use baseball to attract more development. Those cities can justify the cost of pursuing professional baseball. Such cities as Fort Lauderdale, which are not in a rapid growth situation, may, however, have to reevaluate whether it is worthwhile to remain competitive in the baseball bidding.

PART IV

The Use of Stadiums
for Downtown Redevelopment

All cities, whether they are large or small, old or new, have downtowns. Suburban communities, as well as small towns and villages, have town centers, central business districts, or commercial corridors that correspond to the concept of a downtown. All downtowns face threats, even though the literature tends to focus on the plight of the downtowns of large cities. Many cities are struggling to rebuild and revitalize their downtowns. Others are seeking ways to prevent deterioration of their downtowns.

Downtown redevelopment efforts are decades old. Although they always have been, and continue to be, intergovernmental efforts with private sector participation, recent analyses emphasizes the entrepreneurial creativity of local officials and their private sector partners. Cooperation between local government and private sector interests is presented as the critical element in the deals that are made to redevelop and revitalize downtowns, given the diminution of the federal government's role in urban redevelopment.

A few cities (e.g., St. Louis, Cincinnati, Indianapolis, New Orleans) have recognized that major league sports stadiums are important to downtown redevelopment. In May 1990, Cleveland voters narrowly approved (by a margin of 3.4 percent) a new baseball stadium and sports arena designed to be the centerpiece of a downtown redevelopment project that will include restaurants, hotels, and shops. Part IV examines how minor league stadiums can play a similar role.

The Logic of Downtown Stadiums

The twin economic goals of urban redevelopment are to expand the tax base and to increase economic activities downtown. This implies the need to develop projects that will attract people downtown and that will be synergistic with the downtown's economy and built environment.

The traditional strategy for attracting more people downtown has been to locate government facilities, office buildings, and financial institutions downtown. The explosion of downtown office building construction in the 1980s is evidence that this strategy continues. Small towns, especially, have kept their government operations in the traditional downtown as a symbol of their commitment to downtown and its merchants, even as annexations change their population settlement patterns.

A city with a downtown of only office buildings, banks, and government facilities has a downtown that is busy from 9 A.M. to 5 P.M. during the week but is virtually a ghost town at all other times. Many are critical of such cities for at least two reasons. First, they argue that a 9-to-5 presence cannot sustain any significant retail activity, which is necessary to support and attract downtown residential development and such economic activity as tourism. Second, critics suggest that cities should have ambience and personality. This is acquired in large measure from a variety of (high and low) cultural attractions and entertainment forms. Local officials must pay attention to a city's "personality" as well as its physical being.

Downtown redevelopment efforts have therefore expanded to include projects that promise to keep office workers downtown after 5 P.M. and to bring nonresidents downtown not only during the week, but also after hours and on weekends. Entertainment and recreational activities are essential to doing this. For example, Atlanta's redevelopment of the Underground and Phoenix's efforts to develop cultural arts facilities downtown are recognitions of this fact, as is the construction of downtown sports facilities.

Minor league baseball represents an addition to the recreation and entertainment mix that a city offers its residents and visitors. Nearly all of a minor league team's games are played at night or on the weekends. A downtown stadium housing a minor league team therefore has the potential of attracting a large number of people downtown at times they ordinarily would not be there.

A minor league team only plays approximately seventy dates during the summer months, however. A downtown stadium must be used for purposes other than minor league baseball games if it is to fulfill its economic development role. The more events staged in the stadium, the more the locality is exploiting the stadium for economic development purposes. This is true, however, only if the stadium's location encourages those attending stadium events to engage in other economic activities.

For example, attendees are more likely to shop or stop for a drink after the game if the stadium is close to stores and restaurants, instead of isolated from the rest of downtown.

Once the decision to build a stadium is made, it must be decided if it is to serve a development function. If so, location and design decisions will be critical to the stadium's success as a development project, as distinct from serving merely as a home to a sports team and providing good sight lines for fans. For example, the selection of Camden Yards as the site for the Orioles' new stadium in Baltimore was intended to reenforce the city's Inner Harbor as an attraction for residents and nonresidents. The stadium has been designed to model the old-time ballparks that tended to fit comfortably into their neighborhood environs.

The Political Economy of Downtown Redevelopment: Retail Centers and Minor League Stadiums

Frieden and Sagalyn (1989: 41), in their analysis of the decline and reemergence of downtown retail centers, note that most redevelopment projects of the 1960s sought isolation from other (sometimes undesirable) downtown activities. Those were large, single-function projects designed to be separate from downtown. In contrast, the authors find that the success of downtown retail centers in the 1970s and 1980s was based in part on the fact that they were designed to fit into and complement downtown areas. The minor league sports stadiums discussed in this section were designed to be inviting to spectators, to be used for events other than minor league baseball, and, most important, to accomplish other objectives related to downtown development.

Frieden and Sagalyn (1989: 281) find that even the most successful retail centers were the result of ad hoc decision making rather than rational urban planning: "To call the composite of projects a corporate center strategy is to dignify it beyond the reality of piecemeal, trial and error decisions." We can draw the same conclusion from cases in this section and cases throughout the text. Stadium decisions tend to be the result of taking advantage of opportunities as they arise rather than strategic planning.

Nevertheless, this does not mean the absence of planning or of a logic that serves as the foundation for specific decisions. Frieden and Sagalyn (1989: 281) note that "the logic of city development produced a series of ventures that were possible because they were anchored in some way to the jobs and businesses that were growing downtown." The cases in this section demonstrate that city officials in Harrisburg, South Bend, and Durham had a vision of what a downtown stadium can do for revitalization efforts. The mayor of each city envisioned a specific role for his stadium. Location in each case was the critical factor in making the stadium work for the city. In Harrisburg and South Bend, the evidence suggests that the stadiums are doing what was expected. In Durham, voters did not permit the opportunity.

The downtown retail center projects described by Frieden and Sagalyn were true public-private ventures. Developers invested large sums of money and much time in the projects, as did local governments. The introduction to this book presented a summary of the criticism by urban scholars of development projects of all types. These critics charge that urban redevelopment sacrifices neighborhoods and a sense of place and enriches developers and other private sector interests at the expense of the poor and the public interest (e.g., Logan and Molotch, 1987). Frieden and Sagalyn (1989: 247–48), while recognizing some basis for these charges from a moralistic perspective, reach a different conclusion: "we found no private takeovers of downtown negotiations; instead both sides used the bargaining opportunity to extend their influence. Developers certainly shaped the terms of the deals that cities offered them. But at the same time city negotiators politicized decisions that used to belong to the private sector.... The new methods of project management, in short, gave cities a place at the bargaining table that they could use to promote the public interest."

Although academic observers are critical of development projects, there was relatively little community-based political opposition to downtown retail center projects. Frieden and Sagalyn (1989: 248–52) state that city officials learned to defuse antirenewal protests by finding sites that did not threaten homes and by paying for the projects with off-budget funds. An acceptable location avoided imposing direct costs on a concentrated group of residents. Off-budget financing avoided the linkage between increased taxes and project costs, spread costs over a long time horizon, and obfuscated the true project costs and source of payments. Frieden and Sagalyn (1989: 153) also note the importance of a political climate (in the 1970s) that "gave city negotiators the freedom to wheel and deal."

In sum, the projects that Frieden and Sagalyn describe were true public-private partnerships, carried out in a favorable political climate. The benefits (e.g., new jobs, attractive buildings, and increased tax revenues) they promised for the community were easily communicated to, and understood by, the public. Their costs were diffuse and inexact. The development of minor league stadiums as described in Part IV, however, was of a different character and did not have such favorable circumstances.

In most cases, the relationship between a team and a city is more of a tenant-landlord relationship than a true partnership. In the downtown stadium projects of Harrisburg and South Bend, for example, private sector involvement early in the process was minimal. It is the stadium lease, as exemplified by South Bend's fifty-page document, that forges a relationship, rather than concurrent risk taking in the stadium project itself. The case of Durham, on the other hand, promised a partnership between the team, the area's corporate interests, and local government, but voters rejected the proposed downtown stadium project.

The projected costs of minor league stadiums are much more exact than those of the larger and more complex downtown retail centers. Nevertheless, the public, using the major league analogy to judge minor league stadium projects, will believe that any errors in calculating minor league stadium costs will be on the low side due to the well-publicized cost overruns of major league stadiums. The public is less likely to agree the benefits of a minor league stadium are high priority. The public remains skeptical, even when a stadium project is packaged as part of a downtown development project.

The political climate of the 1980s and 1990s was different from that of the 1970s. Deal making and public-private ventures are still in vogue, but taxpayers are much more aware of hidden costs, especially those of off-budget financing plans. The "taxpayers' revolt" became more intense in the 1980s and remains strong in the early 1990s. Projects that appear to be luxuries and that cannot pay for themselves are given much closer scrutiny by the public than was the case in earlier years. The trend away from bond issues, which require a popular vote, and toward certificates of participation is, in part, a recognition of this fact (Wright, 1990; "States Hike Use of Lease-Debt, COPs Financing," 1989).

The Harrisburg and South Bend stadium projects, like most of the retail center projects described by Frieden and Sagalyn, were never presented to the voters for approval. If they had been put to a vote, they likely would have failed. In the former case, few thought the stadium was a workable idea, and in the latter case, political opposition was intense. The Durham stadium project reached the voters and failed.

In Harrisburg and South Bend, strong mayors forged ahead once they arrived at a vision of how a minor league stadium could benefit their plans for downtown revitalization. In both cases, the mayors championed the project and presented a consistent and explicit rationale that related the stadium to downtown revitalization plans. In the case of Durham, which is governed by a city manager form of government, no such champion emerged in the early stages of the debate, and the city changed mayors during the stadium debate. The rationale for a downtown stadium was not strongly made in the public arena until after other issues had been raised by opponents to the project.

The cases in this section provide examples of the use of minor league stadiums to assist downtown revitalization. The politics of such projects threaten their very being, and the economics of the completed projects are uncertain.

Harrisburg, Pennsylvania   10

Harrisburg, a city of approximately 52,000 citizens, is located on the Susquehana River in central Pennsylvania. It is the central city of a region of seventy-five boroughs and townships within a three county area. Although the city lost population throughout the 1980s, the region increased its population of 464,221 in 1986 to 492,629 by 1990 (an increase of 6 percent).

Harrisburg, under the leadership of Mayor Stephen Reed, became a national success story in the 1980s. In 1980–81, after three decades of decline, Harrisburg was one of the most distressed cities in the nation. It had lost its credit rating and faced bankruptcy. By 1988, the city had become the leading city in economic growth among those with a population of 50,000–75,000.

Between 1982 and 1988, more than five hundred projects were begun, representing more than $700 million in new investment. The number of businesses on the tax rolls nearly doubled, from 1,908 in 1981 to 3,300 in 1988. The market value appreciation of taxable real estate climbed from $356 million to $726 million between 1983 and 1988.

The city's turnaround gained national recognition. In a national poll of banking institutions in 1986 and 1987, Harrisburg was identified as the second best investment city in the eastern United States. In 1986, the United States Conference of Mayors selected Harrisburg as one of its eight "profile cities" in recognition of its success in economic development. In 1985, the National Municipal League selected Harrisburg as an "All American City."

Baseball Comes to Harrisburg

Mayor Stephen Reed took office in 1981. Within a year, the mayor launched a number of innovative projects designed to reverse the city's declining fortunes and to develop alternative revenue sources for the city. The mayor's Energy and Revenue Development Program resulted in several projects that produced revenue for the city from the sale of steam and electricity to the Pennsylvania Power and Light Company.

In late 1983, the mayor announced his plans for improving the city's waterfront. The plan focused on City Island and called for the eventual construction of a seventeen-foot-high gated spillway on the Susquehanna River to replace the existing four-foot-high Dock Street Dam. The project, known as the Harrisburg (nee, Dock Street Dam) Hydroelectric Project, includes a 34.4 megawatt hydroelectric generating facility, a 3,000-foot-long dam with a height of seventeen feet, and a reservoir eight miles long, as well as recreational facilities and riverfront improvements. The estimated cost was set at $262 million.

The riverfront improvements were to occur principally at City Island. City Island is a site of more than sixty acres owned by the city of Harrisburg and is situated in the middle of the Susquehanna River, the west bank of which forms the city's border. The Susquehanna River serves as both a physical and symbolic barrier between the city and its suburbs. The west shore is described in local jokes as the white shore and the east shore as the black shore.

City Island is connected to the city's downtown by a bridge. In the early 1980s, the island had become an eyesore and was perceived by the public to be crime-ridden. For example, a newspaper article in the mid-1980s described it as an evening attraction for male prostitutes. City Island was symbolic of the city's deterioration.

In 1983, the mayor persuaded a minor league team to relocate to Harrisburg, but he failed to raise the money necessary to build a stadium. He could only obtain the promise of a small grant from the state, and efforts to raise private funds generated less than $100,000. In 1983, the city lacked the financial capacity to issue general obligation bonds. It would have been politically impossible to use local tax dollars for a sports stadium when the city was struggling to pay its bills. Because of the city's inability to finance and construct a stadium, the team was lost.

Mayor Reed, however, continued to talk about the desirability of minor league baseball in Harrisburg. His enthusiasm was met with apathy and criticism. According to the mayor and his staff, critics predicted that no team would locate in Harrisburg; if a team did agree to relocate, the city would not be able to build a stadium; and if the city did build a stadium, few fans would turn out for the team. Furthermore, the critics argued, no one would go to City Island to attend baseball games.

City Island was the mayor's announced site for a future baseball stadium. In fact, the mayor planned to use the baseball stadium as the centerpiece and stimulus for the redevelopment of City Island. The mayor viewed the stadium as the anchor for an economic development project that would be highly visible and would attract large crowds of people to the island, making other events and improvements on the island feasible. A desolate area with a bad reputation would be transformed into a festive, vibrant, and attractive park and recreational complex.

A 1984 pre-feasibility study of the Dock Street Dam Project concluded that the city should seek an FERC (Federal Energy Regulatory Commission) licence for the project. The licence was issued in May 1984, and in November 1985, the city issued $215 million of tax-exempt Advanced Funding Bonds for project financing. The bonds were to be repaid from revenues derived from the sale of electric power generated by the hydroelectric facility.

Significantly, the bonds were issued before the federal tax reform of 1986. The city was therefore able to reinvest the bond principal at a higher rate than the city promised to pay the holders of the bonds. In July 1986, the city had to decide whether to terminate the project or to refinance the bonds. The city refinanced the project with a new $391 million bond issue, which was reinvested in U.S. government securities.

Restrictions on the bond issue limited the use of the money to revenue-producing projects that would improve the waterfront. A new stadium on City Island would meet both requirements. The mayor began his search for a minor league team in earnest. He notified Eastern League officials and the Pittsburgh Pirates of his intent to bring a team to Harrisburg.

The Pirates AA team in the Eastern League had been located in Nashua, New Hampshire, since 1980. The team drew more than 100,000 fans during its first year in Nashua, but it experienced declining attendance in subsequent years. Cold weather and an old facility discouraged fans from attending. Also, team officials speculate, the area's residents were turned off by the nationally publicized drug problems of several of the Pirates. City officials in Nashua declined to invest money in the ballpark's concession areas, locker rooms, or press facilities. In 1986, the team attracted only 70,000 spectators. Pirates officials did not object to management's desire to relocate.

When the team failed to make progress in negotiations with officials of Springfield, Massachusetts, it turned to Harrisburg. Eventually, agreements between the team and the mayor and his staff were reached. The Pirates welcomed the move, which brought its AA team to a city that was only two hundred miles from Pittsburgh. Bringing a farm team to a city that is closer to the major league club's host community reduces the travel costs of the player development personnel and the cost of transporting players between the two cities.

Construction of Riverside Stadium on City Island began in 1986. The stadium had to be built in less than twelve months so operations could begin by March 1987. The team had no input regarding the site or the design of the stadium.

Financing the Stadium

Harrisburg's 4,300-seat stadium cost $1.9 million to construct. The bulk of the money that financed the stadium came from the arbitrage earnings of the Dock Street Dam Project bonds. Private donations, mainly from the investment bankers and bond counsel who handled the refinancing, totaled $40,000.

The city also received assistance from the state. It received two recreational grants worth $350,000. This was the first time this type of grant was used for a sports stadium, and the project therefore met bureaucratic resistance. The mayor, however, was able to win Governor Richard Thornburgh's support for the project. Local officials cite the mayor's relationship with the governor, the governor's residency in Harrisburg, and the governor's love of baseball as reasons for the city's success in winning the governor's support.

Harrisburg also was allowed $103,000 worth of tax credits to be used by the Tri-county Commission for Community Action, which is a nonprofit organization. The state allows the tax credits for an economic development project if it benefits low-income citizens. Individuals and private companies can apply the tax credits to offset up to 50 percent of their income or corporate taxes. The tax credits can only be issued by nonprofit organizations.

The stadium was thus built without using any of the city's general revenues and without incurring additional debt. Use of the arbitrage earnings allowed the mayor to proceed with the project without having to gain the approval of the city council or the public. Given the skepticism toward the project, it is not likely the mayor would have won the support of either group.

Minor League Baseball in Harrisburg

Indeed, the skeptics were wrong. The Harrisburg Senators won the Eastern League championship and attracted 233,000 fans during 1987, their first year at Riverside Stadium. The team attracted 216,940 fans in 1988, 200,196 in 1989, 223,533 in 1990, and 233,423 in 1991. The team's attendance in 1988 and 1990 was the highest in the Eastern League. In 1990, out of the twenty-six AA-level teams, the Senators ranked sixth in attendance; in 1991, they ranked seventh.

The team's success in the first year led to a 1,000-seat expansion of the stadium in 1988. The team contributed $120,000 toward the cost of that expansion. In 1989, the city was planning a larger expansion for 1990, and there was cautious talk about seeking a AAA franchise when major league baseball expanded. The team's owners, however, did not seek a Triple-A expansion franchise when applications were requested in 1990. City officials understood that the team had to demonstrate its ability to increase its level of support before it could seek AAA status.

The team's success also made the revitalization of City Island possible. In addition to Riverside Stadium, the city has constructed another sports field, where a minor league football team and community soccer teams play. Concerts also are held on this second field. Riverside Village consists of a number of food stands that attract downtown workers and residents and city visitors to the island. A marina and a riverboat, which presents an hour-long cruise when the river's water level permits, also have been established on the island. The island is fast becoming what the mayor had planned in the early 1980s.

City officials estimate that more than 600,000 people visit the island annually. The island's season is slowly expanding, although most activities take place from April to December. The baseball team remains the principal attraction, but other features on the island are becoming well established in their own right.

The Benefits

City officials identify several benefits that the city has derived from the presence of the Harrisburg Senators. The most important benefit has been the redevelopment of City Island. Its importance is cited as being principally symbolic. The island signals to suburbanites as well as city residents that the revitalization of the city is real. The team and the stadium are prominently mentioned and pictured in the city's promotional literature and the mayor's reports to citizens. The stadium and the island serve as a meeting ground for suburbanites and city residents. City officials are hopeful that a pleasant experience on the island will entice suburban residents to cross the river into downtown for other events and activities.

The economic benefits derived from the team are not discussed as enthusiastically as the symbolic importance of revitalizing City Island. Aside from the economic activity that the team itself generates with its payroll and purchases, several other benefits are mentioned. Many believe the team provides a means of regularly bringing the city's name to cities throughout the Northeast. There is no hard evidence, however, that this has ever been translated into new economic activity for the city or region.

Several interviewees asserted that the team has meant increased business for downtown businesses, especially bars and restaurants. Some, however, wonder how this could be, when many downtown merchants close their doors at 6 P.M. The most popular sports bar in the downtown employs one extra person on game nights. There is no evidence that many downtown establishments have benefited from the team.

Local charities have benefited from the team's financial and organizational support. In 1988 and 1989, for example, the team's management helped raise $15,000 and $25,000, respectively, beyond direct contributions of cash, tickets, and merchandise for local charities.

The city is not seeking to bring in a surplus of revenues from the operation of the stadium. It does expect to avoid operating deficits. Any surplus revenues are to be reinvested in City Island projects or used by the Parks and Recreation Department for its programs.

The Costs

Hosting the Senators has not been without its costs. These costs have been primarily political. Although some wonder if the city entered into a beneficial financial arrangement with the team, no one makes the claim that the team is a drain on the city's treasury. The stadium was built without local tax dollars and appears to be operating without a deficit.

The city, however, has had a combative relationship with its intergovernmental partners concerning the stadium and City Island, and the Senators became the focus of a bitter conflict between the mayor and city council. Although the first of these might be considered a normal by-product of intergovernmental partnerships, the latter clearly imposed costs on the community.

Since one condition for receiving the state tax credits used to construct the stadium was that low-income citizens would benefit from the project, the state was concerned early in the stadium's operation with how the city intended to accomplish this. Written into the original 1987 lease is a requirement that at least three special events be cosponsored by the team and the city during the baseball season for the youth of the community and that the club give to the city "a reasonable number of free admission tickets" to be distributed to the community.

The state accepted this arrangement as meeting the technicalities of the law in the case of Harrisburg, although it subsequently rejected a similar proposal from another community as inadequate. In a renegotiated lease with the Senators, the requirement was deleted.

City officials make the argument that the stadium benefits low-income citizens in two ways. First, officials claim that the team hires from 85 to 90 percent of its personnel from the city and that Riverside Village does likewise. Approximately eight full-time and seventy part-time jobs are filled by the team at the stadium. Many of these employees are low-income residents.

Second, the city cites the increasing use of the stadium by organizations other than the Senators. In the first year of the stadium's existence (which was less than twelve months), the stadium was used fewer than a dozen times by groups other than the Senators. In the second year, this number increased nearly fourfold.

It is not clear to what extent organizations with low-income citizens make use of the stadium, though. The city charges a rental fee of $125 for three hours of use to cover its operating costs, but no one has been turned down for lack of money to pay the fee. Although the issue can be debated, the state appears to have accepted the city's practice and does not seem inclined to challenge the city on this issue.

To win the state recreation grants, the mayor had needed Governor Thornburgh's assistance. In 1989, after Thornburgh left office, the city sought a $1 million grant to fund its proposed 1990 expansion of the stadium, but it was rebuffed. This created ill will toward the new Casey administration because a new minor league stadium in Scranton received $11 million of state support. Although Harrisburg officials claim that Scranton's success is because Governor Robert P. Casey, who was elected in 1988, comes from the Scranton area, Casey's defenders point out that $7 million had already been approved by the Thornburgh administration.

The federal government also posed questions about the use of the stadium on City Island. Federal officials voiced concern that citizens do not have free access to the facilities on the island. Their interest stems from the fact that federal land and water funds have been used for the island. State officials mediated the issue and advised the city how it could meet federal concerns. State officials also claimed they have attempted to persuade federal officials that the current facilities improved the status of the island and that they should not voice opposition.

The confrontation between the mayor and a majority of city council members, ostensibly over baseball, was more intense. Five city council members sued the mayor in 1988, challenging his right to negotiate and sign a lease (which the mayor called a park permit) for Riverside Stadium and other city property without the council's approval. The council objected to several aspects of the Senators' initial lease. Council members expressed concern about the financial return to the city, obligations to make expensive improvements to the stadium, and the city's liability for injuries to fans at the stadium.

The council lost its case in the county court, but it appealed to the commonwealth court in August 1988. The case was still being disputed when the Dock Street Dam Bonds came due for refinancing. The council threatened to withhold its approval for refinancing if the mayor did not renegotiate the lease and agree to pay the legal costs for the council's challenge, which at the time were in excess of $24,000. The mayor acceded to these demands.

The mayor lost in the commonwealth court, but he gained an injunctive stay until his appeal was heard. The Senators were therefore allowed to play their 1989 season uninterrupted. During the controversy, the president of the team suggested there was a possibility of relocation. The conflict came to an end as a result of the mayor's decisive victory in the primary elections in the summer of 1989. Mayor Reed won more than 75 percent of the Republican and Democratic vote, and the slate of council candidates that he was supporting defeated four of the five incumbents who had pressed the lawsuit. The new council members were expected to drop the suit when they took office.

Some city council members also argued the team is an inappropriate expense for the city. They contended that the team brings little benefit to city residents, since most of the fans are suburbanites, and that the attention given to City Island is an example of the priority given to downtown redevelopment at the expense of the city's neighborhoods.

Another criticism was that the Parks and Recreation Department has not been able to care for the neighborhood parks adequately because priority has been given to maintaining City Island. The director of the department refutes that charge by citing the improvements made to local parks throughout the city. Of the $5 million spent on improving parks prior to 1990, $3 million went to neighborhood parks. Sixteen parks have been rehabilitated.

Although the dispute between the mayor and the council had its roots in personal and political differences, the team became embroiled in the conflict. The president of the Senators claimed that the team was not able to engage in long-term planning because of the battles between the mayor and the council. Even if the team is an innocent victim of local politics, some representatives of the public are unconvinced that public expenditures in support of a minor league baseball team are in the public interest.

A Sports Strategy for Harrisburg

Mayor Reed sought a baseball team for Harrisburg to accomplish a specific goal—to occupy a sports stadium that would stimulate redevelopment of City Island. He viewed sports as a means of accomplishing economic and community development goals. The exploitation of professional sports has been carried further by the city. The city hosts a minor league football team, which uses a field on City Island. The mayor has considered hosting minor league teams in basketball and soccer and foresees the possibility of hosting professional lacrosse in the future.

The mayor views the emergence of a sports strategy for the city cautiously. He believes that a franchise failure could be equated with failure on the city's part. The mayor fears that, just as the city exploited the success of its minor league baseball experience, critics and competitors could exploit a sport's failure—to the city's detriment.

South Bend, Indiana 11

Arthur Johnson and C. James Owen

South Bend, Indiana, is located on the south bend of the St. Joseph's River in the north-central part of the state, ten miles south of the Michigan state border. The city's economy, historically based on manufacturing, was hard hit by plant closings and layoffs in the 1960s and 1970s. Local residents identify the loss of its largest employer, Studebaker, in 1963 and the subsequent closings of the Singer Sewing Machine Company and the John Deere tractor factory as major events that marked the city's decline.

Slowly, the city has struggled back toward a stable economy, anchored in part by the University of Notre Dame, which is located at the city's northern fringe, and an American Motors Corporation jeep plant, which occupies part of the vacated Studebaker site. As in most "frostbelt" cities, South Bend mayors were forced by circumstances to emphasize economic revitalization as a major policy goal throughout the 1970s. Economic development also became a priority issue for Mayor Roger Parent when he assumed office in 1980. Parent's dual strategy was to increase employment and the tax base by directly assisting new commercial and industrial development and to promote new economic enterprise indirectly by improving amenities, especially in the downtown area.

A Downtown Strategy and Mayoral Style

During Parent's first term, he championed the development of East Race Waterway (a downtown recreational watercourse) and the construction of an ethanol plant (a gasohol fuel ingredient) on the city's far west side. Mayor Parent established an image as a willful and aggressive entrepreneurial manager by forging ahead on these projects in the face of determined opposition from a citizens' group called Fair

Tax. He thereby set the tone for subsequent downtown expenditure decisions.

Fair Tax is a citizens' association of property taxpayers in St. Joseph County. It is a voluntary association, with few members, no office space or staff, and irregular funding. Fair Tax draws its strength from its president, Joseph Guentert. A retired factory worker at Bendix Corporation and a lifelong South Bend resident, Guentert is a knowledgeable and tireless political activist, who is reputedly personally able to obstruct any tax measure he does not like. Part of his success lies in his understanding of the tax remonstrance process and his ability to generate considerable and often controversial material for local media outlets.

Guentert became a very able adversary of Mayor Parent during Parent's first term. The terms of Parent's relationship with Guentert and Fair Tax were forged during the mayor's quest for the development of the East Race Waterway.

The East Race Waterway was an eighteenth-century mill race supplying power to businesses in the near downtown area. It eventually fell into disuse and was filled in completely by the 1960s. The redevelopment project to reconstruct the East Race is part of a fifty-two-acre East Bank Development Area plan the planners envisioned as a means to stabilize the eastern portion of the central business district and to provide a base for new commercial and residential development. The East Race itself is an 1,800-foot sluice of controlled water flow, with an eleven-foot drop and several permanent and movable barriers for international kayak-rowing competition. The East Race now serves as the only artificial whitewater course in the United States and is one of only three in the world. World-class international competitions have drawn as many as 10,000 spectators to downtown. Many people can now float down the waterway on inner tubes and rafts or in canoes during the summer months.

The East Race is also being used as one of several fish ladders between South Bend and Lake Michigan, which enables steelhead trout and chinook salmon to migrate during spawning season. The goal is to generate additional spring tourist trade by offering a challenging fishing area for anglers in the Midwest.

The mayor's encounter with Fair Tax centered on the bond issue sought to fund East Race. Parent originally sought $5.6 million in park bonds to fund East Race (for which $3.2 million was dedicated) and several other recreational projects. Fair Tax (doing business as Citizens Information Exchange) was able to force a negotiated settlement with Parent at the remonstrance stage and reduced the bond to $3.2 million— just enough to finance the raceway.

Mayor Parent's second major redevelopment project was to locate an ethanol producing plant in South Bend. The proposed $141 million plant, designed to employ 150 workers producing 52.2 million gallons of ethanol per year, was funded largely with federal assistance. The Department of Energy provided construction loan guarantees, and an Urban Development Action Grant was secured for $6 million to construct access roads to the site.

The timely completion of these two major projects enabled Mayor Parent to win reelection in 1984 with little difficulty. Although he clearly alienated some taxpayers in gaining funding approval for his projects, it appeared to a large majority of voters at election time that he had the vision needed for the city and the ability to deliver his priority projects. He thus entered his second term confident that he had community support for continuing his redevelopment agenda.

Most of the mayor's downtown redevelopment efforts, such as the East Race, were focused on the east side of the downtown business district. Blighted areas adjacent to the downtown on its south and west sides showed little improvement during Parent's first term, although he believed the future redevelopment of the Studebaker Corridor was a critical element for the city's southwest quadrant. The 220-acre under-utilized site of the former Studebaker Motor Corporation was viewed as a potentially significant asset in attracting new businesses and industries.

Baseball Comes to South Bend

South Bend in many ways exists in the shadow of Notre Dame University, especially in the area of sports entertainment. Although the university is nationally known for its fall and winter sports, it offers little in the way of sports events during the summer months, however. Local baseball fans were in the habit of traveling to Chicago or Detroit to watch baseball. Interest in bringing professional baseball to South Bend, which had been discussed informally since the end of World War II, began to gather momentum in early 1984, when a group of about thirty avid baseball fans (the Baseball Group)[1] began to explore the possibility. One of them, Charles Minkler, the executive officer of South Bend's regional planning commission, became the key resource in initiating a stadium plan in government circles.

Minkler originally explored the possibility of bringing either a AAA or a AA team to the city. He quickly discovered that no AAA team would be available and that the location of the AA leagues made the relocation of a AA team to South Bend impractical because of the costs of traveling long distances to play other league members. The group therefore turned to the Midwest League, which competes at the A level.

It discovered that the league's president had plans to expand and eventually to split the league into an A league and a AA league. They invited him to South Bend to examine several potential stadium sites, which were mostly high school fields. He encouraged their efforts.

Through the cooperation of league officials, the Baseball Group was put into contact with Robert and Debbie Staley. The Staley family had an historical connection with the founding of the Chicago Bears, a professional football team. The Staleys had recently bought an expansion franchise in the Midwest League for $20,000. Debbie Staley owned 80 percent of the team, which was to be her business to operate.

The Staleys said that they wanted to run the team as a first-class business and that they needed a first-class stadium to do so. They had been negotiating with the athletic director of the University of Illinois to have a stadium built on the campus for use of the university and the Staleys' team. Questions related to the sale of alcohol and the abrupt departure of the Illinois athletic director brought those talks to an end.

During their meetings with the Staleys, the South Bend Baseball Group indicated the city could build a new stadium that the Staleys would approve of. This was indeed "playing it loose," since city officials at the time were still unaware of the meetings. Furthermore, Mayor Parent was not known to be a sports fan.

Securing Mayoral Support

Arrangements were made for the Staleys to meet the mayor in early 1985. The Baseball Group included several strong supporters of the mayor. The Staleys were presented as "quality owners" who were considering purchasing a residence in South Bend if a stadium deal could be worked out. The mayor became the leading proponent of the project once he became convinced that the Staleys were committed and that baseball could fulfill an element of the downtown development plan. He saw a new stadium as a physical anchor on the southwest side and as a link to the Studebaker Corridor.

The Redevelopment Commission had declared three areas near the center of South Bend as redevelopment areas. Two of them, the Central Downtown Urban Renewal Area and the East Bank Area, already had received considerable assistance. The Monroe Sample Development Area, which included the Studebaker Corridor, had been declared a blighted area for development in 1981, but not much had been done there.

Although the Parent administration had thought about how to redevelop the area, no active plan was in place. An urban enterprise zone existed that included the Studebaker Corridor, revolving loan funds had been established, and the South Bend School Corporation recently had constructed its offices in the area, but the area remained blighted and had a reputation for being unsafe. For example, the city's train station that was located in the area had been occupied by a motorcycle gang and had its roof stripped for its copper. The park across the street from the train station allegedly was frequented by transients, winos, and drug dealers.

This park became a part of the thirteen-acre site for the proposed baseball stadium. The city had attempted to sell the park to a private developer several years earlier, but it could not overcome state laws restricting the disposal of parkland. Fewer than ten residential structures existed on the site, and most of these substandard dwellings were abandoned. The mayor identified the thirteen-acre site as the proposed stadium's location and insisted the city would invest its money for a stadium only if that site was selected. From the outset, the mayor approached the project as an urban redevelopment project that would benefit the downtown and create redevelopment opportunities for the Studebaker Corridor.

The mayor announced his intentions in early March 1985 at a press conference held at the Studebaker Museum, near the proposed site. This symbolized the importance the mayor attached to the site as an element of the city's overall commitment to redevelop the Studebaker Corridor.

Not everyone shared his vision. Citizens quickly noted that no one would attend night games downtown, especially at a stadium located in a distressed area across the street from a public housing project. Few in the city were willing to accept the financial burden of a multimillion dollar minor league stadium.

Fair Tax immediately announced its opposition. The organization skillfully painted the stadium proposal as another project of the mayor's that would go awry. Fair Tax linked it to the ethanol plant, which had begun to emit a foul odor shortly after the mayor's reelection and had now become an environmental liability for the mayor.

The Staleys wanted to field their team in 1986, giving the city a year to get financing in place and to design and build the stadium. The mayor assigned a member of his staff to work on the project nearly full-time, and other staff members also devoted a large amount of time to the project. Two tasks were of immediate importance: securing the Staleys' commitment to South Bend and constructing a stadium. To these ends, the city began to research the lease arrangements of other cities with minor and major league baseball teams and the financial implications of

hosting a team. City officials also authorized engineering and architectural studies for a stadium and initiated ways to find the money to pay for
stadium construction.

The Quest for Funding

The most difficult task was to develop an acceptable funding package.
The first financing proposal was to increase the city's tax on food and
beverage sales, as Indianapolis had done to help finance the Hoosier
Dome. This would require approval from the state legislature. City
officials hoped that the Indianapolis precedent would give them a favorable reception in the state capitol.

Their proposal ran into immediate opposition from a South Bend
legislator, who some speculate had mayoral ambitions of his own. Patrick
B. Bauer (Democrat), a South Bend teacher, had been a longtime
member of the general assembly, as had his father before him. The
Bauers were close friends with Charlie O. Finley, an Indiana resident
and a former owner of the major league Oakland Athletics. Bauer
influenced some of his legislator colleagues to oppose the food and
beverage tax by quoting Finley's warning that minor league baseball is a
sure money loser and a bad investment for a city to make. In addition,
the state legislature was on record as wanting cities to adopt a local
income tax, an option provided to local governments since 1973, before
they sought other taxes for pet projects. It soon became clear that South
Bend would not receive state approval for increasing its food and beverage tax for its stadium, so the city dropped its proposal.

The research done by the mayor's staff and the mayor's visits to other
cities convinced him of several things. First, it was clear that minor
league baseball was a profitable business for a franchise owner, but not
necessarily for the host city. This fact led the mayor to conclude that the
city would not enter into any "sweetheart" lease with the Staleys. Second,
the mayor and his staff realized that the revenues from a AAA lease
might be sufficient to finance a new stadium, but that the revenues from
an A lease would not produce sufficient funds to amortize a new stadium.
Third, the mayor became even more convinced that his original strategy
for the stadium would succeed as a redevelopment project, if the funding
could be worked out. He consequently requested an economic impact
study, and a local professor, who was known for the quality of his work
and for his political independence, was retained to conduct the study.

Professor John E. Peck, director of the Bureau of Business and
Economic Research at Indiana University at South Bend, estimated that
the immediate construction phase would generate $7.5 million in income

and 355 jobs in the community. His comparative evaluation of the twelve teams making up the A-level Midwest League at the time indicated that baseball franchise operations would generate $2.5 million in team expenditures and visitor spending annually. Peck concluded that "the extensive direct and indirect benefits that are realized in comparably-sized Midwest League cities—and, which can be projected to accrue in South Bend—leads to the further conclusion that the net economic impact would be decidedly positive" (Peck, 1985: 4).

With design work completed in May 1985 and the economic impact study in hand, the administration decided to switch strategies and fund the stadium with park bonds. The mayor planned to use private donations and redevelopment money for land acquisition; however, the opposition of Fair Tax made local fund-raising efforts a dismal failure. Although the South Bend Chamber of Commerce supported the stadium by a two-to-one vote of its board, at least one major financial institution in the city was strongly opposed. Two local foundations also rejected the city's requests for foundation support.

Petitions favoring the park bonds were never filed. Intense opposition to the project was being fueled by Fair Tax. It was evident to the mayor that the bond issue would not survive a remonstrance. The city council also objected on the grounds that issuing park bonds for the stadium would bring the Parks Department to the debt limits imposed by the state, which would prohibit any future borrowing by the department until the existing debt was retired. Another financing option had to be found.

Earlier in 1985, after Fair Tax defeated a previous bond issue by remonstrance, the city had entered into a lease-purchase arrangement with a San Francisco bank to purchase fire equipment. Under Indiana state law, such lease-purchase agreements are not subject to remonstrance, although they must be reviewed and approved by the State Board of Tax Commissioners. Twice daunted, the mayor and city council agreed to pursue a lease-purchase arrangement with the San Francisco bank to finance the stadium and announced the plan in September 1985. This strategy reminded citizens, especially Fair Tax, of how the mayor had rammed other projects down their throats in his first term. Opposition intensified. Although no remonstrance was possible, public hearings were required. Both sides prepared.

During the latter part of 1985, city officials received a commitment from the Chicago White Sox to provide a South Bend team with a Player Development Contract. White Sox officials were brought to South Bend in January 1986, a few days before the scheduled public hearing, to announce the agreement with the South Bend franchise. The city could now claim that a minor league team was committed to rent its stadium.

The testimony at the public hearing of the Local Property Tax Control Board (advisory to the State Board of Tax Commissioners), which was held in Indianapolis, was heated. Fair Tax packed the hearing room with its members to testify against the proposal and to cheer members who spoke. Representative Bauer repeated Charlie Finley's warning. Chairman Harold Goodnow was quoted by the local newspaper as saying that he "believed that the vote was influenced by the turnout . . . it's the largest crowd we ever had." The hearing officers recommended against the proposal by a four-to-three vote. The recommendation then went to the State Board of Tax Commissioners.

City officials seeking to win the commissioners' favorable vote focused on the governor's office and emphasized the economic development rationale for the project. Meetings were held with the lieutenant governor, an Indianapolis resident who had executive authority for economic development in Indiana. Indianapolis's sports strategy was cited at every opportunity. Ultimately, the governor's staff was convinced of the plan's merits. The State Board of Tax Commissioners, whose three members are gubernatorial appointees, rejected the Local Property Tax Control Board's recommendation and approved the lease-purchase proposal, but with an important caveat.

The commissioners required an additional hearing in South Bend to ensure that the law was being followed correctly. It had been revealed during the previous hearing and review process that the law, which had been written at two different times, was confused concerning the public hearing process.

The second Tax Control Board hearing, held on March 27, 1986, mirrored the first hearing with the same result. This hearing, held in South Bend before seven hundred citizens, lasted for over five hours. The opponents argued that the stadium would not pay for itself and that it did not have public support. They bolstered their case the day before the hearings by releasing a citizens' survey that showed only 34 percent of those polled favored the ballpark, while 54 percent opposed it and 13 percent were undecided.

Mayor Parent argued that although the stadium would not pay for itself out of direct revenue, the ancillary growth projected for the surrounding area would make the stadium a good overall investment for the city. The mayor cited the recent development of property adjacent to the East Race Waterway as an example of the kind of investment the stadium would promote. The mayor also noted that the city had "expended tax funds in the past to support such recreational activities as golf, tennis and a zoo. 'Why shouldn't we spend for baseball?' "

As with the first hearing, the Local Property Tax Control Board recommended against the proposal. Once again, its recommendation was overturned when, on April 30, 1986, the State Board of Tax Commissioners gave unanimous approval to the lease-purchase agreement "with no strings attached."

Fair Tax next turned to the courts for relief. Its request to overturn the State Board of Tax Commissioners' decision was denied by Circuit Court Judge John W. Montgomery. Montgomery considered boxes of evidence presented by Fair Tax but based his ruling in large part on Peck's economic impact study. Fair Tax's appeal of Montgomery's decision failed when it missed the thirty-day filing deadline by one day.

With the State Board of Tax Commissioners' approval upheld in court, the city could proceed with the lease-purchase agreement. Negotiations with the bank became confused, however, because of uncertainty about how such agreements and the proceeds from sports stadiums would be treated in congressional action on tax reform. The agreement ultimately called for an interest payment of 13.42 percent by the city if those payments were taxable or 9.25 percent if they were tax-exempt.

Local officials directed their attention to Washington. Failure to obtain tax-exempt status for their stadium would mean payments to the bank at a rate of 13.4 percent, or more than $1 million a year. The city was not included in the final version of the 1986 tax reform legislation, nor did it succeed in gaining recognition in the subsequent transition rules.

Stadium construction began in August 1986, shortly after the lease-purchase agreement was signed. Within a month, the city was informed that the Staleys had sold the franchise to New York–based owners, who owned several other teams. The purchase price was reported to be $465,000. The sale appeared to confirm the opposition's earlier arguments that the city was being taken advantage of.[2] It led some to believe that the team was without owners and therefore gone. The mayor and his staff understood that lease negotiations would be more difficult because of the new owners' large investment.

The mayor believed he had been double-crossed. He had relied on the Staleys as owners who saw South Bend as a community in which to invest. He objected to the sale so vehemently that he filed letters of protest with the National Association and the commissioner of Major League Baseball. It was pointed out to the city that owners of franchises can sell them whenever they wish, to whomever they wish, depending only on league approval.

The mayor feared that the new owners had been led to believe that they had the city over a barrel (with a stadium, but no lease) and that the city would be willing to negotiate a sweetheart lease. The mayor's response was to refuse to negotiate with the new owners. He was willing to keep the team from playing at the stadium.

The mayor could take this stand because he was not facing reelection. Council members could not, however. Under pressure from city council members, the mayor returned to the negotiation table and reached agreement with the New York owners on July 19, 1987.

Aftermath

The Stanley Coveleski Memorial Regional Stadium was completed in April 1987, too late for the opening of the baseball season and before a formal lease was signed with the new franchise owners. Accordingly, the franchise did not field a team in South Bend until the 1988 season. The stadium was used in 1987 for several amateur sports activities, including American Legion baseball, the U.S. Pan American baseball team tryouts and practice, and local soccer. It seats 5,000 and is expandable.

The final construction cost of the stadium was $5.95 million. The major portion of the cost was met through the $5.25 million financial package with Security Pacific. The remainder was paid from local tax incremental financing and capital improvement funds.

Although the Fair Tax strategy to delay funding approval and thereby kill it when the lease-purchase proposal lapsed failed, its secondary political strategy to defeat Parent was more successful. As the *South Bend Tribune* reported at the time of the State Board of Tax Commissioners' final decision, "Fair Tax could use the court proceedings to keep the stadium issue alive for use against Parent, if he seeks re-election next year."

Parent, however, decided not to seek reelection. The fact that the stadium was not completed, and was still a subject of considerable controversy, at campaign time raised speculation that it had influenced him not to run. Parent, however, insisted his desire to return to the Peace Corps caused him to step aside. His advisors maintain that before the stadium confrontation with Fair Tax, Parent had indicated he would not seek another term.

Critics of Parent and the stadium project, however, are certain that he realized that he could not win and therefore decided not to run again. They point out that only three of nine city council members were returned to office in the 1987 elections. Among those defeated were the city council president in 1985–86, when the controversy raged, and the city council president in 1986–87, who was seeking a fourth term. Both are reported to have blamed the stadium for their defeat in the 1987 Democratic primaries (Baines, 1987: 35). Others, however, deny that the baseball stadium was an important election issue, pointing out that each of the three council members who were returned had supported the baseball stadium.

The South Bend White Sox played their first season in the stadium in 1988. First year attendance of 171,444 was second best in the A-level Midwest League, behind Peoria, which had an attendance of 207,294. The team's 1989 attendance of 203,197 ranked third (behind Durham and Peoria) among fifty-eight teams at the A level, as did its 1990 attendance of 212,485 (behind Durham and Frederick). Its 1991 attendance of 221,071 was fifth among A-level teams.

During the summer of 1990, the South Bend White Sox again were sold. The reported purchase price was approximately $4 million. Thus, within six years, the South Bend A-level franchise appreciated by nearly $4 million. The owners of the franchise made formal application for a Triple A expansion franchise but were not successful.

The new administration, headed by Mayor Joseph Kernan, took advantage of a decline in interest rates and, in 1988, refinanced the stadium through the newly created South Bend Redevelopment Authority. The city now pays an interest rate of 9.42 percent (reduced from 13.42 percent) and expects to save $400,000 over the eight years that remained on the loan at the time of the refinancing. Nevertheless, the city cannot generate enough revenue from stadium operations to pay the annual debt service of approximately $1 million.

In 1988, the team generated $153,000 in gate and concession revenues for the city. Of these funds, $50,000 was dedicated to the stadium's debt service, $26,000 went to the construction of two new obstacles in the East Race Waterway, and $25,000 was used for a neighborhood improvement program. The remainder went for stadium maintenance and improvements. In 1989, South Bend officials estimated that the team generated approximately $200,000 in revenues for the city.

The annual revenue from the stadium's operations has been much greater than anticipated. In July 1989, the city council voted six to three to use $25,000 of stadium revenues for neighborhood organizations. Twenty-five $1,000 grants have been made available to neighborhood organizations for neighborhood projects. This program, called "Next Door Neighbor," is a widely publicized citywide contest in which neighborhood organizations or groups of twenty or more homeowners are invited to submit requests to a panel of nine judges (appointed by mayor and council). It is made clear that minor league baseball is returning money to the community. The goal, according to Mayor

Kernan, is for the public to see the benefits of the stadium and to maintain good feelings about the stadium.

Local officials cite several benefits of having the team play in South Bend. The stadium is a major part of the city's strategy of providing various forms of entertainment in the downtown. The stadium complements the East Race Waterway, the Centennial Center (which is a hotel–convention center complex on the riverfront), and other activities designed to provide local residents with entertainment options and to bring nonresidents into South Bend.

Officials cite the good feelings that abound at the stadium, whether a White Sox game or an amateur game is being played. Local citizens, officials assert, are proud of the stadium and enjoy attending events there. The stadium not only has given local residents a reason for coming downtown, but also provides a positive experience for them when they are there.

Evidence supporting the view that the stadium is popular with local citizens is provided by a survey of local citizens conducted in the summer of 1990. The respondents cited the construction of Coveleski Stadium as Mayor Kernan's most significant accomplishment during his first term. Of course, it was Mayor Parent, not Mayor Kernan, who was responsible for the stadium.

Officials continue to insist that the stadium will provide the link between downtown and the Studebaker Corridor. In 1992, local officials issued a $5 million general obligation bond to acquire, rehabilitate, and demolish a number of properties in the corridor, continuing the implementation of the city's redevelopment strategy.

NOTES

1. The term "Baseball Group" is the authors' term to designate this group of civic leaders who had no formal designation.

2. Interviewees claimed that the Staleys tired of the controversy and resented personal attacks, including hate mail, directed at them by opponents to the stadium project.

Durham, North Carolina 12

Durham, North Carolina, like many American cities, has had to struggle with a radical transformation of its local economic base. The city's traditional textile- and tobacco-based economy declined in the 1960s. This decline was symbolized by the closing of Burlington Mills and the American Tobacco Company, located adjacent to the central business district. Today, Durham's local economy is oriented toward corporations and organizations engaged in service, research, and medical activities.

A development boom began in the city of Durham and Durham County in 1983 and has continued into the 1990s. Development occurred especially in and around Research Triangle Park, which is located in Durham County, beyond the city's borders. Duke University's medical-related research and development has been another key component in the area's economic recovery.

Downtown Durham has not kept pace with overall growth in the region. A 1989 planning study found one resident living downtown. Vacant stores pock the central business district. Durham no longer can claim to be the commercial center of the area, although downtown Durham does remain the government and financial center of the county.

The public and private sectors have launched an impressive revitalization effort to bring life back to Durham's downtown. The city and county jointly contributed approximately $15 million toward the construction of a $30 million civic center–hotel complex and plaza, which was completed in 1989. The city and county also made a commitment to spend more than $41 million on downtown development projects before 1991.

The restoration and expansion of the Royall Center for the Arts, which opened in 1988, and restoration plans for the Carolina Theater, both of which are historic buildings located adjacent to the new civic center, are intended to make cultural arts important in attracting visitors to the downtown. The former project represents a $6.5 million renovation.

The latter project is intended for symphony concerts, stage and dance performances, and tour productions.

A public-private venture resulted in the construction of Durham Centre, a $40 million, twin-tower office building. The first tower, consisting of 220,000 square feet of space, opened in the summer of 1988 across from the civic center and expanded downtown office space by 25 percent. The project was made possible by the city's financing of an 800-car parking deck beneath the office tower at a cost of $11 million.

Not only is new construction taking place, but adaptive use of abandoned mills and factories is occurring. A local developer, Duke University, and Glaxo, a large pharmaceutical firm with its U.S. headquarters in Research Triangle Park, were committed in the summer of 1989 to renovate the abandoned American Tobacco Plant (ATP) complex. The ATP complex is located south of the downtown loop and adjoins the central business district. Total project costs were estimated to be in excess of $100 million to remodel 800,000 square feet and to build 300,000 square feet of new construction.

The principal components of the ATP renovation project were to include Glaxo's construction of a manufacturing plant with 300,000 square feet of new space and 200,000 square feet of the former plant for office and distribution purposes; Duke University's use of 270,000 square feet for administrative functions; the location of the North Carolina Museum of Life and Science in 110,000 square feet of former warehouse space; and the absorption of more than 200,000 square feet for other uses, including residential, office, commercial, and cultural development.

Much activity focusing on downtown development took place in the late 1980s and was planned for completion in the 1990s. The downtown Durham Revitalization Plan, drafted by the joint Durham City-County Planning Department, envisioned the downtown as a center for government, finance, and the arts. The ATP complex was viewed as a key component to the successful revitalization of downtown Durham. Local officials knew that public sector and private sector cooperation would be necessary if the project was to be successful.

Despite this economic activity, interviews with government officials and community leaders revealed a concern for the city's image in the region. The city of Durham is part of a tricity region composed of Raleigh, Chapel Hill, and Durham. Several interviewees volunteered that Durham traditionally has been a "poor cousin" to its neighboring cities.

Raleigh serves as the state capital. Chapel Hill is home to the well-respected University of North Carolina. Durham, according to interviewees, was known for its blue-collar character and manufacturing.

The North Carolina Symphony's move from Durham to Raleigh in the mid-1980s was cited as an example of Durham's lack of respect in the region and harmful intercity competition. Another reflection of this image problem, according to interviewees, is the prohibition against the city's annexing Research Triangle Park that the state legislature has imposed on the city. Although the issue of taxation was an important concern in the legislative debate, Durham residents believe the prohibition is related to the city's image problem.

Durham officials have sought to change the city's image as its economy has changed. They officially have adopted the name The City of Medicine to reflect the presence of Duke University, Glaxo, and several health-related firms. The city hosts the prestigious American Dance Festival, which Raleigh attempted to lure away in the late 1980s.

Durham also has a rich tradition in minor league baseball. It served as the headquarters of the National Association of Professional Baseball Leagues from 1933 to 1947. Its minor league team, the Durham Bulls, was one of the most successful minor league teams in the 1940s, 1950s, and 1960s. For a variety of reasons, including poor management and the deterioration of Durham Athletic Park (DAP), the team fell upon hard times at the end of the 1960s. The team's owner advertised the last game of the 1971 season with a full-page advertisement in the local newspaper that read, "Final game of a long, disastrous—just plain awful season" (Morris, 1979).

Only 40,447 fans paid to see the team that year, which was the last year for minor league baseball in Durham, until Miles Wolff brought professional baseball back to the city in 1980. Wolff paid the A-level Carolina League $2,417 for franchise rights and the city spent $25,000 to renovate Durham Athletic Park. Wolff also owns a Rookie League team and is the publisher of *Baseball America,* a national publication devoted to minor league baseball that has a circulation of approximately 62,000.

The Durham Bulls received national publicity in 1988 with the success of the movie *Bull Durham.* A year earlier, Raleigh officials sought to lure the Bulls from Durham. Failing in that attempt, Raleigh officials supported an attempt to displace the A-level Bulls by seeking permission from the National Association to bring a higher-level team into the Raleigh-Durham territory.

Interviewees consistently stressed that minor league baseball in the form of the Bulls was one thing Raleigh and Chapel Hill did not have. The Bulls were recognized as important to the city's image and an important possession in the intercity rivalry in the region. The possibility of losing the team to Raleigh was therefore taken seriously by local officials.

The Need for a New Stadium

Durham Athletic Park serves as the home for the Durham Bulls. The ballpark, which was built in 1938, reeks of nostalgia and fits the stereotype of a minor league ballpark. The National Association, in its 1989 evaluation of the stadium, rated the clubhouses for the players as fair (3 on a 5-point scale) and space for umpires as poor. The stadium's lighting met Class A standards, but not those of AA or AAA. Parking for fans was rated as poor. In his general comments, the evaluator concluded, "It is hard to keep putting cosmetics on the old gal, but she looks good!"

The Downtown Durham Revitalization Plan (1989: 45), referred to earlier, recognized that even with recent extensive improvements to the stadium, "inadequate parking, restrooms, and public areas create severe operational problems for the management and frustration for the fans." The plan noted the desirability of building a new multipurpose stadium to house the Bulls and to allow the team's ownership to gain a franchise in a higher-level league. The plan briefly referred to sites near the Durham Freeway, a local highway adjacent to the downtown core area, and included a stadium in its list of first-priority items.

Durham Athletic Park seats 5,000 fans. The Bulls seat additional fans on a grass embankment overlooking the outfield fence. The Bulls broke A-level attendance records by drawing 271,650 fans in 1988, 272,202 fans in 1989, and 300,499 fans in 1990. The team consistently outdraws many AAA teams and until 1991, when Frederick topped Durham's attendance, had led all A-level teams in attendance since 1985. For example, its 1989 and 1990 attendance was better than that of eleven of twenty-six AAA teams. Sellouts and overflow crowds are a common occurrence. Fire marshals have, at times, forced the Bulls to turn away fans because they threatened to exceed stadium capacity. Clearly, the Bulls are a success and could attract more fans in a larger stadium.

Miles Wolff made his desire for a new stadium known to local officials several years ago. He never made it an issue and did not threaten to relocate. Wolff was committed to Durham. The issue of a new stadium did not reach the local government's formal agenda, however, until Raleigh made known its interest in the team.

Raleigh interests approached Wolff in 1987 to discuss relocating the Bulls to Raleigh. Wolff, who makes his residence in Durham, suggested moving a Single A team to Raleigh under his ownership and keeping the Bulls in Durham as a AA or AAA team. The Raleigh representatives rejected that idea.

In 1988, Raleigh interests requested a waiver of the National Association's thirty-five-mile territorial rule and permission to "draft" the territory so they could bring a team to Raleigh. Drafting occurs when a higher-level team locates in an area and displaces an existing team of a lower classification. An arbitration committee composed of six members of the National Association's executive committee and the National Association's commissioner rejected the Raleigh request. The threat remained, however, that Raleigh could attract a AA or AAA franchise and win permission to "draft" the Bulls' territory the next year.

The Raleigh threat touched a nerve among Durham officials and community leaders. The desire to prevent a rival community in the region from either stealing the Bulls or displacing them motivated Durham officials to move the stadium to their formal agenda in spring of 1988. Mayor Web Gulley, who chose not to run for reelection in 1989, had moved the stadium from among his top four or five priority items early in his four-year term to the top two or three priority items at the end of his term.

The remainder of this case focuses primarily on the development of the stadium issue in Durham as of summer 1989. It was during 1988–89 that the issues related to the use of a stadium as a downtown development tool took shape. The case's epilogue reveals the results of Durham's efforts to build a stadium for the Bulls.

The Durham Stadium Project Steering/Advisory Committee

In the early summer of 1988, the Durham Stadium Project Advisory/ Steering Committee was formed by a small group of corporate leaders, with the blessing of public officials and Miles Wolff. The group was chaired by Richard Wright, vice president of People's Security, which is the developer and primary tenant of Durham Centre. Wright, reflecting a tradition of corporate community involvement in Durham, recounts that the group suggested it was "his turn" to take leadership of a community project.

The committee initially was intended to be a short-term vehicle for ensuring the sale of skyboxes in a new stadium. A Bulls employee was loaned to the committee and served as its staff. He was housed in an office at People's Security.

The goals of the committee, as written on an undated draft of a proposed membership list, were:

> To render private sector opinion-counsel to parties at interest in building a new Durham baseball facility.

To determine level of private sector support for various methods of funding for construction of new park.

If project approved, develop marketing plan for successful implementation.

The focus of committee activity during 1989, however, was the city and county legislative bodies. According to Wright, the committee was to help the local governments answer three questions: "Do you want to build a facility? What method of financing should be used? Where should the facility be built?" Another leader of the advisory committee stated that the group's purpose was to serve as a catalyst to gain public support for a new facility.

The committee had its preferences. It urged the construction of a new stadium. The committee secured pledges to make certificates of participation a viable means of financing rather than general obligation bonds, which required voter approval. The committee also favored a downtown site adjacent to the ATP complex.

The committee's activities at this time tended to be low-key and involved direct contact with local officials. The one exception to this method of operation was the printing of an advertisement in the local newspaper to thank city and county officials for their "continued and positive leadership and support of our efforts to 'save the Durham Bulls.'" The committee identified the stadium project as a "cornerstone for revitalization efforts" and focused on the Raleigh effort to "take the Durham Bulls away from Durham."

Raleigh officials protested the charge to the National Association. The National Association's commissioner wrote a letter to the committee, identifying erroneous assertions made in the advertisement, explaining that no one could take the team away, and urging that no inflammatory remarks be made during the campaign for a new facility.

The committee appeared to be successful in its early efforts to win council support for its preferences, but it failed in the long run.

Site Selection

Four locations emerged as potential stadium sites in early summer 1989. Each site carried with it a number of advantages and disadvantages.

An eleven-acre site, known as the Hayti site, bordered the L.L. Bean Expressway. *Durham Morning Herald* editors declared it was "the cheapest and best site for a ballpark" ("Bulls Future at Risk?" 1989: 4A). This, in fact, was Wolff's original preference for a site. The property once was the core of a thriving black commercial corridor. Eventually, the corridor went into decline, and urban renewal cleared the site of buildings in the 1960s. Black leaders in the community continued to recall a pledge local officials made at the time to revive the area.

The site is city-owned and would not require extensive improvements. Parking is located within walking distance of the site. The expressway gives the site excellent visibility and access. Building a stadium on the Hayti site, however, would do little for downtown redevelopment, since the site is somewhat isolated from the central business district. To make the stadium compatible with surrounding land uses, an existing funeral home would also have had to be relocated, against the owners' wishes.

The most important obstacle was the fact that black leaders objected to using the site for a stadium. They remained committed to having the city fulfill its pledge to return black-owned commercial activity to the area. As a result, city council members agreed not to consider Hayti.

The Commerce Center/Briggs Avenue site was another possibility. This parcel, which is located within the city limits but away from the central business district, had been opened up for an industrial park in the mid-1980s. The site was expected to attract light industrial activity quickly because it is located on the way to the Raleigh–Chapel Hill region, which is experiencing rapid growth. It had not done so as of the summer of 1989.

The site is attractive as a stadium site because it would locate the Bulls closer to the Raleigh–Chapel Hill market, it has easy access and good visibility, it could accommodate adequate parking, and the site was prepared for immediate construction.

The significant disadvantage of the Briggs Avenue site is its distance from downtown. A stadium constructed at the Briggs Avenue location would not support any downtown-related activity. Those interviewed were even skeptical that a stadium would help attract industrial activity to the site. They saw no auxiliary benefits of using this site for a stadium.

A third potential stadium site began to receive public attention in July 1989. Local officials met with the stadium architect (hired by the advisory committee) to discuss renovating Durham Athletic Park after the local paper printed two pages of letters, which generally were opposed to a site that had received much publicity and appeared to be favored by the advisory committee and local officials.

Renovation of Durham Athletic Park, however, did not receive a great deal of serious attention. The architect stated from the beginning that it was the least likely of three alternatives. He cited problems with access, infrastructure, roadway systems, parking, and visibility. The most serious problem was that the Bulls would probably have to play elsewhere while the renovation took place. Costs of renovating DAP were estimated to be $6–10 million.

The principal motivation for attempting to maintain DAP as the Bulls' home is the fact that fans love the stadium. Local officials, however, argued that after extensive renovation the ballpark would be quite different from what the fans were trying to save.

The fourth site was the early favorite of local officials and the preferred site of corporate leaders. It also proved to be the most expensive. The downtown University Ford site is the setting of an automobile dealership. It consists of eight acres and is located adjacent to the downtown core but is separated from it by railroad tracks. It also is directly adjacent to the ATP complex. North Carolina Mutual Life Insurance Company, which is a longtime corporate resident of Durham, also occupies a portion of the site.

City planners described the automobile dealership's use of the site as a "black hole" in the redevelopment plans for downtown, given the projected redevelopment of the ATP complex. Local officials favored the site as a means of bringing to the downtown an activity that was capable of drawing large numbers of people. A stadium would complement several of the contemplated activities in a redeveloped ATP complex. The parking required for the stadium also could be used during the day by the businesses operating in the ATP complex. In terms of downtown redevelopment, this site was viewed as the best of the four sites.

The corporate actors also preferred this site. Richard Wright noted that his bank had a large investment in downtown, which would be protected by having the Bulls as a neighbor. Glaxo was to be a partner, with an investment of $50 million in the ATP project. A stadium next to the ATP would bring thousands of people into contact with the commercial tenants of the project other than on weekdays, ensuring the success of the project.

There were several financial implications of the site. The city estimated that total costs would reach $20 million. The newspaper, which had favored the Hayti site, predicted total costs would reach $40 million. The newspaper estimated property acquisition to be $10 million, compared with less than $3 million at Briggs Avenue or the existing DAP and even less at Hayti.

During early discussions of the Ford site, North Carolina Mutual emphasized its special status as a landowner in the city's twenty-year-old redevelopment plan for the area. The terms of the original agreement gave North Carolina Mutual the right to veto any use not included in the original plan. Although the proposed stadium was a permitted use, activities planned for the ATP complex were not. Shortly after North Carolina Mutual announced its possible unwillingness to end the redevelopment agreement, it was announced that the company was seeking a swap of buildings that would net it $1.9 million. In effect, the company was requesting that the city purchase a building valued at $3.7 million for tax purposes; prepare it for occupancy, including asbestos removal; and trade it for $900,000 in cash and the existing North Carolina Mutual building valued at $882,000. North Carolina Mutual representatives argued the company would have to relocate because the proposed stadium would take too much of its parking area.

The more serious and more expensive problem was relocating the Ford dealership, which was a successful dealership. The owner took a firm negotiating position. His demands, in addition to a high purchase price, were that the city buy land for the dealership's relocation, prepare it, and give it to him. City officials emphasized the legal restrictions they must work under regarding deals of this nature, but they were certain they could find some means of relocating the dealership and had identified an acceptable site by the end of the summer.

The other significant cost factor was the construction of a parking deck to serve the stadium and ATP and a pedestrian walkway to connect the stadium with downtown, traversing the railroad tracks. The cost of the parking deck was estimated to be well above $10 million.

Local officials and the corporate leaders thus favored the downtown University Ford site because of the spinoffs that a new stadium located next to the ATP and the downtown would produce. It came to be viewed by planners, city officials, and corporate leaders as a critical component of the ATP. The projected cost of the stadium project, however, made it a focus of public debate and controversy, as did the proposed method of financing.

Financing

The stadium project was designed to be a joint effort by Durham County and the city of Durham. City officials during the period under review took the lead role. Members of the city council and the Durham County Board of Commissioners had to make two decisions concerning the financing of the proposed stadium: How much should they spend for the stadium? How should they finance that amount? The answer to the first question would be determined, in part, by site selection. The answer to the second question would be influenced primarily by the answer to the first question.

The advisory committee had its own thoughts on financing and worked closely with city staff. If the preferred site was to cost $20 million, the committee promised to find investors willing to loan $17 million of that amount to the city and county in the form of certificates of participation. Certificates of participation are a device whereby local governments can borrow money without going to voters for approval.

The advisory committee lobbied city and county legislators to use certificates of participation. Committee members believed there was a chance of losing a referendum, despite the Bulls' popularity. They recognized that a stadium for the Bulls was not a top priority for all citizens. In the summer of 1989, interviewees feared that the black community might oppose the stadium. The city had been on the verge of being polarized by a dispute involving a black police chief weeks earlier. Some also feared that antigovernment sentiment would affect any referendum.

A referendum also costs money and takes time. Committee members believed that three to four months of construction time could be saved by avoiding a referendum. Glaxo offered its construction team to work on the stadium. The earliest a referendum could be held was March 1990, whereas a summer council vote on certificates of participation would allow the city to move forward before then.

Finally, the committee's corporate leaders agreed to purchase certificates at AAA bond rates, which was a level higher than the city's AA+ rating. The consequence of this would be to lower the interest rate and, therefore, the annual debt service the city would have to pay. Glaxo pledged $6 million and People's Security pledged $7.5 million. This was the largest civic venture Glaxo had ever undertaken. People's Security does not purchase general obligation bonds and could use its money differently to make a larger return. Another bank originally pledged to purchase $2 million worth of certificates, but it later withdrew that pledge as a result of tax-law considerations. The committee's leaders continued to search for an investor or investors to bring the total pledges up to $17 million.

A second part of the financing puzzle was a proposed lease arrangement with the Bulls. Although it had not been finalized at the time of the city council's vote on financing, agreements on most issues had been tentatively reached. The city would receive from the Bulls a minimum of $200,000 per year according to the proposed lease. This is an amount well above what most communities receive from their teams and well above the $8,000 rental fee and 7 percent of concession revenues the city of Durham was receiving from the Bulls. Concession revenue paid to the city in 1987–88 and 1988–89 amounted to $32,818 and $45,600, respectively.

On June 27, 1989, in a joint meeting of city and county officials, with about sixty Bulls fans, who arrived in buses provided by Wolff, in attendance, the use of $17 million of certificates of participation was approved. City council members voted eight to four in favor of it. A stadium site was to be recommended by city staff within sixty days. Opponents, who wanted a site selected before financing issues were decided, noted the need to fund other priorities and called for a referendum on the project.

Without making any commitment to participate in the project, county commissioners voted three to two to begin negotiations with the city over how the costs would be shared. This issue is a perennial problem for local officials. City residents believe they are taxed twice—by the city and again by the county—for the same projects. County residents resent paying for what they perceive to be city projects. Both sets of local officials were therefore under pressure to ensure that the cost sharing was equitable. The task of finding that formula fell to the mayor and the chairperson of the county commissioners.

No site was approved within the sixty-day framework, and no agreement was reached on a funding formula before the mayor left office. Community organizations were critical of officials throughout the process for not including them in the planning and for bypassing the voters. In August, the city council, under heavy criticism from community organizations and a conservative coalition, reversed itself and decided not to issue certificates of participation. Instead, the council members approved a referendum for general obligation bonds to finance the stadium. In an effort to avoid the double taxation issue, the stadium project was presented as a county project. The referendum would therefore be countywide.

Epilogue

In March 1990, the voters of Durham County defeated a proposal to issue $11.28 million worth of general obligation bonds to build a stadium at the downtown University Ford dealership site. The American Tobacco Project quickly unraveled with the defeat of the stadium proposal and was no longer viable in late 1990.

The proposal lost overwhelmingly 12,984 (59 percent) to 9,051 (41 percent), with 23.8 percent of the eligible voters voting. Residents in the city of Durham narrowly approved the referendum, but residents outside the city heavily opposed the proposal.

Although many explanations have been offered for why the referendum failed, the foundations for its failure were laid during the months examined above. Three errors were made early in the history of this issue. First, in a city with a tradition of community activism, the community organizations and the public in general were ignored by those managing the issue, especially the advisory committee. In part, this is explained by the fact that the committee originally did not see itself as the public advocate for the stadium. Its leaders preferred to deal quietly with elected officials and city staff rather than negotiate with community leaders in open forums. Its one effort to communicate with the public led to a minor controversy.

Second, no clear champion, or advocate, of the stadium emerged to lead the quest for the downtown stadium. Several proponents can be identified—the mayor, a councilman, advisory committee members—but no one seemed to emerge as the true leader before August 1989. The Bulls owner, Miles Wolff, who disliked becoming involved in politics, also maintained a low profile on the issue. Wolff chose to provide support to the advisory committee rather than lead the charge himself. In fact, Wolff was opposed to putting the issue to a referendum after the city council reversed itself. Unlike other team owners, Wolff did not threaten to relocate or to leverage the city.

The failure of a champion to emerge meant a lack of focus in efforts to justify the stadium, especially the proposed downtown site. City officials and corporate leaders clearly saw the downtown site as critical to downtown redevelopment plans. The plan adopted by the city council envisioned a downtown stadium as an important component to downtown redevelopment. Nevertheless, as of summer 1989, it was difficult to find this rationale in public forums, and it had not shaped earlier debate. Instead, the newspaper's opposition seemed to be dictating the terms of the debate.

By the time the economic rationale of the downtown site was brought into the referendum debate, enough other issues—competing priorities, especially from capital needs for schools and water and sewer infrastructure; city-county taxation; the position of black leaders on the stadium issue; the quality of the financial management of the city; and the desirability of keeping DAP—had been raised to confuse and undermine the credibility of the redevelopment rationale for the stadium. The Raleigh threat, which had given the issue its original impetus, seemed to fade away in the public's mind with the passage of time.

Steve Bryant, owner of the Columbus (Georgia) Mudcats in the AA Southern League, announced his intention to move his team to Zebulon, North Carolina, for the 1991 season. Zebulon, a town of 2,000 citizens, is located approximately fifteen miles southeast of Raleigh. In April of 1990, the National Association ruled that the Bulls could not relocate to the proposed regional sports complex in Research Triangle Park between Durham, Raleigh, and Chapel Hill in Durham County that James Goodmon, a Raleigh broadcasting executive, was planning to develop.[1]

Goodmon's site was thirty-two miles from Bryant's proposed ballpark in Zebulon, and, therefore, the association ruled, within Bryant's thirty-five-mile home territory. However, the National Association's executive committee, on appeal, made an exception to the thirty-five-mile limit for the Bulls. The executive committee gave permission for the Bulls to move to the proposed regional complex, but not within a thirty-mile radius of Zebulon's stadium.

By the end of the 1990 season, Goodmon had obtained an option to purchase the Bulls from Wolff, who had become frustrated with the stadium saga. Goodmon exercised his option in 1991 and continued to pursue his plans to build a stadium in the county. Owners of the Zebulon and Durham franchises were among those considered for a AAA expansion franchise, but neither was included among the five finalists. As the 1992 baseball season opened, a great deal of uncertainty surrounded the Bulls' future location.

NOTE

1. Goodmon had taken out newspaper advertisements during the referendum campaign opposing the bond issue.

PART V

The Use of Stadiums for New Development

The flight of residents and businesses from the center city to suburbia is a familiar story. The center city remains the financial, governmental, and cultural center of its metropolitan region, but suburban communities are the regional loci of retail and commercial activity and house more citizens than any other type of jurisdiction.

Football, hockey, and basketball teams at the major league levels have experimented with suburban locations. However, team owners in major league baseball, with a few exceptions, have been reluctant to leave the center cities. This is less true at the minor league level.

Growth in the form of new development characterizes much of suburban America. Opening up new land for development also occurs within center cities, especially in the South and West. Cities in these regions have annexed many miles of undeveloped land. Part V reports the use of minor league stadiums to promote new development in two suburban communities and a western city. (The case studies of Hoover, Alabama, and York County, South Carolina, are continuations of the Birmingham and Charlotte franchise relocation cases of Part III.)

Officials and developers in the case study communities of this section, as in the previous section, possessed a development logic for their stadium ventures that was similar to the one used by developers of retail centers. Team owners in the case studies of this section took advantage of the available land, just as developers took advantage of available suburban land to build shopping malls with plenty of parking space. Team owners also moved their teams in pursuit of their markets, just as retail stores followed their customers to the suburbs.

Suburban stadiums are designed to attract people to their sites so that other development property can be sold. The stadiums give the sites visibility, glamour, and traffic they would not otherwise have. They promise to bring thousands of people past the new businesses that do locate in their developments. Although this can be a successful marketing approach for commercial and retail developments, the Colorado Springs case suggests that it may be a questionable strategy for residential developments.

When stadiums are used to open new land for development, stadium projects have the potential of benefiting all parties to the deal. The team owners receive a new stadium that is attractive to fans; the developers (and team owners, if they have a business interest in the site) receive infrastructure and an anchor for their development; and the local government gains a sports team, a new sports facility, and the potential of adding developed property to the tax rolls in future years.

The stadium projects described in Part V are real estate deals. The cases describe land swaps and large development projects, commercial and residential, that depend on the success of the stadium. The stadiums in Hoover and York County provided the rationale for extending infrastructure to the undeveloped stadium sites. The infrastructure was critical to opening these tracts of land to new development. Also, local officials in each of the case study communities believed it important to impose planning requirements and land-use regulations on the projects. They viewed this as a means of managing future growth and protecting the public's investment.

The costs of a new minor league stadium are within the fiscal capabilities of many wealthy suburban communities. The politics of suburban America, however, do not favor such amenities as minor league stadiums if they negatively impact the tax rate. For example, team owners in this section had few acceptable options when it became clear that center city officials were not going to meet their demands or negotiate further and that few suburban communities were interested in building a stadium once the costs became known. From the very beginning of negotiations, York County and Colorado Springs could therefore refuse to finance stadiums and still continue negotiating with team owners, as long as team owners did not consider locating outside the region. Even in the case of Hoover, the site's developer assumed much of the construction cost and risk of ownership on a temporary basis, until a lawsuit was settled.

When owners find an attractive location, they may be willing to assume much or all of the cost of stadium construction. This, however, means that they will have to develop revenue sources other than the stadium, as George Shinn realized. As in the case of Florida communities developing spring training sites (see the Fort Lauderdale case), minor league owners are thus beginning to search for stadium deals that have land development potential. That search is bound to lead to the suburbs.

On the one hand, these cases reflect the competition between center cities and suburbs for economic activity. On the other hand, they are case studies of regionalism at work. Hoover and York County interviewees, as well as those from Birmingham and Charlotte, consistently spoke in terms of intercity cooperation regarding their teams, and they denied ill will existed as a result of the relocations.

Hoover officials, for example, stressed their desire to carry their share of the financial burden for metropolitan cultural resources. This is a common plea that center city officials make to their neighbors. Center city officials usually want to retain the resource, however. The Chamber of Commerce for the Charlotte metropolitan area routinely speaks in terms of regionalism. It now must support the Charlotte Knights in York County, South Carolina.

York County, South Carolina 13

According to George Shinn's attorney, Spencer Stolpen, Shinn's concept of a stadium project for his Charlotte Knights was transformed by the realization that revenues from a minor league baseball stadium could not support the land costs of an acceptable stadium site. Shinn then began to think of the stadium project in terms of a larger real estate project. Not only was he looking for a suitable stadium site, but he was seeking a site with sufficient acreage to be commercially developed beyond a stadium.

York County, South Carolina, is part of the Charlotte-Mecklenburg metropolitan area and is located just across the state border south of Charlotte. It was among the top five potential stadium sites identified by Shinn and his consultants. Several of the potential sites would have taken too long to assemble or proved to be too expensive. Early in 1988, Shinn considered acquiring the 2,600-acre Heritage USA, which was located in the northwest corner of York County. Heritage USA was Jim Bakker's base for his PTL operations. Shinn became acquainted with York County officials in exploring the possibilities of Heritage USA as a stadium site.

York County

In 1988–1989, York County was the fastest growing county in the Charlotte-Mecklenburg area. It is in the process of making the transition from a rural farm economy to an urban economy. The interstate highway, I-77, is a major north-south thoroughfare, running from Charlotte through York County. Development along the I-77 corridor has been limited only by an inadequate water and sewer infrastructure. It was clear to everyone that this portion of the county would be developed rapidly once adequate water and sewer service was in place. In 1988, no one knew when that would occur.

Prior to 1988, the northwest portion of York County along the I-77 corridor, which is suburban Charlotte, was served by three privately owned utility companies, the limited water and sewer systems of the towns of Fort Mill and Rock Hill, and the city of Charlotte in the form of the Charlotte-Mecklenburg Water and Sewer District.

In the early 1970s, a recreational theme park, Carowinds, was completed near the state border just north of Fort Mill in York County. At the time, the city of Charlotte agreed to provide water and sewer services to Carowinds. This enabled limited residential and commercial development around the park. Heritage USA also was developed in the same area and was serviced by the city of Charlotte under the same agreement.

In the early 1980s, the city of Charlotte made known its desire to withdraw as a provider of water and sewer services to the York County area, except for Carowinds. This forced York County officials to begin to search for a way of providing services to residents and businesses in the area.

In 1985, the county obtained ownership of the private water and sewer systems that served the Carowinds area, and it entered into an agreement with the city of Charlotte, whereby water and sewer services would be continued to the existing service area for not more than ten years. After 1995, York County would have the responsibility of providing water and sewer services, without the assistance of the city of Charlotte.

The cost of providing the infrastructure to do this promised to be greater than that of any other project the county had undertaken. It seemed certain that property taxes would need to be not only increased, which required a countywide referendum, but increased significantly to pay for the infrastructure. County officials not only were politically fearful of raising taxes, but also were skeptical that such a proposal would be approved by the voters.

In sum, by 1988, the I-77 corridor from Charlotte to Rock Hill was prime for development, limited only by inadequate water and sewer infrastructure. York County officials had accepted an obligation to provide water and sewer service by 1995, but they were uncertain about how to meet that obligation. The bankruptcy of PTL and the demise of Heritage USA complicated the county's financial picture.

The Stadium Agreements

As Shinn searched for a suitable stadium site, he sought commitments from local officials to build the stadium. His request was rejected by some. Others, including York County officials, would only consider building a stripped-down facility, costing at most $4–6 million. Shinn, however, wanted a modern stadium capable of being expanded for a National Football League franchise or a AAA baseball team or a Major League Baseball team. Such a stadium would cost at least $10–15 million. York County officials made it clear they would not build such a stadium.

In early 1988, Shinn entered into a joint-venture agreement with a York County landowner, Doyle Jennings. Shinn agreed to purchase 320 acres of Jennings's land in Fort Mill Township. The negotiations with York County officials for a stadium began in earnest with this agreement and continued for the next eight months.

When it became clear that York County would not build the stadium that Shinn wanted, he proposed to build the stadium himself and then donate it to the county and lease it back. In return, Shinn asked the county to provide the stadium and the surrounding land with adequate water and sewer services and access roads. Because of Jennings's tax concerns, an agreement with the county had to be finalized before the end of 1988. This placed county officials under severe time pressure.

County officials agreed only to the concept that Shinn had proposed and insisted on time to study the proposal. On that basis, with no firm commitment from the county, Shinn proceeded with designing the stadium and buying more parcels of property adjacent to the Jennings property. Shinn eventually assembled more than four hundred acres of land. He negotiated two agreements with county officials. The first was a master agreement for the development of the entire parcel of land, and the second served as the stadium lease and management agreement.

The master agreement called for Jennings to donate to the county approximately thirty-two acres, upon which Shinn would build a $12 million baseball stadium. The stadium was to be a 10,000-seat facility, capable of being expanded to a capacity of 75,000 for either major league baseball or professional football. Shinn was obligated by the agreement to convey the completed stadium to the county and then lease it from the county for use by his minor league baseball team.

The agreement also obligated Shinn to build a 4,000-seat arena adjacent to the stadium to serve as the principal office and training facility for his National Basketball Association team, the Charlotte Hornets (see the Charlotte case study). It also obligated Shinn to reserve ninety acres near the stadium site for the construction of a football stadium, if he gained an NFL franchise and if the NFL required that it play in a football-only stadium.

The agreement recognized the necessity of having the York County Council approve the master plan for the development of the entire four hundred acres of land as a planned unit development. The master agreement also called for the county to construct the necessary infrastructure for the facility, including access roads, parking areas, and water and sewer lines to the stadium. The cost of providing infrastructure to the stadium and the surrounding property was estimated to be $5,657,383, which was to be secured by a 1989 bond issue.

The stadium lease was a fifteen-year lease arrangement. It called for Shinn to pay the county $1 a year in rent. The county, however, was permitted to impose a per ticket surcharge of twenty cents, thirty cents, and forty cents in the first, second, and third five-year periods, respectively. The county also would receive 50 percent of all net parking revenue beginning in the sixth year of operation.

In the first years of operation, the county will thus receive a minimal amount of money from the baseball team. In later years, that amount will increase (to perhaps as much as the county staff's optimistic estimate of $350,000 by the eleventh year), but it will not come close to matching the estimated annual cost of $600,000 in debt service after 1992. The financial benefits for the county, instead, will be derived from the projected development of the surrounding property and the I-77 corridor, facilitated by the infrastructure planned for the stadium project.

Although members of the county council were not unified in their view of the proposal, council president Murray White, who championed the proposal, forged a majority by mid-November. Supporters of the project made it clear that they viewed it as an economic development project, which offered a solution to the water and sewer dilemma the county was facing in the I-77 corridor. White and others argued that the I-77 corridor would be developed at some point in the future. Shinn's proposal had the effect of accelerating that development, while permitting the county to manage it from the outset.

The county was able to secure a commitment to finance most of the roadwork from the local economic development board that dispenses state highway funds for development projects. The chairman of the county board was a resident of Fort Mill and an early supporter of bringing Shinn to the county.

Advocates argued that tax revenues and fees from new development, which would occur as a result of Shinn's plans and the new infrastructure, would be sufficient to pay the costs of the project over time. Politically, revenue bonds could be used for the project without going to the voters for approval.

Opposition came from different sources. Many felt that the wealthy Shinn should not be subsidized with public money. This view was echoed by several members of the county council. The leader of the opposition had previous legal problems with Jennings, and some believed his opposition to the project was motivated by a personal grudge against Jennings.

More seriously, the stadium proposal became an issue, albeit not a critical issue, in the November 1988 county council elections. White was accused of having a conflict of interest because of his family's ownership of land near the project. He also was criticized for giving greater priority to the stadium than to the county jail, which had been the subject of local controversy prior to the election campaign.

White's opponent was a supporter of Pat Robertson's candidacy for the 1988 Republican party presidential nomination. He received a great deal of support from Robertson's organization and from those in the county who supported Jimmy Bakker and the PTL. White and others interviewed for this case agreed that his defeat was a result of the high turnout of his opponent's religiously oriented supporters rather than White's strong support of the stadium.

Even though White lost his reelection bid, he continued to serve as council president until the end of 1988. On November 29, 1988, the York County Council gave its initial approval of the master agreement. On December 19, 1988, the York County Council held an eighty-minute public hearing attended by approximately 125 people. The *Charlotte Observer* reported that opponents and advocates who spoke were well supported. The newspaper described a noisy and spirited meeting. At the end of the hearing the council unanimously approved the project. Not all council members were enthusiastic in their support, however. One councilwoman "closed her eyes and pinched her nose as she voted."

Within a year the York County Council also negotiated utility service agreements with the town of Fort Mill and the city of Rock Hill. These agreements were designed to permit the county to meet its obligations to Shinn and to provide a framework for future expansion of services to the I-77 corridor. An agreement between the county and Fort Mill permitted the county to construct, own, and operate a water distribution system within certain unincorporated areas of the township. The stadium served as the center of this planned construction. The subsequent agreements were designed for wastewater management in the area and committed the county, Fort Mill, and Rock Hill to work in a cooperative manner.

Those interviewed stressed that county officials conceptualized the stadium project as an economic development project that helped them address the infrastructure problems of the I-77 corridor. Furthermore, they believed that the complicated deal conveyed a message that officials of rural York County could negotiate with private sector entrepreneurs and play the economic development game successfully.

Ground was broken for the stadium in February 1989. During the 1989 baseball season, the (renamed) Charlotte Knights played in a temporary stadium erected next to the construction site of the permanent facility. The team's 1989 attendance was 157,720, which was sixth in the ten-team AA Southern League but an improvement by more than 55,000 over its 1988 attendance in Charlotte. The team opened its 1990 season in the permanent facility and increased its attendance to 271,682, which led all AA leagues, as did its 1991 attendance of 313,791. As a result, Charlotte was selected as one of two AAA expansion franchises to begin play in 1993.

Shinn had dropped out of the competition for an NFL franchise by the spring of 1990, but he continued to believe that if Charlotte was granted an NFL franchise and the plans of Jerry Richardson (his competitor for an NFL franchise in Charlotte) to build privately a football stadium in uptown Charlotte fell apart, his stadium could be expanded in time to accommodate the Charlotte NFL franchise. In the meantime, Shinn was granted a franchise in the fledgling NFL minor league, the American World Football League. That team played its games in Raleigh but folded after one year. Shinn represented Charlotte in the competition for a National League expansion franchise, but Charlotte failed to make a final list of six contenders.

One new business had relocated from North Carolina to the project site as of January 1991. County officials estimated that the new business would employ approximately 150 people and represented an investment of approximately $11 million.

Hoover, Alabama, was incorporated in 1967 and is one of thirty-two incorporated communities that surround the city of Birmingham. One interviewee, in the summer of 1989, described it as the "hottest area in the state" in terms of development. Its 1970 population of 1,393 increased to 19,792 by 1980 and to 29,130 by 1986. This reflects a 1991.2 percent growth rate for the years 1970–86, which is the highest in the Birmingham metropolitan area. Hoover's population in 1990 was estimated to be 39,788.

This growth is due to a combination of aggressive annexation actions and in-migration. Hoover's 315 single-family housing permits in 1988 were the most of any jurisdiction in Jefferson County. Their average value of $113,869 was the third highest of all jurisdictions in the county. Similarly, the city's 98 multifamily-unit permits issued in 1988 were the second highest number issued (Birmingham issued the most) and second in total value.

Hoover is the site of the largest enclosed shopping mall in the South (and the longest skylight in the western hemisphere). The Riverchase Galleria, which opened for business in 1986, is a complex of 3.3 million square feet of retail/hotel/office space covering 135 acres of land. It features 1.75 million square feet of retail space. Approximately 300,000 shoppers travel to the Galleria each week. The Galleria not only gives Hoover a regional identity, but also fills the city's coffers with tax dollars.

Hoover's community leaders no longer perceive the city as "just a suburb of Birmingham." They are intent on becoming a partner with Birmingham in the metropolitan area and a "major league city" in the state.

Baseball Comes to Hoover

Officials of several communities in the Birmingham area expressed interest to Art Clarkson when he called for proposals to build a stadium for the Barons (see the Birmingham case study). Hoover, however, was the only community that continued to show interest when the costs were calculated. In Hoover, Mayor Frank Skinner initially developed the idea to respond to Clarkson's request for proposals. Skinner's desire to explore the possibility of building a minor league stadium was met with a great deal of skepticism from his city council.

Skinner persisted, however. He spoke with Clarkson and his consultant Miles Creel, who was associated with a Hoover consulting firm. He asked the city council's finance committee chair, Geoff Huddleston, to explore the matter. Huddleston grew less skeptical after speaking with Huntsville, Alabama, officials about their stadium and with Clarkson. Huddleston soon became an advocate of the idea and the city council's liaison for the stadium project.

Other members of the city council, who were not uniformly supportive of the mayor, remained skeptical. Council president Billingsley, who was a banker, was certain that Clarkson was seeking to leverage the city of Birmingham into the best stadium deal he could get in the center city. Billingsley did not think the idea was viable since he knew a stadium could not pay for itself, which, at the time, was a necessity for some council members.

When the interest of other suburban communities weakened and Clarkson's relations with Birmingham officials worsened, Clarkson realized that if the team was to relocate, it would have to be to Hoover. Relocation to Hoover was in keeping with Clarkson's perception of where his target market was located. It was not certain, however, that Hoover officials would agree to build a stadium for the Barons.

Creel, in an effort to develop community interest in a stadium project, made contact with officials at Harbert Land Corporation, which is located in Hoover. Harbert Land Corporation forms joint ventures to develop large tracts of land. The company is the developer of Hoover's Riverchase, a 3,000-acre joint venture with Equitable Insurance Company and the site of the Galleria. Creel, Clarkson, Harbert officials, and a representative of HOK Sports Facilities Group[1] made a helicopter flight over Hoover to examine the area for potential stadium sights. Their first choice proved to be unavailable; their second choice was a tract of land owned by USX Realty.

USX owns approximately 150,000 acres of land in Jefferson County, which represents about 20 percent of the land in the county. The company, however, traditionally has not shown a great deal of interest in developing its land. Harbert officials were therefore skeptical about the prospects for negotiating a deal with USX for the site they had identified.

They soon discovered, however, that a new philosophy about land development was emerging within USX.

Harbert representatives contacted Hoover officials to promote the idea of a stadium. Although the mayor and Huddleston had other sites in mind, Harbert representatives argued that those sites would not have the spin-off effects of the USX property. Clarkson and Creel made a presentation to city officials asserting that a stadium project would promote growth.

Discussion and negotiations continued for nearly a year. The city negotiated with Clarkson for a stadium lease and management agreement and with Harbert and USX Realty for the disposition of the land. The support of city council members grew as the proposed project evolved. Once basic agreements had been reached with Harbert, USX Realty, and Clarkson, the mayor led a public meeting on February 12, 1987, to inform the council formally of the project's details. On February 16, the city council gave its unanimous approval to the stadium project and lease agreement. The city was now committed to providing a stadium for the Barons in time to open their next playing season, in April 1988.

The Deal

The agreement with Harbert and USX Realty was a complex arrangement. The formal purpose of the arrangement was to develop an industrial park on the 1,300-acre site, which would be annexed into the city of Hoover. The joint venture agreed to seek zoning of its park as a planned unit development. The master plan called for the industrial park to be developed in the vicinity of the stadium. The site would contain retail, office, and residential development when it was completely built.

The city of Hoover agreed to purchase seventy acres of land in the tract for $600,000. This was estimated to be $16,429 per acre below the appraised market value (of $25,000 per acre) of the land. The joint venture also agreed to donate to the city 40.8 acres of land contiguous to the seventy-acre parcel. The city agreed to construct a municipal building on the forty-acre parcel within ten years.

In addition, the city agreed to construct a baseball stadium, referred to as a multipurpose stadium, on the seventy-acre site. It also agreed to fund, in part, construction of a four-lane, divided-median access road to the stadium and to share the cost of developing utility service into the park. Finally, the city agreed to construct a sewer system in the industrial park to be connected to a Jefferson County sewage treatment plant.

The project promised to open a large tract of land to future development. All interviewees agreed, however, that the site eventually would have been developed without the stadium agreement. Its location near I-459 and only a few miles from Riverchase made it a prime development site. The city's general plan had identified the area for future industrial and commercial development, but the lack of infrastructure had delayed its development. Private developers would have had to punch in roads and pay for infrastructure as they developed the site. The proposed project's impact was to accelerate development of the site and the surrounding acreage by a number of years.

Those involved in the decision making deny that stimulation of new development was the most important motivation behind the decision. Each of the interviewees from Hoover claims that city officials believed it was time to make a contribution to the metropolitan area. They were willing to become a partner with Birmingham by sharing in the costs of providing a recreational outlet for the citizens in the metropolitan area. Hoover, like their suburban neighbors, had not been financially supporting the cultural activities and facilities located in Birmingham.

More important for future growth, the 1,300-acre tract of land provided Hoover an escape from being completely surrounded by other jurisdictions. The parcel of land provided an arm that could be used as a base to annex unincorporated areas of the county in the future.

The deal also provided Hoover with a highly desirable site for a new school. Hoover was about to create its own school district, and a site for a high school was needed. The forty-acre parcel, upon which the city was obligated to build a municipal building, was expected to serve as the location for a new high school and a complex of athletic fields, including a field for high school football.

Finally, interviewees emphasized that this represented a onetime opportunity. If Hoover did not build the stadium then, it would not likely have another chance to do so. Although baseball began as a low priority for city officials, they realized they had to make the commitment to the project or forfeit the chance to host the Barons.

Financing and Constructing the Stadium

When the Hoover city council approved the stadium project, the city's financial position was very strong, due, in part, to the success of the Galleria. Before the council vote, the mayor asserted that even if the stadium "should fall in a hole," the city could afford to take the risk of building the stadium without endangering other city projects.

The stadium design was enhanced beyond Clarkson's original concept. The stadium was designed to seat 10,000 fans and to be expanded in two stages, if necessary, to accommodate 28,000 additional fans. It was to include a full-service restaurant and twelve skyboxes.

The cost for the stadium alone was projected to be $10 million. The total project cost was expected to be in excess of $12 million. The nonstadium costs included the purchase of land ($600,000); construction of a one-and-a-quarter-mile, four-lane road to the stadium through the site and underground utilities ($1.45 million); and the installation of sewer mains and a pump station ($500,000).

The city planned to finance the majority of the costs with $7.5 million worth of general obligation warrants, at an interest rate of 8 percent for twenty years. Warrants, like certificates of participation, are loans that pledge a revenue source as a means of repayment and do not require a vote of the citizenry, as do general obligation bonds.

The decision to use warrants, rather than general obligation bonds, as the financing method was not controversial among city council members. Council members did not expect any controversy over the stadium issue or the method of financing. The city had used warrants previously to build its city hall and a sewage treatment plant that was a part of the Riverchase annexation package. In fact, according to the Hoover City Council president, putting bond issues to a vote is not customary in Alabama.

Also, time was of the essence. The city had to begin stadium construction immediately to have it ready for the opening of the baseball season in April 1988. A bond issue vote would delay the construction schedule. Deciding to use warrants was therefore an easy decision for the council to make.

The city had secured other revenue sources in addition to the warrants. The Alabama Industrial Access Bond Authority had approved a $1.25 million bond to finance the construction of the road to the stadium. The authority provides funding for roads that support industrial development. City officials won approval for the financing by use of "their relationship with the state government administration" and by arguing that the road was being built to support the planned industrial park rather than the stadium.

The city had to have at least one company committed to the industrial park to qualify for the funding. A local printing company received a great deal of publicity when it made the commitment to relocate to the park; however, it later withdrew its commitment when it was forced to make an unexpected major equipment purchase after a printing press broke down. This endangered the state funding, but two other firms eventually committed themselves to the industrial park and salvaged the road financing. The joint venture agreed to pay for the cost of installing utilities in excess of $200,000 up to $400,000 and to share equally with the city any costs over $400,000.

Stadium revenues were to offset projected annual debt service of more than $1 million. The city projected first-year revenues of $650,000 from the stadium's operation. This included half of the proceeds from the sale of ten skyboxes at $15,000 each. In the long run, however, sewer tap-on fees and tax revenues from the new development were expected to cover most of the project's costs.

Stadium construction was fast-tracked. That is, it was built at the same time that it was being designed. Work was bid and completed in stages rather than as a complete project. Harbert's construction team was involved from the beginning.

The city quickly began clearing the site and working on the foundation. Almost as quickly, two citizens filed a lawsuit that prevented the issuance of the warrants to finance the project. The lawsuit challenged leasing the stadium to the Barons on the grounds that public funds were being used for the financial benefit of private interests, contrary to the state's constitution, and it opposed issuing warrants on the grounds that warrants are, in fact, general obligation bonds requiring the approval of the electorate.

If the lawsuit proved successful, a common financing method throughout the state of Alabama would be eliminated. For Hoover officials, the legal challenge meant that they had to find an alternative financing method while the case was making its way through the state judicial system or halt construction and miss their April 1988 target date for completion, which would leave the Barons without a playing field.

City officials decided to finance the construction from the city's general fund. As the general fund dwindled to nothing, it became evident that the project was in danger. The mayor then proposed bidding the project out in such a manner that the construction firm itself would finance the construction costs until the city was able to issue the warrants. The city and the successful bidder would agree to a maximum cost for the project. If costs exceeded the ceiling, the construction firm would be responsible for the overrun. If the city lost the court case, the construction company would be in danger of receiving its money over a much longer period or owning the stadium.

Such a construction-finance proposal was put to bid. Only one firm, Harbert, responded. Harbert had the financial means to accept the risk and already had a stake in the project's completion and success. The stadium project therefore moved forward under this arrangement. The city, with its general fund depleted, borrowed short-term to finance its municipal operations and capital expenditures that would have been financed from the general fund.

The city's position was upheld by the trial court in June 1987, but the decision was appealed to the Alabama Supreme Court. On December 31, 1987, that court, by a split vote, decided in the city's favor. It denied a motion for rehearing in mid-January, which ended the litigation.

The litigation proved costly to the city in several ways. Warrants were eventually issued at a rate of 1 to 1.5 percent higher than the projected 8 percent. Short-term borrowing that otherwise would not have occurred was necessary. Depletion of the general fund meant that other projects could not be initiated. The city council had made its stadium decision on the assumption that all revenue from a new sales tax would be available for other projects. The mayor, however, vetoed the sales tax, a portion of which was earmarked for the newly created school system. Thus, a larger share of the general fund money had to be devoted to the school system. As a result of these decisions, a new library and a new park were delayed by a year or more.

At the time this research was conducted, the city expected to experience revenue shortfalls in 1989 and 1990, primarily because of the expenditures for the new school district. The shortfalls were expected to be covered by previous years' surpluses. In fact, the city's revenues in 1989 and 1990 increased by 14 percent and 15 percent respectively. Although no shortfalls occurred, expenditures from the general fund for the new school district made for a tight budget.

The Economics of a New Stadium

Hoover Metropolitan Stadium opened April 16, 1988. More than 10,000 fans attended the Birmingham Barons' opening night, and thousands more were turned away. From all perspectives, the stadium has been a success, but not without problems. Approximately fifteen months after the stadium opened, Hoover officials and Art Clarkson were engaged in a dispute over who was responsible for $180,000 worth of construction expenditures for concession areas and the team office. Clarkson also believed that the electric bill for stadium lighting was excessive. Both sides, however, thought that these were minor disputes in a $12 million project.

More significantly, city officials, in the summer of 1989, were concerned that only two skyboxes had been sold and that the stadium restaurant was not operating. In January 1991, only six of the skyboxes were sold, and there were no immediate plans to make the restaurant operational. The restaurant is probably not feasible until the planned development for the industrial park occurs, since the stadium is located several miles from the business area of Hoover and is not convenient for lunch trips. The restaurant will need more than seventy events in the stadium to be a successful nighttime operation.

City officials justified the stadium as a multipurpose stadium. They expect that nonbaseball events will be conducted at the stadium throughout the year. According to the lease, the team's ownership is responsible for attracting these events. Few events have been booked in the stadium, however.[2]

At the time of this research, the most successful event at the stadium was an Alabama Symphony Orchestra performance. The orchestra normally attracts several hundred people when it plays in its downtown Birmingham home. For a July 4 performance at the stadium, the orchestra drew several thousand people. A Dizzy Dean World Series and a recreational vehicle show were two other events held at the stadium and in its parking lot in 1988–89.

Since then, the symphony orchestra has returned to the stadium a few times, but it remains fearful of the risk of bad weather. The stadium's inner concourses have been used for a Halloween haunted house, and its road and parking lots are used for an annual community Christmas parade and festivities. City officials report that it has been difficult to book rock concerts for the stadium because of promoters' close ties with existing venues in the area.

City officials were fearful not only that revenue from the stadium would be less than expected if Clarkson was not more aggressive in attracting events, but also that the stadium would not be the community resource it was intended to be. Little thought appears to have been given to the potential conflicts of interests of Clarkson as promoter and team owner or to how community organizations could make use of the stadium, given a minimal charge of $2,500 to cover operating expenses.

The first-year stadium revenues to the city were $286,283. Nearly all of this amount came from the Barons. Revenue projections for 1989, which would be the stadium's first full year of operation, were $600,000. In fact, total revenues from the stadium amounted to $307,929 in 1989 and $287,966 in 1990. Although the city does not keep separate expenditure accounts for the stadium, it is certain that stadium revenues exceed operating costs but do not approach the more than $1 million annual debt service.

From the perspective of Clarkson, who by 1989 had become the majority owner of the team, the stadium was a success. According to Clarkson, the team produced a $100,000 pretax loss playing at Rickwood Field in 1987. Playing in Hoover, the team produced a $100,000 pretax profit in 1988. This financial turnaround occurred despite the fact that the rent paid by the Barons increased from $10,000 to $300,000. Attendance nearly doubled from 1987 to 1988, from 139,808 to 269,831. In 1989, the team drew 270,793 fans. Its 1988 attendance led all AA-level teams, and its 1989 attendance was second highest at the AA level, as was its 1990 attendance of 256,247 and its 1991 attendance of 313,412.

In February 1990, Clarkson sold the Barons to a subsidiary of Suntory Limited, Japan's largest privately owned corporation, for a reported $3.6 million. A spokesperson for Suntory stated at the press conference announcing the sale that the primary reason for the purchase was to "get experience in the sports business and to learn how to promote sports business in Japan" (Grant, 1990: 2).

For Harbert and USX Realty, the stadium provides a lead tenant for their industrial park. The stadium draws thousands of people to the industrial park, giving the property visibility and recognition. Most important, the property now has the necessary infrastructure for development. Without the stadium, the joint venture probably would not have been undertaken, and the infrastructure would not exist.

City officials speak with pride about the stadium. It was named Hoover Metropolitan Stadium to identify it as an asset of the Birmingham metropolitan area. Officials give no indication that they believe they stole the center city's team. The city of Hoover and its Chamber of Commerce give the stadium high visibility in their publications. The stadium has brought attention to Hoover from within the state and the region, as well as nationally from the baseball industry. The team was among five finalists for a AAA expansion franchise but failed to be selected.

This is the significance of the stadium for Hoover. Although it promotes development and the site provides a base for future annexations, the stadium's success adds to Hoover's image as an important community within the Birmingham metropolitan area. It will not make or break Hoover's financial health. The Galleria will.

NOTES

1. HOK is an architectural and design firm located in Kansas City. It advertises itself as "the nation's most experienced sports architect." The firm has served as architect for several major league stadiums, including those in Baltimore and Chicago; St. Petersburg's Suncoast Dome; numerous

spring training facilities; and minor league stadiums in Buffalo, South Bend, and Kane County, Illinois, among others.

2. Stadium rental fees received by the city from nonbaseball events totaled $2,722 in 1990.

Colorado Springs, Colorado   15

Colorado Springs, Colorado, is the home of the United States Olympic Committee (USOC). The USOC and several national sports federations have their offices in the Hotel Broadmoor complex. Broadmoor also is the site of an indoor ice-skating rink and a ski area. The indoor ice rink is operated by the hotel. For tax reasons, the hotel gave the ski area to the city in the mid-1980s, and the city began operating Ski Broadmoor in 1987.

A large segment of the city's population of 281,140 is retired. Interviewees described city residents and their government as fiscally conservative. The city's mayor and city council members are not paid, for example. Nevertheless, over the years, the city has been willing to take advantage of several unique business opportunities. As a result, the city government owns and operates its own hospital, part of the road that takes tourists to the top of Pike's Peak, and a shopping center. Several of the tenants in the shopping center are nonprofit organizations, including a small number of national sports federations.

In 1978 and 1979, the city hosted the first two National Sports Festivals and has cooperated with the USOC in planning an Olympic Hall of Fame. As of the summer of 1989, the Hall of Fame project had been delayed because of inadequate funding. Interviewees, however, hinted at strained relations between USOC officials and the city government and suggested that the city took the USOC for granted.

The city has no formal sports strategy. It is in danger of losing several of the national sports federations to cities, such as Indianapolis, that are pursuing an aggressive sports policy. There is resentment on the part of some national sports federation officials who are housed outside of the USOC complex because they must pay rent for their offices while those within the USOC complex do not.

There is no arena in the city capable of seating more than 6,000 people. In April 1989, a $37.5 million bond issue to finance a $50 million indoor arena was defeated 34,597 to 14,965, at the same time that bond issues for roads and a police operations center were approved. The arena proposal was justified as necessary to cement the city's ties to amateur sports and to compete with other cities for sporting events.

The Colorado Amateur Sports Corporation (CASC) is the principal organization pursuing sports events for Colorado Springs. There is no formal relationship between the local government and CASC. The city will host the 1993 World Fire and Police Games, which have thousands of participants. The initiative for attracting the games came from local fire and police representatives, not city government.

An A-level team, the Sky Sox, in the now defunct Western League had played in Colorado Springs from 1950 to 1959. In 1985, city officials discussed with Joe Buzas (see the Fresno case study), owner of the Portland Beavers of the AAA Pacific Coast League, the possibility of relocating his team to Colorado Springs. City officials agreed to renovate Spurgeon Field to AAA standards for Buzas. Spurgeon Field is located in Memorial Park, which is in a residential neighborhood near downtown.

City officials proposed financing the renovation with a $6 million bond issue. In August 1985, voters defeated the bond issue by a vote of 21,837 to 13,364. Voters residing near the park especially tended to vote against the bond issue. City officials believed that residents in the vicinity of the park were concerned about potential parking and noise problems. One interviewee suggested that supporters of a local soccer league opposed the referendum because they feared they would lose a soccer field to an expanded parking lot in the park if the bond issue passed. Officials of the Parks and Recreation Department denied that any plans existed for taking the soccer field. City officials interpreted the defeat as a vote against using the site for professional baseball rather than as a vote against bringing baseball to Colorado Springs.

Hopes for bringing professional baseball to the city dimmed with the defeat of the bond issue, but they were not abandoned. The mayor and other advocates remained interested in the idea. City officials were willing to respond to inquiries and hints of interest, although they did not aggressively seek a team.

Baseball Comes to Colorado Springs

In 1987, city officials learned of David Elmore's interest in relocating his AAA Pacific Coast League Hawaii team. Elmore, a businessman in Hawaii and owner of several minor league teams, had high operating expenses in Hawaii and limited revenue sources.

Elmore's Hawaii team was not allowed to sell advertising on the outfield fence and did not retain parking or concession revenues. The team was dependent on its broadcasting package and ticket sales for revenues. According to the team's general manager, Fred Whitacre, the previous owner of the Hawaii team had lost touch with the community, and attendance had fallen off prior to Elmore's purchase of the team. In addition, the University of Hawaii had developed a strong baseball team with local talent, which continued to play games in an Alaskan summer league. Fans reportedly showed more interest in these players than in the minor league team. In 1986, the Hawaii Islanders drew 84,134 fans, which was the lowest attendance in AAA baseball, and only 11,000 more fans than the university's baseball team attracted with a schedule of twenty-eight fewer home games. Elmore reportedly lost an estimated $450,000 that season.

Elmore's expenses were inflated because the team had to pay for half of the traveling costs of visiting teams. According to Whitacre, the visiting teams had to be presented with a check for half of their round-trip airfare as they deplaned in Honolulu.

Elmore contacted several cities on the mainland in search for a site for his team. The site had to be an economically viable one and acceptable to Pacific Coast League officials. Elmore had previous business dealings in Colorado and, according to several interviewees, seemed to favor a Colorado site for personal reasons.

Colorado Springs officials made it clear to Elmore, when he sought public financing of a stadium early in their talks, that they could not invest a large amount of public money to build a stadium. The 1985 bond issue defeat was very much on their minds. The city referred Elmore to Gregg Timm, who was president of AMWEST, one of the companies of developer and home builder David Powers.

Timm, a former minor league player, for several years had been very interested in bringing a team to Colorado Springs. He had discovered that Colorado Springs qualified as a AAA city according to baseball's criteria. He wrote all AAA teams, except Hawaii, inquiring about their interest in relocating. He and Powers envisioned a stadium and its team as the anchor tenant in a large residential development being planned by AMWEST. He received no positive replies. When the city and Buzas were negotiating in 1985, he remained apart from those talks because the city had selected Spurgeon Field as a stadium site.

In 1987, however, there was no possibility of a city-financed stadium, especially at Spurgeon Field. Timm was informed by the city manager that the mayor and city council wanted the team to locate in Colorado Springs. Timm and Elmore began to do site and cost analyses.

According to Timm, only one site already master-planned for recreation appeared large enough for a stadium. That site was in the midst of a 2,000-acre AMWEST development called Stetson Hills. Only a few houses had been sold by 1988. The potential site, master-planned in the early 1980s, called for a baseball field and a soccer stadium eventually to be built for local residents.

Colorado Springs residents traditionally have been oriented to the mountains on the city's western side. Stetson Hills is on the city's eastern side, 8.5 miles from its downtown. AMWEST officials believed that a stadium would give visibility to their development and attract people to that part of the city.

The city, represented by the city manager and the director of the Parks and Recreation Department, entered into serious negotiations with Elmore and AMWEST officials in early 1987. It is not clear to what extent the mayor and council were kept informed about these negotiations.

City council members were informed of the negotiations in closed ("legal") meetings as early as May or June. Council members gave their approval to a concept of using funds from a dormant account restricted to tourism projects to meet Elmore's demands for public participation in the financing of the stadium. Few if any details, however, were provided in these meetings, according to city officials. Negotiations moved toward closure in October and November.

In the midst of negotiations with Elmore, the city council became concerned about another issue. The city had acquired and began operating Ski Broadmoor in 1987. A manager for the project had been hired, and he began to spend money to promote the ski area. Council members informed the city manager and the director of the Parks and Recreation Department that Ski Broadmoor was not to operate at a deficit. When it was revealed in late fall that Ski Broadmoor had a deficit of $300,000, the city manager was forced to resign and the director of the Parks and Recreation Department was fired.

Ski Broadmoor was a much higher priority for council members than the baseball stadium was. The outcome of the controversy left the city without its lead negotiators in the baseball stadium deal. Elmore needed an agreement if he was to relocate his team for the 1988 season, but the city manager had not signaled city council members that the decision was urgent.

Negotiations became confused and floundered. The new negotiators for the city found some of the commitments made to Elmore by the city manager and the Parks and Recreation director unacceptable. For example, the city manager had agreed to landscape the area around the stadium by holding an Arbor Day ceremony at the stadium and planting at the stadium all the seedlings normally distributed on Arbor Day.

In mid-December, three days after the city manager resigned, the city attorney called all the parties together in an effort to save the deal. Final agreement was reached during this meeting. Little or no consultation occurred with relevant city agencies, such as the Department of Parks and Recreation Advisory Board. It was not certain the site had been checked regarding flood plain regulations. No communication occurred with county officials to determine if they had any questions about the project.

City council members were briefed for the first time on the details of the agreement on Thursday, December 17, in closed session, and they met again in closed session on Friday. The mayor, at a Friday news conference, suggested that there were still questions about the agreement, but that the council could take up the issue at its informal (and open) Monday session and might vote on the agreement at its formal meeting on Tuesday.

The local newspaper was informed Friday that the council's Monday agenda was available. It was not until Monday morning, when a reporter picked up the council agenda, that reporters realized the details of the proposed stadium agreement were available.

The Tuesday, December 22, meeting was attended by nearly 150 citizens. Nearly all of those who spoke before the council vote were supportive. This included representatives from the USOC and CASC. Supporters had been organized. The two citizens who voiced objections did not have business ties in the community, as most of those who voiced their support did.

The city council approved a joint-use agreement for a new stadium that Elmore agreed to build and the expenditure of $500,000 by a vote of eight to one. Construction was scheduled to begin January 4 and was to be completed April 21.

The Agreement and the Financing of the Stadium

The agreement called for AMWEST to deed a fifteen-acre parcel in Stetson Hills to Elmore, and for Elmore to construct a stadium on the site. The site sits within a ninety-acre tract that was planned as a community park. The city's parkland ordinance requires developers either to donate land to the city on a formula basis for use as a park or to pay a parkland dedication fee. The city agreed that the use of the stadium for minor league baseball was in keeping with the definition of parkland use, and it gave AMWEST a $234,000 tax credit in lieu of paying the parkland dedication fee.

The city also agreed to pay Elmore $500,000 as its share of the project. City financial participation was critical to Elmore and was perceived by city officials as a potential deal-breaker. Since the state's constitution forbids the use of public money for private interests, the city was required to receive something of value in return for its $500,000.

The joint-use agreement calls for the stadium to be used by the city 180 days of each year through the year 2002. The city has the right to use the stadium, including its parking lot, for any public purpose, except commercial events that might compete with Elmore's use of the stadium. Also, no event can damage the field (including restriping), nor can any baseball event alter the size or configuration of the diamond or involve players younger than high school age. Any baseball event sponsored by the city must either be "a tournament, play-off or championship game for established leagues or conferences or be a special or exhibition game for other teams."

The city had levied a tax on alcohol and hotel/motel rooms (a "bed and bar" tax) in 1976 to help finance a proposed convention center. Voters, however, defeated the bond issue for the project. The city then repealed the tax, but not before money had been collected. The tax revenues that were collected were placed in a fund restricted for activities to promote tourism.

Over the years, the city council rarely resorted to using this fund. When it did so, the council merely spent part of the accumulated interest for minor projects. To pay Elmore, the council appropriated all of the funds ($440,905) in the account and $59,095 from a lodgers- and automobile-tax fund (a "bed and car" tax) to meet its obligations. No money from the general fund was committed to the project. The stadium project therefore had to be justified in terms of being capable of attracting tourists, which the council formally did to protect itself in case of a legal challenge.

The city's $500,000 contribution was contingent upon Elmore's obtaining financing for the stadium project and construction progress being made. The stadium had to be built within three months for the team to open its 1988 season in Colorado Springs. Elmore began his search for financing.

Timm and Elmore turned to the state government. The Colorado Housing and Finance Administration (CHAFA) had been created to assist housing in the state. CHAFA recently had been given the authority to finance economic development projects. Timm and Elmore proposed a $1.5 million CHAFA bond issue to finance the stadium as an economic development project. They spoke with the governor's office about the project, and shortly thereafter a skeptical CHAFA board of trustees approved the bond issue by a unanimous vote. Dave Powers sat on CHAFA's board, but he reportedly did not participate in any of the board's discussions of the project. Nor was he present when the vote on the proposal was taken. Some, however, believe the project would not have been considered if he had not been a member of the board.

The bonds did not sell. Interviewees suggested that they were never marketed. Some suggested that the underwriter was inexperienced with this type of project; others suggested that the CHAFA board was not enthusiastic about the project. The local newspaper explained that zoning, which restricted the site and the surrounding acreage exclusively to park use, created concerns among lenders and made the bonds difficult to market. If the stadium failed, investors would not be able to use the site for alternative commercial purposes without having the site rezoned. Also, local banks were reluctant to make a $1.5 million loan to Elmore without security beyond the stadium itself. The local economy was in trouble, as were many of the local banks' real estate deals and the banks themselves.

The deal was in trouble, and the stadium was not likely to be built. By early March, little except land clearance had been accomplished. When it became obvious that the new stadium could not be constructed in time, the Sky Sox moved their first eight home games, scheduled for April, to Yuma, Arizona, and selected Spurgeon Field as a temporary site for the team to begin its 1988 season in Colorado Springs.

On March 15, 1988, a local resident, who had been among those who tried to attract baseball to Colorado Springs in 1985, agreed to finance the stadium with a $1.5 million loan. He was given a 20 percent equity position in the stadium corporation (not the team). Gary Loo, the local resident, was viewed by all as a savior.

Aftermath

The Hawaii Islanders relocated to Colorado Springs for the 1988 baseball season. The team, with the help of CASC, began selling season tickets in January of 1988, before it was certain that the stadium would be built. The team changed its name to Sky Sox, in an effort to evoke the memories of the earlier minor league team in Colorado Springs.

The Sky Sox stadium was fast-tracked and completed in eighty-one days, ready for use in June, at a cost of $3.4 million. The Sky Sox opened their 1988 season on the road. They played eight "home" games in Yuma, Arizona, and nineteen home games in Spurgeon Field, where no beer sales were permitted.

According to Timm, sales in Stetson Hills were helped by the stadium at first. Within a year, however, Stetson Hills was tied up in the courts as a result of AMWEST's bankruptcy, the savings and loan crisis, and a number of other problems. Dave Powers had left town. In the summer of 1989, the stadium, twenty minutes from downtown, was surrounded by acres of vacant land, with a few houses in sight.

Elmore has unusually high expenses because of the debt service on the stadium. Nevertheless, according to Whitacre, the team was near the break-even point in 1989. Attendance for 1988 was 168,248 (with thirty-five games in the new stadium) and 203,955 for 1989. Its 1989 attendance was seventh of ten Pacific Coast League teams and twenty-second of twenty-six AAA teams. Its 1990 attendance of 201,642 was ninth in the Pacific Coast League and twenty-third in AAA baseball; its 1991 attendance of 174,731 was last in the league and among AAA teams.

City officials admit that the Ski Broadmoor controversy hampered negotiations and that there was too little time in which to carefully think through the negotiations. The final agreement, in fact, was not very different from what had been agreed to by the former city manager. Local officials soon discovered that the 180 days of use was of little value, given the weather conditions of Colorado Springs and the restrictions on how the city can use the stadium. In 1989, the first full year of the stadium's use, the city had few plans for how it would make the stadium a community resource. Interviewees kept raising the question, "What did we get for $500,000?"

In the summer of 1989, city officials and Elmore's representatives were negotiating the responsibilities for, and cost of, completing the landscaping around the stadium. It had been discovered that the stadium's final certificate of occupancy had never been issued, partly because the landscaping had not been completed. The team's officials believed the city was responsible, and the city believed the team was responsible since the agreement did not commit the city to landscaping. City officials admitted that the misunderstanding was a consequence of how the negotiations were brought to closure in 1987.

There was speculation that the city might impose an admissions tax on professional sports in the city in an effort to generate a monetary return from the stadium. This would impact a semipro football team and the Sky Sox. The greatest concern was that an admission tax would affect Colorado College hockey games and other amateur sports contests.

In sum, the Colorado Springs experience echoes many of the same themes of earlier cases. We find a low-priority item for city government becoming a highly visible project that receives approval under great time pressure. We find state government involvement, even though this was to be a privately built stadium. The short notice given to the public, whether a matter of circumstance or not, brought discredit to the council and mayor. The adumbrated process and the use of public funds for the privately owned stadium were the focal points of what little opposition evolved.

The stadium brought about no new development, in part because of local economic conditions. However, it was not a part of any overall city plan and will play no role in the development of the city. In fact, interviewees suggested that if city officials had consulted their planning staff they would have received a negative recommendation concerning the site. It remains to be seen whether the stadium becomes a true community resource or whether it remains simply the home of the Sky Sox.

Conclusion

The Political Economy of Minor League Baseball

The case studies presented in this book provide insights into the politics of development in small and medium-size communities and the politics of the "stadium issue." The case studies permit us to conclude, as does Stone (1987), that politics matters. Although there are differences among the cases, there are also commonalities. More often than not, there are issue entrepreneurs; triggering events; the evolution of the stadium issue from a low-priority issue to one of high visibility and priority for local officials; intergovernmental cooperation and conflict; the pressure of team-imposed deadlines on local governing bodies; complicating side issues; electoral challenge to (and often defeat of) local officials who championed a stadium proposal; and legal challenges to stadium decisions.

The case studies reveal themes and relationships that appear regularly in the development literature and suggest that the politics of development in small and medium-size communities mimics that of their larger urban counterparts. They also suggest that the politics of the stadium issue reflects the politics of capital projects in general. For example, the following generalizations can be drawn from the text:

1. Intercity competition and concern for image characterize the local economic development environment.

2. Private sector activities are intimately tied to public sector decisions, but local governments are limited in their ability to control development outcomes.

3. Local economic development efforts take place in an intergovernmental context that is as capable of constraining projects as it is of facilitating them.

4. Fiscal and land-use issues are critical to local development projects.

5. Although development efforts often are dominated by private

sector interests and meet little public scrutiny, intense resistance from citizen groups in a community is not uncommon.

The tension between the demand for popular control and the promotion of the economy is a constant in each of the case studies. Local officials attempted to keep the stadium issue off the public agenda until their negotiations with the team owner were complete and agreement among elected officials was reached. Public hearings were of little importance. In some cases, they drew a great deal of attention, but they did not affect the final decision. In other cases, public hearings were held with little notice or fanfare.

Local officials searched for ways to finance stadiums that would not use general-fund revenues or raise taxes. The pledge not to use taxpayers' funds for a minor league stadium was common and led to a search for "off-budget" sources. The case studies provide examples of the use of arbitrage earnings, hotel-room taxes, lease-purchase arrangements, guaranteed loans, certificates of participation, and other means to finance stadiums. Each of these financing strategies avoided the need to gain voter approval.

The call for a referendum best illustrates the effort to impose popular control over development efforts. The issue of a referendum was raised in Buffalo, South Bend, Hoover, Colorado Springs, Durham, and Charlotte. Referenda are time-consuming and cost money. Often an embarrassingly small percentage of eligible voters turn out to cast their votes, and those who do participate tend to be opposed to government action. This is not to deny a proper role for referenda in American democracy. It is a recognition that the tension existing between development politics and democracy cannot necessarily be resolved by resort to referenda.[1]

Ideally, this tension is best resolved by the development of a community plan, or development strategy, in an open democratic manner. The plan should be a guide for local officials when making development decisions. The importance of such a plan is that it can be used to reach a consensus on community goals. It will not eliminate competing interests or the politics of development. The process of creating such a plan can be an important opportunity for full citizen participation that often cannot be provided effectively for specific projects.

The incremental nature of urban politics and organizational capacity requirements make such rational planning very difficult, however (Yates, 1977; Eadie, 1989). For example, with the exception of Indianapolis, the case study communities had neither a planning process nor a development strategy formally based on the business of sports, even though several of the communities were (or expected to become) heavily invested in sports.

Even in the absence of a comprehensive plan, however, many of the case study communities applied a development logic to stadium projects. This helped them make appropriate choices among potential sites, assisted them with other decisions, guided them in establishing negotiating positions with intergovernmental partners and the team owner, and made it easier to justify the project to the public.

The public ultimately must evaluate the success of a stadium project in terms of the specific goals that were used to justify the project. If the only justification offered during debate over a minor league stadium is a nonspecific assertion of economic growth, the public will have little trouble in labeling the stadium a failure in future years.

The Economics of Minor League Stadiums: Identification of Goals

One conclusion of this study concerning the value of a minor league team to a community is that although a minor league team contributes to a local economy, its contribution is small relative to a community's total economy, especially in larger cities. The economic impact of a minor league team is not sufficient to justify the relatively large public expenditure necessary for a minor league stadium. This conclusion is implicitly supported by the absence of any significant local corporate funding of stadium construction costs in the case study communities. The exceptions were Durham, Hoover, and Colorado Springs. In these cities, corporate participants had a stake in the development of the stadium or its site. In some communities (e.g., Harrisburg and Charlotte), fund-raising drives were less than successful. In nearly all cases, the local business community supported the effort principally by buying space for signs on the outfield fence, renting skyboxes, and purchasing season tickets or buy-outs of specific games as promotions, instead of making an up-front investment in the facility.

When state government gave financial assistance, projects were handled in an ad hoc manner, which maximized the local government's ability to exercise its political leverage. In the majority of these cases, local officials (or private developers) were successful more because of their political influence than because of the economic worthiness of the project. It is questionable whether state funding would have occurred solely on the basis of the economic impact of the project.

A second conclusion concerning the value of a minor league team to a community is that even though the economic impact of a minor league stadium is likely to be minimal and its economics are quite different than those of a major league stadium, a minor league stadium can fulfill important development functions. If it is to produce outcomes that contribute significantly to local economic development, a minor league stadium must be planned using a development logic that complements other community development planning objectives. These outcomes, however, rarely will be measurable directly in terms of economic growth. More often, they will enhance other aspects of a community's development efforts.

The goals for a minor league team and stadium identified here provide a practical foundation for such a development logic. They can also serve as benchmarks for evaluating whether local officials have attempted to protect the public interest in their negotiations with team owners.

The Goal of Operational Viability

Operational viability refers to the stadium's potential to be self-supporting, exclusive of debt service. This is determined for the most part by the nature of the stadium agreement that is negotiated by local officials and the team owner. A stadium lease (or joint-use agreement or a management agreement) details the financial and nonfinancial relationship between the two parties and assigns both parties specific responsibilities. It should achieve three fundamental objectives: obtain a long-term commitment from the team, ensure sufficient revenues in rental payment to make financial self-sufficiency likely, and formally recognize the community's right to use the stadium for nonbaseball events (which will be discussed later).

OBTAIN A LONG-TERM AGREEMENT
TO PROTECT THE COMMUNITY'S INVESTMENT

One goal that must be pursued when a community expends public dollars for a minor league facility is to protect that investment. This can be accomplished in a variety of ways, including community or municipal ownership of a team. As noted in Part I, however, community ownership can prove to be unstable and is likely to succumb to generous purchase offers that were common in 1989–90. Local officials can better control the fate of minor league baseball in their communities through municipal ownership, as exemplified by Visalia, California, and Lucas County and Franklin County in Ohio.

The city of Visalia regained its minor league team, which had relocated in 1972, in 1978 when it bought a franchise in the California League for $5,000. The purpose of municipal ownership of the team was to bring baseball back to Visalia. The city's deputy city manager oversaw the team's operations as part of his duties, and a general manager was responsible for day-to-day operations. A baseball advisory board was set up, but it did not play an important role in the team's operations. City appropriations were made to run the team, and team profits were returned to the city's treasury. The team's financial losses were to be absorbed by the city.

The city sold the team in 1982 to local owners. To ensure that the team would not relocate, the agreement with the new owners contained a clause that required the city's permission to relocate and gave the city the right of first refusal if the team was sold. The resale of the team did occur in 1988. A year later, at the time of this research, negotiations were still being conducted concerning the applicability of the clause to the new owners.

A modified form of municipal ownership is exemplified by the Toledo and Columbus, Ohio, teams. In these cases, nonprofit corporations hold the franchise. The corporations, however, are tied closely to their respective county governments. Their governing boards are appointed by the county governments, and a percentage of team profits is returned to the counties or to one of the counties' agencies. In the case of Columbus, significant amounts have been held in reserve for major stadium improvements. Team profits financed the purchase of the stadium's artificial turf, for example. In case either franchise is sold, all revenue would go to its county.

The nonprofit organizations are used as a means of keeping local political conflicts from interfering with the teams' operations. They serve as an effective buffer between the elected officials and the teams' operators. Both counties were successful in persuading the U.S. Internal Revenue Service that their teams met the definition of a nonprofit organization.

Municipal ownership is rare, however. It is unlikely that public officials today would invest the large sums of money required to gain a franchise.[2] A more common technique used to ensure a long-term presence of a team in a community is to tie the team to its playing facility for a specific period of time, usually the length of the stadium's debt service.

Local officials try to tie a team to the facility by imposing financial penalties for relocating before the expiration of the lease, or they seek the right to purchase the team if it is put up for sale. Hoover is to receive $250,000 for each year remaining on its lease if the Birmingham Barons relocate. South Bend will receive a minimum of $50,000 and a maximum of $150,000 per year, depending on when the relocation takes place. The later it takes place, the lower the penalty. The city of Colorado Springs will receive a portion of its $734,000 investment (which includes the tax credit given to Elmore) if there is a premature termination of the agreement. The amount refunded depends on when termination occurs, with each year of use valued at $50,000. The Fort Lauderdale lease calls for the city or the team to pay a penalty if either one prematurely terminates the agreement.

Other terms have been negotiated by the case study communities to protect their stadium investments. Buffalo negotiated the right of first refusal if the team is put up for sale and the owner receives an offer. Buffalo can purchase the team for 95 percent of the purchase offer, all other conditions being equal. Colorado Springs has the right of first refusal to purchase the stadium (not the team) if it is offered for sale. The proposed lease in Durham would have given the city the right of first refusal for 98 percent of the value of a bona fide offer, but it would have prohibited the city from reselling the team to the person or group making that offer.

MAXIMIZE REVENUE, MINIMIZE COSTS

Another aspect of operational viability is to minimize the net cost of operating the stadium and to earn enough revenue to cover the stadium's annual operating costs. Local government financial projections for minor league stadiums commonly predict that operating costs will be met with revenue from the stadium's operations. In the case of successful teams with leases that call for a payment based on a formula tied to the team's success, the prediction may be accurate. As reported in Part I, however, this is a rare occurrence.

Financial data from the case study communities generally were not available. One reason for the lack of data was that several of the stadiums were not yet built (e.g., Frederick, York County) or were not in operation for a full year (e.g., Hoover, Colorado Springs) at the time of the research. Also, accurate records on cost are not always kept. Field maintenance costs, for example, often are not recorded specifically for a ballpark, but instead are subsumed into the total operating budget of the Parks and Recreation Department. In Colorado Springs, sales-tax data are confidential and were therefore not available for analysis.

The case study communities reflect the diversity of stadium rental arrangements described in Part I. Some do not share in the stadiums' revenue, while others, such as Buffalo and South Bend, have tapped into it. The suburban communities of Hoover and York County negotiated a share of parking revenues, but they do not benefit from concession sales. The team becomes a full partner with the community when rental payments are based on gross revenue (rather than net revenue), as they were in South Bend and would have been in Durham if the referendum had passed.

The Goal of Targeted Development

The case studies establish that a stadium, by virtue of location decisions, can be used to advance economic development through redevelopment activity or new development opportunities. This suggests the presence of a need or opportunity and the existence of a plan or development logic. It suggests that the stadium is expected to have a positive impact on a specific geographical area. The stadium in such a plan is given a specific purpose (e.g., serve as an anchor) apart from merely increasing economic activity in the community.

For such spin-off benefits to accrue to a community, however, the stadium must be of sufficient size and contain the necessary amenities to attract large crowds of residents as well as nonresidents. These requirements make stadiums costly. Downtown locations, where secondary effects can be expected, are likely to be more costly than outlying sites. Larger, more attractive stadiums are more expensive than mere shells with smaller capacities, which can be erected at minimal cost. If owners do agree to a location that they do not perceive to be in their interest, they may demand compensation in the form of a more generous lease.

If new development is the goal, more is needed than building a stadium in the middle of a corn field and waiting for businesses to grow around it. The area in which the stadium is to be built must be selected with care. Necessary infrastructure must be in place or put in place. Consumers must be nearby or about to move into the area. A stadium, by itself, will not attract businesses or residential development, as the Colorado Springs case demonstrates.

Neither will a stadium alone reverse urban decline. In Buffalo, South Bend, and Harrisburg, other redevelopment activities already were occurring when their stadiums were constructed. A downtown stadium should complement activities already in place or planned for the immediate future. It promises to keep those who are already downtown and to attract residents and nonresidents who normally would not venture downtown.

In sum, a stadium can assist in achieving specific development goals. In doing so, the stadium will benefit the local economy. Without an appropriate plan or development logic, however, the benefits that a stadium is capable of producing either will not be realized or will be too diffuse to have a meaningful impact.

The Goal of Enhancing the Community's Image

Another goal is the enhancement of the community's image. Interviewees in each case study community expressed concern about the community's image. They believed the community either lacked any image or possessed a negative image. Several communities were struggling to overcome a period of economic decline. A minor league team can be used to promote the community, and a new stadium can be exploited to send positive signals to different audiences.

Interviewees referred to two distinct audiences when speaking about a community's image. One audience is external. A minor league team promotes a city's name throughout the region in which it plays. Its name is in the newspapers of larger cities and nearby communities on a daily basis. Local officials, economic development specialists, and tourism officials invest a great deal of time, effort, and money promoting a community's name and visibility. A minor league team is a means to accomplish this goal.

A new stadium and the process by which it comes about also can convey messages to nonresidents. The stadium can serve as a symbol of the community's commitment to growth, business, the quality of life of its residents, and a number of other positive goals. For example, Hoover officials wanted to be accepted as Birmingham's metropolitan partner; York County officials wanted to be viewed as competent and sophisticated public servants capable of making complicated deals with the private sector; and Frederick officials simply wanted their city to be recognized by others.

A second audience is the community's residents. Local officials want residents to have a positive attitude toward their community. Interviewees mentioned that their stadiums created civic pride among residents and were a pleasant place to spend leisure time. The creation of civic pride is particularly important where there has been a long period of decline leading to negative attitudes and despair among local citizens and where there is intense competition with nearby communities.

Local officials must aggressively exploit the team and a new stadium to enhance the community's image. The mere presence of a team or the existence of a new stadium is not sufficient to create or enhance a community's image beyond its borders or to instill community pride in local residents.

Local government agencies, especially the mayor's office, economic development agencies, tourist-related offices, and the Chamber of Commerce and other business organizations must actively picture and identify the team and its stadium in their promotional literature and presentations. A variety of community events also can be planned around the stadium or the team to create a positive image and the desired identity.

For example, one can walk into the Harrisburg city hall and find city brochures with action pictures of the Harrisburg Senators on their front cover and mayor's reports highlighting the success of the Senators and City Island, the stadium's location. Indeed, the team's business offices were temporarily housed in city hall, until adequate space could be provided at the stadium. The city's Fourth of July celebration focuses on the riverfront, City Island, and the team. This contrasts sharply with several of the case study communities, where no recognition of the team by the city was evident.

Maximizing the visibility of the team or stadium is not sufficient, however. The specific image must also be taken into account. For example, some cities fear that hosting a minor league team at a lower level suggests they are in a sense second-rate (e.g., Fresno and Fort Wayne officials were not interested in hosting A-level teams). A specific strategy directed toward well-defined goals must be developed and implemented to exploit the team and the stadium in a manner that will communicate the desired message to residents and nonresidents.

Some may object to local government's promoting a minor league baseball team. The team is a competitor with other local businesses for the consumer's entertainment dollar, but the community and the team are joined in a partnership, in a costly venture. The success of the stadium will depend on the success of its primary tenant, which is the team. The team also carries the city's name and, in a sense, is transformed into an agent of the city when it is provided a stadium and a negotiated agreement is accepted by local officials.

The Goal of Increasing Recreational Opportunities

Another goal is to provide additional recreational amenities for residents. Recreation is an important component of a community's quality of life. Minor league baseball in the 1990s is developed and marketed as low-cost entertainment. Indeed, it is common to be able to obtain tickets during particular promotions at no cost. Minor league baseball also is marketed as family entertainment. Parents in the case study communities dropped children off during games and picked them up after games. In some of the case study communities, it appeared that the minor league stadium had replaced the local shopping mall as the teenage mecca.

Minor league teams provide an opportunity for the baseball fan to view professional baseball "up close," to identify future stars and to follow their careers, and to get a glimpse of current major league players who occasionally are assigned to a minor league team for rehabilitation purposes or who are in the last stages of their careers.

The stadium, however, should be more than a place to view seventy minor league baseball games in the summer. It should be conceptualized as a community resource that provides many different types of recreational opportunities. In other words, the stadium, not the team, is the vehicle for enlarging residents' recreational opportunities.

As such, the stadium should be viewed as a part of the community's infrastructure. A new stadium is a capital improvement, much like a library, museum, bridge, or airport. It will have a life of more than two decades, if properly maintained. Officials in several of the case study communities appeared to have this view when they noted that if the team did relocate, the community would still have a facility that could be used for many different activities for a number of years.

The goal of making the stadium a community resource typically is pursued by designing a multipurpose stadium and building into the lease agreement the recognition that nonteam events will take place or a requirement that a minimum number of nonteam events take place in the stadium or on its grounds (e.g., parking lots). The lease agreement must balance the interests of the team with those of the community. For example, the Frederick team agreed to play games in nearby Hagerstown if necessary to accommodate certain types of amateur baseball games. In Colorado Springs, the city "purchased" 180 dates. In South Bend, the city has fifteen priority dates, and in York County, the team must accommodate fifteen "community service events."

No case study community had yet achieved the goal of making the stadium a true community resource, however. Several of the case study communities permit the team to manage the stadium, including the booking of events. This must be well thought out and specific obligations be placed on the team if it is to be an effective strategy, as Buffalo, Colorado Springs, and Hoover quickly discovered. A financial incentive may not be sufficient to motivate the team owner to bring in the number and type of events that local officials envisioned. Furthermore, weather conditions beyond the baseball season may curb the use of the stadium.

If the stadium and team are to be evaluated as true community resources they must serve the entire community. One cannot help being struck by the absence of blacks and other minorities in the stands at minor league baseball games. Several team representatives acknowledged this is a concern throughout professional baseball. Former Baseball Commissioner Bowie Kuhn has charged that "the major leagues have persistently ignored blacks as a source of attendance" (Miller, 1990). One study found that only 6.8 percent of the spectators at major league baseball games were black (Miller, 1990: 309–10).

The lack of minority fans is not a government concern. If minority citizens do not choose to attend baseball games, it is their choice. When a public-private partnership has made a minor league stadium possible, however, local officials should not only ensure that no discrimination takes place in the employment practices of the team and the stadium operator or in the sale and distribution of game tickets, but also ensure that the team owners and stadium operator make positive efforts to benefit the entire community.

Several of the case study communities have written affirmative action goals into their stadium agreements with the teams. Local officials in South Bend claim to have an "informal understanding" that the team will hire low-income residents of the stadium neighborhood. State officials in Pennsylvania scrutinized how Harrisburg complied with regulations designed to ensure that grant money benefited low-income residents.

Evaluations of the success of a minor league stadium must consider the project in the overall context of a community's economic development as well as how it enhances the community's quality of life. The case studies in this text have demonstrated that minor league stadiums can play important economic development roles. The critical factor in evaluating success, however, is how well the stadium serves the community's nonbaseball recreational and entertainment needs. When officials utilize a stadium during the months baseball is not played, not only will a community's quality of life be enhanced, but the economic development function of the stadium will be maximized as well. The key to ensuring that minor league baseball is "worth it" is that a stadium does both.

NOTES

1. California provides an excellent example of the problems encountered when citizen initiatives and referenda are used to make public policy regarding land use and development issues. (See Caves, 1988; Melious, 1988; and Glickfeld, Graymer, and Morrison, 1987.)

2. Elizabethton, Tennessee, owns a franchise in the Rookie-level Appalachian League. In 1989, it attracted 17,952 fans, which was the second lowest attendance in the league. In 1990, it had the lowest attendance in the league, despite being a championship team. The team is administered by the city's director of Parks and Recreation Department, and it reportedly is operating at a deficit. The Scranton Red Barons of the AAA International League are

owned by Lackawanna County and operated by the Lackawanna County Multi-Purpose Stadium Authority. The team is the most recent example of municipal ownership.

Appendix A

The data used in this analysis are of two types. First, data are reported from a mail survey of 148 cities that hosted minor league baseball teams in 1988. The survey was conducted for the International City Management Association's (ICMA) Sports Consortium during December 1988 and January 1989. Cities with teams in AAA, AA, and A leagues and in two Rookie leagues, the Appalachian and the Pioneer Leagues, were included in the sample. Telephone calls were made to each city to determine to whom the survey should be mailed. Respondents include city managers, directors of parks and recreation departments or their equivalent, and facility managers.

The overall response rate was 64.2 percent (n = 95). More than half of the local governments hosting teams at each league level returned questionnaires. Response rates by league levels are displayed in Table A.1.

Table A.1: Survey Response Rate by League Level

League Level	Number of Teams in League	League Sample Size (N)	Response Rate (percent)
AAA	26	17	65.4
AA	26	16	62.5
A–regular season	58	41	70.7
A–short season	20	11	55.0
Rookie	18	10	55.5
Total	148	95	64.2

Second, the core of the book is a series of case studies that present information systematically collected from eighteen communities having experience with professional baseball at the minor league level.[1] During the summer of 1989, the author interviewed nearly two hundred local and state government officials, community leaders, and representatives of minor league teams in thirteen

Table A.2: Case Study Communities

Community	Community Size[a]	League Level	Other Information
Birmingham, Ala.	265,968		Team relocated to Hoover.
Buffalo, N.Y.	328,123	AAA	Team breaks minor league attendance records; city seeks major league team.
Charlotte, N.C.	395,934		Team relocated to Fort Mill, S.C.
Columbus, Ohio	632,910	AAA	County owns team.
Colorado Springs, Colo.	281,140	AAA	New stadium is privately owned; team moved to city in 1988 from Honolulu.
Durham, N.C.	136,611	A	New stadium loses in referendum.
Fort Mill, S.C. (York County)	4,000	AA	Team moved from Charlotte in 1989; stadium is privately built, publicly owned.
Fort Lauderdale, Fla.	149,377	A	Negotiations prevented relocation of minor league team and spring training.
Fort Wayne, Ind.	173,072		City refused to finance stadium; franchise did not relocate to Fort Wayne.
Frederick, Md.	33,000	A	New stadium built; team moved from Hagerstown in 1989.
Fresno, Calif.	354,202		Teams relocated in 1987 and 1988.
Harrisburg, Pa.	51,000	AA	Team moved from Nashua, N.H.; new stadium built in 1987.

Table A.2 (Continued)

Community	Community Size[a]	League Level	Other Information
Hoover, Ala.	30,000	AA	Team moved from Birmingham in 1988; new stadium built.
Indianapolis, Ind.	741,952	AAA	Team is community-owned.
Maumee, Ohio (Toledo)	16,000	AAA	County owns team.
Old Orchard Beach, Maine	6,400		Team relocated in 1989.
South Bend, Ind.	105,511	A	New stadium built in 1988.
Visalia, Calif.	61,000	A	City-owned team 1977–82.

[a]Data from *Municipal Year Book, 1988* (Washington, D.C.: International City Management Association, 1988) and 1990 census data.

communities. Relevant government documents were obtained and reviewed, and media reports were analyzed. The assistance of several colleagues was enlisted to complete case studies in five additional localities. The cases are brought up to date as of January of 1992 wherever it is relevant to do so.

The sample of case study communities (see Table A.2) includes local governments that host teams at the A, AA, and AAA levels of minor league baseball; communities with a diversity of size, geographic location, and economic health; cities with different forms of government; and communities with a mix of professional sports experiences.

The case study communities were not selected randomly. They were selected partially on the basis of their responses to the ICMA survey. Communities that indicated they were attempting to use their teams for a specific development purpose or that recently built stadiums were of special interest. Other jurisdictions were selected to explore specific issues or examine unique policy responses (e.g., franchise relocation, strategic planning). The study included only communities whose officials indicated a willingness to cooperate.

A multiplicity of case studies is presented to provide different perspectives on a particular theme. Analysis of the case studies permits the development of prescriptions, as well as answers to the research questions identified in the introductory chapter (see Yin, 1984).

NOTE

1. The experience of three of these communities—Visalia, California; Lucas County (Toledo), Ohio; and Franklin County (Columbus), Ohio—is presented only briefly in the conclusion.

References

Altaner, D. 1988. "Cities Raising Stakes with Pitch to Teams." *Ft. Lauderdale Sun Sentinel,* March 6.

Artiaga, Sal. 1989. Personal communication to the Durham Stadium Project Steering/Advisory Committee.

Baade, Robert. 1987. *Is There an Economic Rationale for Subsidizing Sports Stadiums?* Chicago: Heartland Institute.

Baade, Robert, and Richard Dye. 1988. "Sports Stadiums and Area Development: A Critical Review." *Economic Development Quarterly* 2 (August): 265–75.

Baim, Dean V. 1990. *Sports Stadiums as "Wise Investments": An Evaluation.* Chicago: Heartland Institute.

Baines, Don. 1987. "Class A Controversy." *Chicago Tribune Magazine,* July 26, pp. 10 ff.

Bamberger, Rita J., and David W. Parham. 1984. "Leveraging Amenity Infrastructure: Indianapolis's Economic Development Strategy." *Urban Land* 43 (November): 12–18.

Barnekov, Timothy, and Daniel Rich. 1989. "Privatism and the Limits of Economic Development Policy." *Urban Affairs Quarterly* 25 (December): 212–38.

"Baseball 1990." 1990. *Broadcasting* 118 (March 5): 35–45.

Beebe, Michael. 1989. "In Stadium Conflict, the Issue Is Money." *Buffalo News,* August 27.

Blakely, Edward J. 1989. *Planning Local Economic Development.* Newbury Park, Calif.: Sage Publications.

Bluestone, Barry, and Bennett Harrison. 1980. *Capital and Communities: The Causes and Consequences of Private Disinvestment.* Washington, D.C.: Progressive Alliance.

Bowman, Ann O'M., and Michael A. Pagano. 1991. "Urban Development Outcomes." Paper delivered at the annual meeting of the American Political Science Association, Washington, D.C., August 29–September 1.

Broward County Convention and Visitor Bureau. 1988. *Marketing Plan 1988–89.* Fort Lauderdale, Fla.: Broward County Convention and Visitor Bureau.

Bryson, John M., and William D. Roering. 1988. "Initiation of Strategic Planning by Governments." *Public Administration Review* 48 (November/December): 995–1004.

Buffalo Sabres. 1989. "Position Statement on Aud Renovation." Mimeo.

"Bulls Future at Risk?" 1989. *Durham Morning Herald,* March 30.

Burris, Joe. 1989. "Maine Diamond Shines No More." *Boston Globe,* June 23.

Buss, Terry F., and F. Stevens Redburn. 1987. "The Politics of Revitalization: Public Subsidies and Private Interests." In *The Future of Winter Cities,* edited by Gary Gappert. Newbury Park, Calif.: Sage Publications.

Caves, Roger W. 1988. "Electoral Land Use Planning: The Case of Growth Initiatives in California." Paper presented at the annual meeting of the Urban Affairs Association, St. Louis, March 9–12.

Center for Regional Studies. 1987. "The Buffalo Economy: A Social and Economic Overview." Center for Regional Studies, State University of New York at Buffalo.

Chicago Department of Economic Development. 1986. *The Economic Impact of a Major League Baseball Team on the Local Economy.* Chicago: Chicago Department of Economic Development.

City Fort Lauderdale, 1986. Department of Parks and Recreation Memo No. 86–92(SF), Yankee Impact on Stadium and City, June 6.

———. 1988a. *City Budget 1988–89.* Fort Lauderdale: City Fort Lauderdale.

———. 1988b. City Commission Conference Minutes, September 20.

Cohen, Ted. 1989. "Harmony Flees When Councilors Talk Rock." *Portland Press Herald,* August 2.

"Colleges, Most Players Drafted." 1990. *Baseball America,* June 10, p. 35.

Coopers and Lybrand. 1988. *Analysis of the Buffalo Memorial Auditorium Renovation Project.* Prepared for Development Downtown, Inc., December 6.

Creeth, Terry K., ed. 1989. *The Indiana Factbook.* Bloomington: Indiana University School of Business.

Davis, Lance E. 1974. "Self-Regulation in Baseball, 1909–1971." In *Government and the Sports Business,* edited by Roger Noll. Washington, D.C.: Brookings Institution.

DeBare, Ilana. 1989a. "Raiders Would Bring Capital $1.4 Billion Boost, Study Says." *Sacramento Bee,* September 2.

DeBare, Ilana. 1989b. "Some Economists Skeptical that Raiders Mean a Bonanza." *Sacramento Bee,* September 3.

DiCesare, Bob. 1988. "Pitching for the Majors." *Buffalo Magazine,* April 10, p. 34ff.

Doto, P. 1988. "Yankees' Demands for Training Complex Blasted by Officials." *Ft. Lauderdale Sun Sentinel,* December 20.

Downtown Durham Revitalization Plan. 1989. Durham, N.C.: Durham City-County Planning Department.

Eadie, Douglas C. 1989. "Building the Capacity for Strategic Management." In *Handbook of Public Administration,* edited by James L. Perry. San Francisco: Jossey-Bass.

Elkin, Stephen. 1987. *City and Regime in the American Republic.* Chicago: University of Chicago Press.

Fainstein, Susan S., Norman Fainstein, Richard C. Hill, Dennis R. Judd, and Michael P. Smith. 1986. *Restructuring the City.* Rev. ed. White Plains, N.Y.: Longman.

Fairbanks, Phil. 1989. "Field Packs a Wallop for Image: Impact on Pocketbooks Varies." *Buffalo News,* July 17.

Feagin, Joseph. 1988. *Free Enterprise City: Houston in Political and Economic Perspective.* New Brunswick, N.J.: Rutgers University Press.

Fink, James. 1988. "Pilot Field Is One in a Line of Bisons' 14 Home Parks." *Buffalo News,* April 11.

Florida Department of Commerce, Division of Tourism. 1987. *The Economic Impact of Major League Baseball Spring Training on the Florida Economy.* York, Maine: Davidson-Peterson Associates.

Foschio, Leslie. 1976. Testimony at Inquiry into Professional Sports. U.S. Congress House Select Committee on Professional Sports, Hearings, Pt. I: 507–24.

Fosler, R. Scott. 1988. "The Future Economic Role of Local Governments." *Public Management* 70 (April): 3–10.

Frensen, Mark. 1989. "Private Public Partnership in Indianapolis." Erasmus University, The Netherlands. Mimeo.

Frieden, Bernard J., and Lynne B. Sagalyn. 1989. *Downtown Inc.* Cambridge, Mass.: Cambridge University Press.

Fulton, William. 1988. "Desperately Seeking Sports Teams." *Governing* 1 (March): 34–40.

Gammons, Peter. 1990. "Making the Grade." *Sports Illustrated,* July 23, pp. 41–43.

Glickfield, Madelyn, LeRoy Graymer, and Kerry Morrison. 1987. "Trends in Local Growth Control Ballot Measures in California." *Journal of Environmental Law* 6 (Fall): 111–58.

Grant, Jane A. 1990. "Making Public Choices: Local Government and Economic Development." *Urban Affairs Quarterly* 26 (December): 148–69.

Grant, Rubin. 1990. "Japanese Buy Birmingham Club." *Baseball America,* March 25, p. 2.

Greater Buffalo Development Foundation. 1988. "Erie County Cultural Arts Fiscal Assessment." Mimeo.

Haider, Donald. 1990. "Place Wars: Marketing the Competitive Advantages of Places in a Global Economy." Paper presented at the annual research conference of the Association for Public Policy Analysis and Management, San Francisco, October 18–20.

Hart, Stuart, Daniel Denison, and Douglas Henderson. 1989. "A Contingency Approach to Firm Location: The Influence of Industrial Sector and Level of Technology." *Policy Studies Journal* 17 (Spring): 599–623.

Heaney, James. 1988. "Nine Years in the Making." *Buffalo Magazine,* April 10, pp. 14ff.

Henderson, Cary. 1980. "Los Angeles and the Dodger War, 1957–1962." *Southern California Quarterly* 62 (Fall): 261–89.

Henderson, J. 1989. "Yankees Plan Expansion of Minor-League Complex." *Tampa Tribune,* June 22.

Hendon, William S., and Douglas V. Shaw. 1987. "The Arts and Urban Development." In *The Future of Winter Cities,* edited by Gary Gappert. Newbury Park, Calif.: Sage Publications.

Henschen, Beth M., John Pelissero, and Edward Sidlow. 1989. "Professional Sports Franchises, Economic Development and Municipal Government: A Contemporary Policy Dilemma." Paper presented at the annual meeting of the Midwest Political Science Association, Chicago, Illinois, April 13–15.

Horowitz, Ira. 1974. "Sports Broadcasting." In *Government and the Sports Business,* edited by Roger Noll. Washington, D.C.: Brookings Institution.

Hudnut, William H., III, and Judy Keene. 1987. *Minister-Mayor.* Westminster: John Knox Press.

Hyman, Mark. 1991. "Vincent Says Leaner Times Lie Ahead." *Baltimore Sun,* February 12.

Indianapolis Indians. 1988. *Annual Report.* Indianapolis: Indianapolis Indians.

Johnson, Arthur T. 1983. "Municipal Administration and the Sports Franchise Relocation Issue." *Public Administration Review* 43 (November/December): 519–27.

———. 1985. "The Sports Franchise Relocation Issue and Public Policy Responses." In *Government and Sport: The Public Policy Issues,* edited by Arthur T. Johnson and James H. Frey. Totowa, N.J.: Rowman and Allenheld.

———. 1986. "Economic and Policy Implications of Hosting Sports Franchises: Lessons From Baltimore." *Urban Affairs Quarterly* 21 (March): 411–34.

Jones, Bryan, and Lynn Bachelor. 1986. *The Sustaining Hand: Community Leadership and Corporate Power.* Lawrence: University of Kansas Press.

Judd, Dennis R. 1988. *The Politics of American Cities.* 3d ed. Glenview, Ill.: Scott, Foresman.

Judd, Dennis, and Michael Parkinson. 1989. "Urban Revitalization in the United States and the United Kingdom: The Politics of Uneven Development." In *Regenerating Cities,* edited by Michael Parkinson, Bernard Foley, and Dennis Judd. Glenview, Ill.: Scott, Foresman.

Justice, R. 1989. "A New Florida Has Spring in Its Step." *Washington Post,* March 21.

Kahn, Roger. 1985. *Good Enough To Dream.* Garden City, N.Y.: Doubleday.

Kantor, Paul. 1988. *The Dependent City.* Glenview, Ill.: Scott, Foresman.

Klobuchar, Amy. 1986. *Uncovering the Dome.* Prospect Heights, Ill.: Waveland Press.

Lake, Thomas H. 1982. "A Commitment to Our City." *Annual Report to the Board of Directors, The Lilly Endowment Foundation, Inc., Indianapolis, IN.* Indianapolis: Lilly Endowment, Inc.

Lamb, David. 1991. "A Season to Remember." *National Geographic* 172 (April): 40–73.

Levathes, Louise E. 1987. "Indianapolis: City on the Rebound." *National Geographic* 172 (August): 230–59.

Levy, Frank S., Arnold J. Meltsner, and Aaron Wildavsky. 1974. *Urban Outcomes.* Berkeley: University of California Press.

Levy, John M. 1990. "What Local Economic Developers Actually Do." *Journal of the American Planning Association.* 56 (Spring): 153–60.

Logan, John R., and Harvey L. Molotch. 1987. *Urban Fortunes.* Berkeley: University of California Press.

Mack, Paul, Ain Haas, Jane Holdeman, Doytgo Hamilton, Carol Hegland, Harold Karabel, Dorothy Mack, Tim Maker, Tom Shaffer, and Victor Wallis. (1980) *Indianapolis: Downtown Development for Whom?* Indianapolis: Downtown Development Research Committee.

Malloy, Edward. 1977. *The Impact of Baseball on the Pittsburgh Economy.* Pittsburgh: Pittsburgh Chamber of Commerce and the Department of Economics, University of Pittsburgh.

Markham, Jesse W., and Paul V. Teplitz. 1981. *Baseball, Economics and Public Policy.* Lexington, Mass.: Lexington Books.

Market Decisions. 1987. *Old Orchard Beach Downtown Revitalization Plan.* South Portland, Maine: Market Decisions.

McEwen, Bill. 1988. "A Whole New Ball Game for City." *Fresno Bee,* October 28.

Melious, Jean O. 1988. "Growth Management by Local Initiative: 'Grass Roots' Planning in California." *Land Use Law* 40 (May): 3–8.

Miller, James E. 1990. *The Baseball Business.* Chapel Hill: University of North Carolina Press.

"Minor League Baseball: A Major Resurgence." 1991. *Washington Post,* July 11–12.

Molotch, Harvey. 1976. "The City as a Growth Machine: Toward a Political Economy of Place." *American Journal of Sociology* 82 (September): 309–32.

Mollenkopf, John. 1983. *The Contested City.* Princeton, N.J.: Princeton University Press.

Moore, Thomas, and Gregory Squires. 1991. "Two Tales of a City: Economic Restructuring and Uneven Economic Development in a Former Company Town." *Journal of Urban Affairs* 13(2): 159–73.

Morris, Ron. 1979. "Where Did Minor Leaguers Go?" *Durham Herald,* August 6.

Noll, Roger ed. 1974. *Government and the Sports Business.* Washington, D.C.: Brookings Institution.

Nunn, Samuel. 1977. "Suburban Cities, Professional Sports, and the Recapturement of Economic Activity: The Case of Arlington and Irving, Texas." Master's thesis, University of Texas at Arlington.

Okner, Benjamin. 1974. "Subsidies of Stadiums and Arenas." In *Government and the Sports Business,* edited by Roger Noll. Washington, D.C.: Brookings Institution.

Olsen, John B., and Douglas C. Eadie. 1982. *The Game Plan.* Washington, D.C.: Council of State Planning Agencies.

Orange Book. 1990. St. Petersburgh, Fla.: National Association of Professional Baseball Leagues.

Peat, Marwick, Mitchell and Company. 1987. *Report on the Economic and Tax Impacts of the Camden Yards Stadium Development.* Prepared for the Maryland Stadium Authority. New York: Peat, Marwick, Mitchell and Company.

Peck, John E. 1985. "An Economic Impact Analysis of South Bend's Proposed Class A Baseball Stadium." South Bend: Bureau of Business and Economic Research, Indiana University at South Bend. Mimeo.

Peirce, Neal. 1981. "Economics of Amenity: Private-Public Partnerships in Indianapolis." *Journal Gazette* (Fort Wayne, Ind.), June 8.

Peterson, Paul E. 1981. *City Limits.* Chicago: University of Chicago Press.

Pitt, D. 1990. "Millions of Dollars at Stake in Spring Training States." *New York Times,* February 11.

Policinski, Gene. 1978. "Indianapolis Outgrows Its Small-town Image" *Planning* 44 (April/May): 13–15.

Regional Center General Plan: Indianapolis 1980–2000. 1982. Indianapolis: Indianapolis Department of Metropolitan Development.

Riess, Steven A. 1980. *Touching Base: Professional Baseball and American Culture in the Progressive Era.* Westport, Conn.: Greenwood Press.

———. 1989. *City Games.* Urbana: University of Illinois Press.

Robinson, Carla, and Patricia Wright. 1990. "Community Interests and Stadium Development in Chicago and Atlanta: A Tale of Two Cities." Paper presented at the annual meeting of the Urban Affairs Association, Charlotte, N.C., April 18–21.

Rosentraub, Mark S. 1977. "Financial Incentives, Locational Decision-Making, and Professional Sports: The Case of the Texas Ranger Baseball Network and the City of Arlington, Texas." In *Financing Local Government: New Approaches to Old Problems,* edited by M. S. Rosentraub. Fort Collins, Colo.: Western Social Science Association.

Rubin, Herbert J. 1988. "Economic Development Perspectives: The View of the Practitioner." Paper presented at the annual meeting of the Urban Affairs Association, St. Louis, March.

Rudolph, Barbara. 1988. "Bonanza in the Bushes." *Time,* August 1, pp. 38–39.

Sanders, Heywood T. 1987. "The Politics of Development in Middle Sized Cities: Getting from New Haven to Kalamazoo." In *The Politics of Urban Development,* edited by Clarence Stone and Heywood T. Sanders. Lawrence, Kans.: University Press of Kansas.

Sanders, H. T., and Clarence Stone. 1987. "Developmental Politics Reconsidered." *Urban Affairs Quarterly* 22 (June): 521–39.

Schaffer, William, and Lawrence Davidson. 1985. *Economic Impact of the Falcons on Atlanta: 1984.* Suwanee, Ga.: Atlanta Falcons.

Schmenner, R. 1982. *Making Business Location Decisions.* Englewood Cliffs, N.J.: Prentice-Hall.

Selman, J. 1989. "TSA Gives Yanks 2-year Extension." *Tampa Tribune,* June 20.

Sharp, Elaine B. 1990. *Urban Politics and Administration.* New York: Longman.

Shils, Edward B. 1985. *Report to the Philadelphia Professional Sports Consortium on Its Contributions to the Economy of Philadelphia.* Philadelphia: Spectacor.

"Star of Snowbelt, Indianapolis Thrives on Partnership of City, Business, Philanthropy." 1982. *Wall Street Journal,* July 14.

"States Hike Use of Lease-Debt, COPs Financing." 1989. *City and State,* November 6.

"Statistical Overview of the State." 1989. *Florida Trend* (Spring): 49–54.

Steinbreder, John. 1990. "No Ordinary Joe." *Sports Illustrated,* July 23, pp. 65–67.

"Steinbrenner Demands Off Base." 1989. *Ft. Lauderdale Sun Sentinel,* May 3.

Stone, Clarence. 1987. "Summing Up." In *The Politics of Urban Development,* edited by Clarence Stone and Heywood T. Sanders. Lawrence, Kans: University Press of Kansas.

Stone, Clarence, and Heywood T. Sanders, eds. 1987. *The Politics of Urban Development.* Lawrence, Kans.: University Press of Kansas.

Stough, Roger R. 1987. *The Indiana Tourism Report: An Assessment of Visitor Expenditures on the Indiana Economy in 1987.* Indianapolis: Tourism Development Division.

Sullivan, Neil J. 1987. *The Dodgers Move West.* New York: Oxford University Press.

———. 1990. *The Minors.* New York: St. Martin's Press.

Touche Ross and Company. 1985. *Professional Sports Action Plan.* Newark, N.J.: Touche Ross and Company.

———. 1988. *The Economic Impact of the Phoenix Cardinals on the Local Tempe Economy.* Newark, N.J.: Touche Ross and Company.

U.S. Congress. 1952. *Study of Monopoly of Power,* Pt. 6, *Organized Baseball.* Hearings of Subcommittee on Study of Monopoly of Power, House Committee on the Judiciary. Washington, D.C.: Government Printing Office.

U.S. Department of Commerce. 1986. *Regional Multipliers.* Washington, D.C.: Bureau of Economic Analysis, U.S. Department of the Commerce.

Vlahou, T. 1988. "2-year Agreement with Yankees Set for Vote Today." *Ft. Lauderdale Sun Sentinel,* October 25.

———. 1989. "Yankees Contract Hits Snags." *Ft. Lauderdale Sun Sentinel,* May 1.

Warner, Gene. 1988. "Stadium Plays Big League by Batting in the Bucks." *Buffalo News,* July 17.

Warren, Robert, and Mark S. Rosentraub. 1986. "Information, Space, and the Control of Local Decisions." *Journal of Urban Affairs* 8(4): 40–50.

White, Joseph B. 1988. "Factory Towns Start to Fight Back Angrily When Firms Pull Out." *Wall Street Journal,* March 8.

Whitt, J. Allen. 1987. "Mozart in the Metropolis: The Arts Coalition and the Urban Growth Machine." *Urban Affairs Quarterly* 23 (September): 15–36.

William L. Haralson and Associates. 1988. "Feasibility of Developing a Stadium for Minor League Baseball in Fort Wayne." Mimeo.

William M. Brooks. 1987. "Report of Structural Findings for J. Euless Ball Park Seating." Mimeo.

Wolf, Steve. 1984. "It's the Maine Attraction." *Sports Illustrated,* July 9, pp. 42ff.

Wolman, Harold, and Larry Ledebur. "Concepts of Public-Private Cooperation." In *Shaping the Local Economy,* edited by Cheryl Farr. Washington, D.C.: International City Management Association.

Wright, Deidra. 1990. "The Municipal Bond Gets Competition." *Public Administration Times,* July 1, pp. 1ff.

Yates, Douglas. 1977. *The Ungovernable City.* Cambridge, Mass.: MIT Press.

Yin, Robert. 1984. *Case Study Research—Designs and Methods.* Beverly Hills: Sage Publications.

Index

Arthur T. Johnson is an associate professor of political science at the University of Maryland Baltimore County. He is the author of a number of articles and essays on public sports policy and is co-editor (with James Frey) of *Sport and Government: The Public Policy Issues.*

Books in the Series Sport and Society

Go Big Red! The Story of a Nebraska Football Player
George Mills

Sport and Exercise Science: Essays in the History of Sports Medicine
Edited by Jack W. Berryman and Roberta J. Park

Minor League Baseball and Local Economic Development
Arthur T. Johnson

REPRINT EDITIONS

The Nazi Olympics
Richard D. Mandell

Sports in the Western World
Second Edition
William J. Baker